Reading the Postmodern Polity

Reading the Postmodern Polity
Political Theory as Textual Practice

Michael J. Shapiro

University of Minnesota Press
Minneapolis   Oxford

Library of Congress Cataloging-in-Publication Data

Shapiro, Michael J.

Reading the postmodern polity: political theory as textual practice / Michael J. Shapiro.
   p. cm.
  Includes index.
  ISBN 0-8166-1964-6 (hc) — ISBN 0-8166-1965-4 (pb)
  1. Political culture. 2. Political science.
JA75.7.S43 1992
306.2—dc20
                            91-12382
                            CIP

A CIP catalog record for this book is available from the British Library.

Published by the University of Minnesota Press
2037 University Avenue Southeast, Minneapolis, MN 55414
Printed in the United States of America on acid-free paper

For Hannah

Contents

Acknowledgments

These essays have all led more than one life. Begun, in most cases, as seminar lectures, colloquium presentations, and/or conference papers, they became journal articles or contributions to anthologies or both. Here they are revised, considerably in the case of the introduction, and somewhat in the case of the rest, to make their mutual association as neighborly as possible. From the beginning, the work on each has been facilitated both by colleagues who have provided the original invitations that provoked and thematized them and the students, colleagues, and audience/participants who provided the critical reactions that led to some of the revisions. I am grateful to "my editor," Lisa Freeman, for encouragement and guidance in turning the collection of essays into a book and to Rick Ashley, Frank Beer, Hans-Georg Betz, Aryeh Botwinnick, Bill Connolly, Fred Dallmayr, Sakari Hänninen, Manfred Henningsen, Brad MacDonald, Dick Merelman, John O'Neill, Stephen Riggins, Adam Sorkin, Keith Topper, Geroid O'Tuathail, Rob Walker, Stephen White, and Doug Williams, all of whom were involved in summoning the original versions of the essays by inviting me to participate in colloquia, conferences, anthologies, and the like. Welcoming invitations, real or imagined, are a necessary starting point, but the refining process requires forms of resistance. I usually find criticism aversive at its point of initiation, but because I am more or less academically civilized, I can, with some effort, appear edified if not grateful when challenged. However, once the initial pique has passed and I am able to abide more calmly with the challenges, it becomes evident that I am indebted to all of them at least as much as to the welcoming invitations. I therefore gratefully acknowledge all the edifying criticism, which has ranged from such terse remarks as, "for whom are you writing anyway?" (my answer to that changes from day to day, although I always want to say "everyone") to more prolix commentaries on my ideas, vocabulary, sentences, juxtapositions, and arguments. Thus for various degrees of support and resistance, I wish to thank Stanley Aronowitz, Jane Bennett, Paul Chilton, Bill Connolly, Bill Corlett, Fred Dallmayr, Tom Dumm, Kathy Ferguson, John Fiske, Manfred Henningsen, Henry Kariel, George Kateb, Sonja Kruks, Warren Magnusson, Peter Manicas, Deane Neubauer, Doug Williams, and various anonymous hecklers. And I want to extend special thanks to Stanley Elkin for his generous and rapid response to my queries about *The Magic Kingdom* and for his subsequent reactions to the initial version of my reading of it in "Terminations . . ." (chapter 9).

Thanks are owed to Lynne Reinner Publishers, Notre Dame University Press, and SUNY Albany Press, as well as to the following journals, for permission to reprint essays that appeared in their publications in earlier versions: *Alternatives, History of European Ideas, International Political Science Review, International Studies Quarterly, Political Theory,* and *Strategies.*

CHAPTER 1

Language and Power
The Spaces of Critical Interpretation

Critical interpretation appears in many forms, but virtually all of them—
from the mildly critical, as in some versions of the liberal democratic and
hermeneutic, to the more critical, as in Marxist, Frankfurt/critical, and
poststructural—derive their political significance from an attempt to disclose the operation of power in places in which the familiar, social, administrative, and political discourses tend to disguise or naturalize it. Thus we
learn from Marx and his successors that social processes that appear simply
to involve the creation and exchange of value also embody relations of domination and subjugation. And we learn from Gramsci, Adorno, and modern
culture theorists that although it would appear that simple matters of taste
drive the production and consumption of both high and popular culture, it
is the case, rather, that, with the exception of some resistant forms, music,
theater, TV weather forecasts, and even cereal box scripts tend to endorse
prevailing power structures by helping to reproduce the beliefs and allegiances necessary for their uncontested functioning.

The analyses in this book draw their inspiration from many different critical approaches, but this chapter is aimed at isolating some aspects of the
genealogical mode of critical interpretation, for it is the one most emphasized in many of the chapters to follow. Genealogical interpretation (or anti-
interpretation)[1] is most familiar as an approach to power in the later historical investigations of Michel Foucault. His investigations can be
distinguished from other forms of critical interpretation on the basis of both
his textual and spatial practices, significantly interrelated elements whose
connections are elaborated below.

As a form of textual practice, the Foucauldian genealogy is driven by a
commitment to a process of disruptive inscription, where the *process* aspect
is especially important. This commitment is obliquely expressed in the con-

1

cept of patience with which Foucault began his essay on Nietzsche. Noting that genealogy is "gray, meticulous, and patiently documentary," he outlined a mode of inquiry aimed at the continuous disruption of the structures of intelligibility that provide both individual and collective identities for persons and peoples and that construct the spaces as well as the more general assumptions of the order within which they are confined.[2]

More of the specifics of this textual practice are illustrated in chapters 2 and 3. Briefly, Foucault's writing has a defamiliarizing effect. By producing unfamiliar representations of persons, collectivities, places, and things, and by isolating the moments in which the more familiar representations have emerged, his texts disclose the instabilities and chance elements in meaning-producing practices. For example, in order to show how arbitrary and fragile are the interpretations constituting the person, Foucault substitutes violent imagery for the more benign representations of social learning process found in sociological discourse. In a phrase such as, "The body is the inscribed surface of events,"[3] intrinsic to the approach are the grammar, which renders the person as the passive receptor of meanings rather than its initiator, and the figuration, which represents persons as bodies rather than in terms of the cognitive orientations familiar in approaches that locate the impetus of the social bond in purposive mentalities.

The critical posture achieved with such linguistic impertinence is not justified with a parallel attempt, characteristic of some forms of critical theory, to seek the authentic essence of the self hidden by mystifying representations. Unlike, for example, most Marxian-inspired critical analyses, genealogy does not presume the validity of a particular construction of the self and the order, such as one in which the self masters "nature" rather than succumbing to self-defeating ideologies of subjectivity (a version associated with critical theory). Whereas the general tendency of critical theory is toward critique of ideology, based on the presumption of an authentic model of intelligibility, the genealogical imagination construes all systems of intelligibility as (in Nietzschean terms) false arrests, as the arbitrary fixings of the momentary results of struggles among contending forces, struggles that could have produced other possible systems of intelligibility and the orders they support.

What makes genealogy "patient" is therefore the ontology within which it functions. Rather than presuming an underlying system of order, a form of life in which the self can achieve authenticity or nonalienation, it assumes that Being is fundamentally disordered and that every interpretation of the order is an arbitrary imposition or a violent practice. There is no natural limit summoning the process of inquiry.

> We must not imagine that the world turns toward us a legible face which we would have only to decipher; the world is not the accomplice of our knowledge; there is no prediscursive providence which disposes the world

in our favor. We must conceive discourse as a violence which we do to things, or in any case as a practice which we impose on them.[4]

Within this ontology, the question that has been familiar within traditional interpretive practices (from Kant onward), Who is man?, is displaced by the question, Which one? — which possible self is being imposed on the basis of what attempt to naturalize and thereby maintain the order? For genealogy, *every* form of life creates its modes of subjectivity or kinds of human identity and its systems of meaning and value in a struggle with other possible forms of life.

This ontology is intimately associated with genealogical historiography. The typical modern version of history, influenced by Hegel, tends to regard the present as a moment whose meaning is based on a trajectory reaching into the past. Everything that has emerged as substantial in earlier periods maintains vestiges of its existence in the present, according to this view. The genealogical (or postmodern) approach, by contrast, views the present as peculiar.

Against the Hegelian view of the contemporary self as a product of a continuously more edified form of self-consciousness, the genealogist inquires into the different periods in which different forms of the self emerge — for example, the dangerous individual or "criminal" who does not show up until the middle of the nineteenth century (an example detailed in chapter 2). Within such a view, knowledge of the self is not a process of accretion but rather a form of power, a way of imposing an interpretation or, within Foucault's figuration, of imposing a topography on the body. It is a form of subjugation rather than part of a process of enlightenment.

Put in spatial terms, what is understood about the self at a given time is a matter of local practice, where "local" partakes of temporality as well as spatiality. A given historical period has forces at work producing interpretations and overcoming rival ones. The present is not a product of accumulated wisdom or other dynamics reaching into the distant past. It comes about as one possible emergence from an interpretive agonistics. It is the arbitrary result of modernity's configuration of self-producing forces. "We are," Foucault has noted, "much more recent than we think."[5] Genealogical patience thus resists the moralizing exhortation to recover authenticity in the past or to transcend an inadequate present by either imagining a natural attunement between the self and order produced by a process of mutual adjustment over the centuries or imagining a future situation with a more shared communicative competence (a la Habermas, a position addressed in chapter 2). Instead it is aimed at offering a history of the body, which reflects a history of the exercise of power. This is not the form of power described in traditional histories of political theory, which have emphasized power as a possession of an individual sovereign or class, a form of power analyzed by focusing on geopolitical space rather than the topology of the body, but a power that functions through discursive strategies and tactics, through the identities produced in the forms of knowledge and interpretation that normalize human subjectivity in various historical periods.

Genealogy and the Practice of Political Theory

To situate genealogical strategies with respect to more traditional forms of political theory it is important to note that inasmuch as all discourse is spatially situated, all forms of political theory that are comprehensive and totalizing presume elaborate spatial strategies. To say this is to invoke a recognition that "space" designates not only the boundary practices dividing a given society into recognized public and private, industrial and leisure, political and administrative, and other domains, but also the temporal practices that give both shape and definition to various historical epochs and thereby contribute to the meanings of written and oral statements circulating within them.

The historical dimension of this relationship between spatial and discursive practices requires the kind of specification it achieves in a recent investigation of the differences in the relationship between people and animals in both peasant and bourgeois classes. Focusing especially on "transformation of La Pensée Bourgeois"[6] over the past few centuries, the analyst concentrates on the way the bourgeois class came to distinguish itself by ascribing callousness, brutality, and indifference to the peasant and proletarian classes in their treatment of animals.[7] What appears immediately peculiar about this bourgeois claim is that one can discern no consistent pattern of generalized kindness in *their* treatment of animals. They have been alternatively kind and cruel, depending on the species of animal and the sphere of activity. While the bourgeois class has tried to legitimate its moral and cultural supremacy by seeing itself "as treating animals in a much more civilized and sensitive way . . . than the callous proletarians who flogged their horses or the ignorant peasants who maltreated their dogs,"[8] there have remained such paradoxes as "that of an industrialist who was a member of *The Society for the Friends of Small Birds*" and "could be moved to tears about the problems of the little thrush but may have shown a marked indifference to the sufferings of his own workers."[9] And certainly such people did not have this sentimental regard for all animals, only those domesticated as pets or held up as special examples for aesthetic appreciation.

However, the paradox dissolves when one heeds spatial practices. Bourgeois life has come to embody a "sharp division of labor between spheres of production and non-production."[10] Kindness and sensitivity have operated not at the work place but in the domain of leisure and domesticity, and the animals participating in this latter sphere have enjoyed the kind of "humane" treatment of which the bourgeois class has been so proud.

More generally, then, to be able to regard a discursive commitment—in this case claims about the comparative degrees of humane treatment of animals by different classes—as unambiguous and uncontestable, one has to treat the spatial practices necessary to predicate such a claim as natural or uncontestable. To express the relationship more positively and comprehensively: a politics of discourse is inextricably tied to a politics of space. Moreover, this intimate relationship between space and discourse is not one between disparate modes. Because "space" is constituted by the way locations are imagined or given meaning, it is always already a largely discursive phenomenon. For this reason the domains or spaces within which conversations take place can be thought of (as noted in chapter 2) as "protoconversations," for they amount to the already established, if now silent, conversations that shape the voluble ones taking place. And because they are a silent force in conversations, they are difficult to draw into discursive processes.

Accordingly, one interested in politicizing elements of a social formation will find spatial practices more resistant than discursive practices to contestation. This proposition is central to the thinking of Henri Lefebvre, who has done for space what Marx did for the commodity by recognizing that it is a "social product."[11] Because space, like all fetishized or reified things, does not yield its productive dynamic up to the immediate exercise of perception, the politics of space is not readily discernible.

> If space has an air of neutrality and indifference with regard to its contents
> and thus seems to be "purely" formal, the epitome of rational abstraction,
> it is precisely because it has already been occupied and used, and has
> already been the focus of past processes whose traces are not always evident
> in the landscape.[12]

While much of "social space"—the practices through which locations are formed and provide the implicit context for human relations (discursive and otherwise)—remains uncontested, there are arenas within which contention is invited. Of interest here are those domains constructed especially for purposes of affording critical reflection on the other nonreflective domains of human interaction, and perhaps the most venerable of these is the theater.

Although the theater is a venerable institution, its relationship with other aspects of social space has been historically inconsistent and problematic. This is brought out in an insight that playwright Arthur Miller achieved during an excursion in Sicily. One afternoon, Miller's driver (a minion of the famous "mobster" Lucky Luciano), who had said nothing for miles, stopped in the town of Siracusa, "and with a gesture behind him said, 'teatro.' "[13] When Miller got out of the car he saw a very large ancient Greek theater, which provoked a long meditation:

> I felt something close to shame at how suffocatingly private our theatre had become, how impoverished by a psychology that was no longer involved with the universalities of fate. Was it possible that fourteen thousand people had sat facing the spot on which I stood? Hard to grasp how the tragedies could have been written for such massive crowds when in our time the mass audience all but demanded vulgarization. If the plays were not actually part of religious observances, it is hard to imagine what it was that fenced them off from the ordinary vulgarity of most human diversions. . . . Surely one sound was never heard in this place—applause; they must have left in amazement, renewed as brothers and sisters of the moon and sun.[14]

To cast these observations within the relevant theoretical problematic— linking space and discourse—what Miller is recognizing is that in the Greek polis there was, at various moments, a virtual correspondence between the- atrical space and social space. By dint of both the size of the audience and the dimensions of social thought being addressed, the Greek playwright was not one standing apart inventing a performance to be applauded, criticized, or remunerated, but was one who stood among the citizens, encouraging a reflection on questions of identity and social practice and on the conditions of possibility for coherent community, given the emotions and passions im- peding such possibilities and the chance events intervening in and mitigat- ing them.

Juxtaposed with this recognition of the space of drama, and thus the so- cial location of the playwright in ancient Greece, are Miller's insights into *his* location in private, commercial space. In addition to seeing the modern theater as relatively distant from most critical personal and political aspects of social space, he recognizes that the theater has become both a commodity and an item in a highly restricted system of prestige. The former aspect of its location, the existence of the playwright in commercial space, is reflected in Miller's remarks on his royalties as he appreciates the fact that his plays are "work" and products being sold. They are therefore occupying com- mercial space as much as social and intellectual space:

> It occurred to me three or four time a day that if I did no work I would still be earning a lot of money, and by the end of the week would be richer than at the beginning.[15]

And he goes on to ask himself what is left of his contact with life now that he is no longer on the outside of commercial success looking in. His prob- lem, he notes, is to keep "trying to maintain contact with the ordinary life from which [my] work had grown."[16]

The latter aspect of theatrical space—its significant drift toward a space enclosed by elite criticism—also hounded Miller. In this connection, he speaks of the significance of the reaction to his work of other playwrights such as Clifford Odets and Lillian Hellman.[17]

This contrast between the spatial exclusiveness of theatrical discourse in modernity as opposed to the drama of ancient Greece that Miller's reflections point up is not paralleled in the case of social and political theory. Certainly the Platonic version of the relationship between intellectual discourse and the discourse of everyday life suggests a radical separation of the two spaces. In the Platonic version, this separation is based on the superior vision of the philosopher, who is thought to be able to see beyond the veil enclosing the immediate life of the polis into the transcendental domain of the "real," of which everyday life is but a pale, symbolic reflection.

One of the best exemplars of the modern version of Platonism was Leo Strauss, who, along with his many students, also held to a radical separation between intellectual and mundane (nonphilosophical) social space. But the Straussian position is not based upon the Platonic imaginative geography, for Strauss saw the "real" not as a special transcendent place of perfection but as lexical, as that which yields itself up to those able successfully to gloss the wisdom of ancient texts.

Ironically, this wisdom points in the direction of a secular enlightenment, but fearful of the dangerous instability that might flow from a mass acceptance of an impious, secular view of reason, Strauss wrote in a code meant to be penetrated only by intellectuals. His textual practice was, in effect, designed to maintain a separation between intellectual and social space. Despite giving up on the ancient and medieval commitments to a vertically shaped world in which there is a marked separation between the sacred and secular or transcendent and mundane worlds, the Straussian position nevertheless incorporates what "the 'ancients' (meaning Plato and Aristotle) knew and [what] we have forgotten . . . that philosophy and society are irreconcilable."[18]

However modified the Platonic separation is within the modern, Straussian format (which is secular and even relativist in its more esoteric level of expression), it is useful for purposes of illustration to analyze the Platonic use of the transcendent as a form of spatial strategy, and the relationship of this strategy to Plato's textual practice. To oversimplify, Plato's strategy consisted in the invention of an imaginary space, a domain of perfect things or referents, on the basis of which he could then judge (or demonstrate in dialogues) the adequacies of conversations purporting to treat both questions of individual propriety and the value and meaning of collective arrangements.

As is well known, Plato's invention of the transcendent is represented as a discursive discovery, so that the transcendent becomes the "real," and the mundane venues of everyday life, the situation of his contemporary conversations, are consigned to the realm of the imaginary. It is this spatial strategy that enables Plato to privilege certain interlocutors in his dialogues (e.g., Socrates) and diminish others (e.g., Thracymachus), for their argumentative success is a function of their varying abilities to create trajectories for their utterances that can aim at Plato's invented/real space. Of course, if Plato is being ironic and intends to accord privilege in the reverse way (as some commentators have argued), the same spatial strategy enables the ironic trope. Moreover, the dialogic structure of Plato's style articulates well with his spatial strategy as his interlocutors become positioned vis-à-vis each other on the basis of the two-domained spatial structure, which renders some referents as illusory (existing in the world of appearances) and others real (existing in the transcendent world).

A variety of modern social theorists pursue variants of Plato's spatial strategy in that they are also involved in inventing imaginary space. For example, Jürgen Habermas's original version of critical theory is based on his invention of a conversational space that is removed from the political conversations of everyday life in order to transcend the ideologies immanent in different forms of interest-driven or partisan positions. Embracing (unlike Plato) nonabsolutist notions of the real, the good, and the true, Habermas envisions the possibility of a form of utopian politics that can only be approached within a conversational space that exists outside of the impositions of partisan forms of power on language.[19] There is a shift in Habermas's more recent perspective toward a different imaginative geography to situate critical discourse. It involves a temporal broadening of the terrain within which discourse is deployed.

In his recent writings, Habermas has lent critical discourse two trajectories, one extending into the past to illuminate the background conditions that enable rational communication, the other extending into the future, anticipating a condition of unforced intersubjectivity, which encourages a form of community in which partisanship is not totally overcome but muted and aimed at reconciliation because the participants are able to transcend their particular solidarity groups.[20] This more recent spatial strategy still involves the invention of a separate space of intersubjectivity freed from the attractions that persons' group commitments exert on them. It amounts, in short, to an attempt to free thought from its social determinants, not through reflecting on them but through aiming them (in a motivational sense) toward a transcendent ideal of intersubjectivity. Ironically, this attempt to build a more free condition in the present is both illusory and politically insensitive. As Pierre Bourdieu has succinctly put it, "It is through the illusion of freedom from social determinants . . . that social determinants win the freedom to exercise their full power."[21]

There is thus still a significant degree of detachment for the conversational space that Habermas invents. He seeks a discursivity that is wholly separated from the field of practices that is productive of and orienting for statements. His spatial strategy amounts to an attempt to replace a false present, one with no utopian or emancipatory aim, with a true or authentic present, one able to dissociate itself from a false past and envision an authentic future capable of sustaining an ideal form of discursivity. Habermas's version of the role of the intellectual is very much like Plato's, but the textual practice is different. Replacing the philosopher's superior vision of a transcendent real, which is conveyed through a process of dialogic argumentation, is a more democratic notion of "competence." This competence is articulated not in terms of a dialogic process, which sweeps aside positions with the wrong trajectory, but in more abstract terms, linking it with the ability to communicate while resisting some contentious aspects of past situations and anticipating a less contentious and fractionated life-world.[22]

This is not the place for an elaborate evaluation of Habermas's position (some of the issues are treated in chapter 2). Here it is worth noting briefly the critical losses associated with his communication and intersubjectivity imagery. His position assumes that speakers have a large measure of intentional control over the meaning of their locutions, that the meanings of their statements are wholly present to them and under their control. This logocentric view of language has been effectively criticized by Derrida (and is also treated in chapter 2).[23] What is most relevant here is that, ironically for one influenced by a classic on rhetorical force, Habermas's view of communication as a relatively nonsituated process deprives discourse of the deep rhetorical force it has by virtue of two of its fundamental aspects: (1) its connection with the historical traditions that have given rise to the meanings of its utterances, and (2) the more immediate force it acquires from the spatial and temporal moments from which it issues.

A recognition of the dependence of intelligibility on such dimensions of positioning requires an attunement to textuality. For example, in Stanley Elkin's novel *The Magic Kingdom,* a story about a group of terminally ill children taken to Disney World (analyzed in chapter 9), this relationship between positioning or space and meaning is made evident. At one point, the children are taken on a river ride on a "tiny steamer that vaguely resembled the *African Queen.*" Their conversational exchange is rife with irony because of both the long tradition of meaning ordinarily associated with the kind of remarks being made and the special circumstances of the location of the conversation. It takes place in a section of "nature" that has been invented. "Nature is amazing," remarks one of the children, and in response the boat pilot says, "I learned all my lore here on the river."[24] What makes both remarks in this fragment of the conversation ironic becomes evident as Elkin describes the setting. As the boatman makes his response it is noted that "with a broad sweep of his arm he indicated the rubber duckies floating on the surface of the water, the mechanically driven wind-up sharks, the needlework palm fronds along the banks."[25]

The ironizing made possible by the invented nature of Disney World is more obvious than in other aspects of Elkin's novel, but his ironic stance is nevertheless a pervasive part of his textual strategy. And once one diminishes the significance of the traditional boundary between the literary or fictional text and the nonfictional one, Elkin's recognition, built into his writing, can be extended to the general relationship between statements and the spaces of their articulation. The fiction–fact boundary tends to dissolve with the recognition that all places have a meaning that is mediated by an imaginative geography. Insofar as space is a set of imaginative practices, all statements can have an ironic dimension. What an ironic gesture requires is a textually registered recognition that the spatial context of an articulation is contestable or in some way peculiar.

Elkin's textual practice is pervasively ironic because it registers his attitude toward location both in space and in time as peculiar human practices, as peculiar acts of imagination rather than as outer structures of the world.

This ironic, distancing view of the world is constitutive of the genealogical imagination, for it is organized by the recognition that such spatial imaginings are often well-entrenched historical scripts, not immediate acts of meaning-giving perception. Therefore, genealogy involves a significant departure from both the emphasis on dialogue or conversation evidenced in the history of political thought and from the view that there can be a space within which the partisan/ideational, interest-laden political impetus of language can be escaped. Conversations always take place in a preconstituted meaning system; they are always in a world. It is in this sense that the spatiotemporal location of a conversation is protoconversational; it shapes the economies of the said and unsaid, as well as providing a structure of intelligibility for the said.

The genealogist seeks to describe such protoconversations, to provide an insight into the power relations existing in the present. This spatial strategy contrasts dramatically with those based on the invention of imaginary spaces that are either transcendent or ideal. Indeed, rather than such extensions of vision, Foucault has argued that forms of power are disclosed when one's vision is shortened to focus, for example, on how the body is constructed by the prevailing interpretations in the present—its "nervous system, nutrition, digestion, and energies"—that is, on all the imposed interpretations that reveal the preoccupations of power.[26]

This seeming paradox—a historian who writes on such domains as medicine, punishment, and sexuality as they have been practiced over several centuries calling for a shortening of vision—disappears when the aim of these histories is understood. The genealogist does not use history to lament the wandering away from a past ideal or the failure to move toward an ideal future, but to point to current dangers—in Foucault's case to warn about the dangers of modern biopower represented in seemingly benign individual and collective identities. A genealogical history loosens the hold of present arrangements by finding their points of emergence as practices and thus by opposing the forces tending to naturalize them.

Genealogy and Policy

This impetus of genealogy can be demonstrated with an example from a public policy episode that occurred several years ago in Australia. The government commissioned an investigation to discover why the aboriginal part of the population manifested what, in world statistical terms, was interpreted as a high infant mortality rate. In another place I subjected their conclusion, in which they blame the "semi-nomadic life of some of the aborigines," to political critique,[27] arguing that it represented a particular politics of explanation. It is a politics that treats as unproblematic the position that it is the aborigines who should adjust their mobility patterns to Western, sedentary medicine rather than the medical system that should adjust its delivery facilities to keep up with aboriginal migration.

A genealogical approach would add a more basic dimension to such a political analysis. Rather than simply pointing to the forms of implicit partisanship in population control politics, it would seek to disclose the politics immanent in the production of the collective identity known as the "population." This has been a key term in Foucault's analysis of modern biopower, as he has traced the modern concern producing the idea of a population and found it to be associated with a change in political treatises on the art of government. He found that these treatises emerged in conjunction with the dual movement of state centralization and the divisive tendencies associated with religious dissidence. By the mid–eighteenth century, this art of government, a problematic evidenced in canonical political theory, had been extended to the economy, and the "population" had displaced the family as both the target of control and its legitimation.

> Population comes to appear above all else as the ultimate end of government, that is the welfare of the population since this end consists not in the act of governing as such but in the improvement of the condition of the population, the increase of its wealth, longevity, health, etc.[28]

This brief genealogy of state problematics places the pressure to investigate the aboriginal mortality rate in a broad political context of governmental management of the collective entity, the "population," which the aboriginal people are necessarily a part of, given the dominance of the interpretive practices (among others) of the European segment of the Australian society.

Foucault's advocacy of a shortness of vision is therefore supplemented by a glance at the past, a glance aimed not at the production of a developmental narrative but at showing what we are now. This "what we are now" is not meant as a simple description of the current state of things. Rather, it is an attempt to show that the "now" is an unstable victory won at the expense of other possible nows. The theoretical regard, the short vision, is therefore aimed at the present, but it is important to note where the gaze is directed *from*.

It is not coming from an imagined transcendent or otherwise dematerialized place. To locate the genealogical spatial strategy in such a way as to include the locus of the theoretical regard, as well as the world within which it is deployed, one needs to avoid the more familiar geographic metaphors—the now and the then, the now and the yet-to-be, the real and the ideal, the symbolic and the real. What must be emphasized instead is the idea of force. The systems of meaning or intelligibility associated with forms of power are seen as forceful interpretations, impositions that succeed within an interpretive agonistics.

In order to show the lines of force that are no longer visible in the present, genealogy goes back to the point of emergence, the historical moment at which an interpretation emerges as dominant. Such a point is, in Foucault's explication of its spatial significance, a "non-place," in which the adversaries representing different positions, for example, different models of space, such as the medieval, vertical spatial practice and the modern, more horizontal one, are in contention.

In order, then, to show the textual practice associated with genealogy, it is necessary to heed the identification of the historically shifting interpretations of space that give the contending discourses their predicates.

Exploring the Space of Writing

In the Middle Ages, the spaces of European societies were imaginative constructions produced within the dominant religious discourses of the period.

> In the Middle Ages there was a hierarchic ensemble of places: sacred places and profane places; protected places and open, exposed places; urban places and rural places (all these concern the real life of men). In cosmological theory, there were supercelestial places, as opposed to the celestial, and the celestial place was in its turn opposed to the terrestrial place.[29]

Accordingly, much of medieval writing, whether religious, political, or biographical, had the effect of retracing and reinforcing the medieval practices of space. For example, medieval biographies placed their subjects within spiritual odysseys whose textual structures reinforced the morality implicit in the design of medieval space.[30]

By the late seventeenth and early eighteenth century, space had become more contentious as commercial impulses produced imaginative cartographies at odds with those that had been generated by spiritually oriented forms of authority. Such a loosening of the dominance of one spatial view invites new forms of thought, so, not surprisingly, various thinkers began to clear an ideational space for commerce by mounting critiques of the political space of the estate-based society. Whereas the estate system was static in that it was conceived as a stipulation of divine will,[31] liberal political economy, as formulated by Adam Smith, recast divine will as a set of dynamic mechanisms regulating the process of production.[32]

The Creator was banished from the world and was replaced by a view of nature that construed it as a series of mechanisms *in* the world regulating the play of interests and exchange of value. A genealogical gloss on this important period in the eighteenth century provides a more politically enabling view of the present. For example, a traditional rendering of the contribution of Adam Smith would emphasize his critical contribution, including not only his above-mentioned move toward desecularization but also his critical departure from the mercantilist view of economy.

The Smithian system was quintessentially critical inasmuch as it took what was regarded as a thing, wealth, and replaced it with the dynamic process through which it was produced. In effect, Smith created, first, a space for conversations about the practices through which wealth is made and, second, a space for a political conversation silenced within the old mercantilist system. By constructing a political economy that shifted the emphasis from a concern with national rivalries to the conditions of production or work, he drew attention to a neglected constituency, the working poor, who could now be the object of conversations about problems of equity.[33]

This opened the way for an analysis of political economy (especially the Marxist) that increasingly was able to theorize the overlap between economic and social/political space. Certainly there is an important degree of desacralization of space associated with Smith's system, for much of his position involved replacing piety with calculation as wealth shifted from a form of bounty to a product of labor power.

However, from a genealogical point of view, the Smithian system can be read more in terms of its continuities within, rather than its departures from, its age. Smith's *Wealth of Nations* is continuous with texts appearing in the seventeenth and eighteenth centuries that reorganized political space. The emphasis in a series of political treatises after Machiavelli, who had focused on the problem of a ruler governing a territory and its inhabitants, was, rather, on "the complex unit constituted by men and things."[34]

This marks the beginning of theorizing the state as a complex governing entity that has to conceive of itself as managing an economy, where "economy" had begun to emerge from its ancient connotation associated with families or households into its modern sense of a field of calculation applied to the new collective identity known as the population.[35]

These political treatises, Smith's included, operated within the unstated problematic that Foucault has called a concern with the "art of government." One might protest that Adam Smith's argument was at odds with positions urging a state control over the economy, but what is important in asserting the continuity of his position is that while Smith may have taken a heterodox position in arguing for less state intervention in controlling commerce, he nevertheless belongs to the reigning doxa;[36] he conceived the problem of governance in terms of the state's relation to the economy in the new, seventeenth- and eighteenth-century sense, and he had adopted, as well, the then-reigning sovereignty problematic, one associated not with ruling territories and their inhabitants but with "men in their relations, their links, their imbrication with those other things which are wealth, resources, means of subsistence."[37]

Text and Space

What remains in elaborating this genealogical strategy is, once again, to specify its textuality and spatiality. In identifying the cluster of texts (to which Smith's practice belonged), Foucault employs the phrase "the governmentalizing of the state."[38] Textually, this move, which substitutes for the static noun "government" the idea that the state has been governmentalized (a temporal process), helps to loosen the grip of the present facticity and allow for recognition of an institutionalized mentality (a "governmentality") realized as a reigning discursive practice, and for the recognition that such practices have won out in the process of struggles. The task, as Foucault has put it, is to "seek to awaken beneath the form of institutions and legislations the forgotten past of real struggles, of masked victories or defeats, the blood that has dried on the codes of the law."[39] Thus insofar as one succeeds in loosening the bland facticity of the present, contention is discerned where quiescence was supposed, and claims to authority become contentious rather than unproblematic. The way is then opened to inquire into the forms of power and authority that the practices of the present help to sustain.

Now how does this gesture work as a spatial strategy? Genealogy is a locational strategy for theorizing, based on a particular view of language. It is a locational strategy for theorizing, but it does not invent utopian spaces, as has been the tradition in the history of political theory. Traditional political theory treats language as referential, and the utopian impulse is an impulse toward an ideal as opposed to an interest-laden referent. But the utopian impulse fails to open the political space that is made available by genealogy. Seeing language not as simply referential but as a stock of discursive assets that constitute sets of enabling and disenabling human identities and enabling versus disenabling social locations, genealogical writing is oppositional. It intervenes in existing discursive economies and disrupts the entrenched systems of value by rendering political what has been passed off as natural or uncontentious. For example, as is elaborated in chapter 2, while Habermas is trying to improve conversations, genealogists remain suspicious of all conversation, because they recognize that systems of intelligibility exist at the expense of alternatives. Therefore to strive to deepen intelligibility and provide more access *within* available conversations is to consolidate the power arrangements that the persistence of such conversations helps to maintain.

From Political Theory to Literary/Political Space

With a focus more directly on the literary dimension of genealogical strategy, the imbrication of textual and spatial practice becomes more evident. This literary dimension emerges dramatically in connection with an intellectual triangle connecting the writings of Franz Kafka, Michel Foucault, and Maurice Blanchot. The comparison takes as its starting point some remarks Blanchot made that bring Kafka's project into a critical intersection with that of Foucault. According to Blanchot, Kafka designated impatience as the gravest fault.[40] We must read this, now, with the recollection of Foucault's concept of patience expressed in his above-quoted remark that genealogy is "gray, meticulous, and patiently documentary."

While there are several important dimensions of the Kafka-Foucault-Blanchot connection, patience is the most significant because it is a code for the concept of *process,* which is central to genealogical analysis. Genealogy aims at incessantly dissolving interpretations. Decrying the leap from the laboratory to the cathedral, it militates against any attempt to arrest inquiry by enshrining a particular interpretation. Genealogy, thus understood, is a process designed to interrupt another process. This is summed up in the translator's gloss on Blanchot's idea of the purpose of literature, which is "to interrupt the purposeful steps we are always taking toward a deeper understanding and a surer grasp on things."[41] Impatience is therefore the impetuous attempt to grasp instead of maintaining the process of inquiry.

Focusing, then, on Kafka with "process" in mind, we are inevitably reminded of *The Trial (Der Prozess)*, the significance of which Blanchot helps us to heed. Kafka's trial is a process of error that is mistaken for truth. Joseph K.'s mistake is his reliance on functionaries (including his lawyer), for he thinks that they stand in the path of certitude—an end to the trial/process. But truth for the genealogist is uncertainty, the dissolving of all finalities, and Kafka, through his writing, sought to escape the maze, the sets of endless passages that depend for their power on a thought of a final authority or sponsorship. Like the Ulysses in his very short version of the Ulysses and Sirens episode (analyzed in chapter 3), Kafka resorted to writing or fiction because he recognized that a consciousness motivated by a search for finality is an enemy rather than an ally. It is a structure of apprehension that tends to merely reproduce the puzzles that power articulates. The resort to fiction, to imaginative constructions rather than to ordinary thinking, provides the escape from the traps set by the search for certitude.

The Foucauldian version of "patience" is based on the same suspicion of finalities, on a recognition that one cannot envision discovering an interpretation that will end interpretation. And, like Kafka's, Foucault's resistance to finalities is represented in his writing. For example, characteristic of his genealogically inspired textual practice is his above-noted treatment of the body as "the inscribed surface of events."[42]

The construction of the "body" as an object-effect of discursive practices rather than as an independent referent of statements accomplishes a powerful reversal. The text does not accord responsibility for statements in some natural aspect of the body but locates it instead in body-making discursive practices. The "real," in this case the body, results from the set of interpretive practices through which the body becomes significant as one thing rather than another. This reversal is not meant to encourage a passive acceptance of authoritative scripts with which selves are fashioned. In particular, what is to be resisted is Western metaphysics' model of subjectivity, which Nietzsche disparaged, the assumption that there is a "stiff, steadfast, *single* individual."[43]

To resist this depoliticizing assumption, the Foucauldian textual practice is a writing against a mode of interpretation that naturalizes prevailing human identities and operates within the pretense that all possibilities are exhausted. It is not the typical critical theory style of writing that is aimed at overcoming an estrangement between an adequate self and a mystified one, constructed within dominant discourses. Foucault, like Nietzsche, assumes that there is an indeterminant range of possible selves and that every institutionalized version of the self represents a political victory.

In keeping with genealogy's commitment to patience, Foucault's style is documentary rather than polemic, for it is not aimed at establishing a particular model of the self. It is aimed instead at opening a broader terrain within which the self (and the order) can be thought. In addition, departing as it does from the elucidation of power characteristic in traditional political theory, Foucault's genealogy identifies a form of power other than that associated with traditional relations between heads of state and their subjects.

This elaboration of the epistemic function of genealogy's textuality provides preparation for raising the question of the spatial predicates of such a textual practice. Where does one reside while engaging in such an analysis? Foucault's case seems to be that genealogical writing, as an imaginative enactment, will reveal and thereby oppose the institutionalized acts of imagination that have sustained existing spaces and thereby reinforced existing forms of power. Those engaged in critical interpretation do not invent places apart from the social order, they write within it. The imaginative function of the critical interpreter is, in Foucault's words, "to create a space of illusion that exposes every real space, all the sites inside of which human life is partitioned as still more illusory."[44]

In the chapters that follow, my analyses are deployed on both fictional and nonfictional texts. But it must be recognized that the production of all texts (as well as their reading or consumption) involves acts of imagination. There are thus no firm boundaries between the genres. If my analysis appears to favor the critical capabilities of what are recognized as fictional texts, it is because in the case of those I have selected, there is an inward gaze; the writing is informed by a recognition of the critical relationship between textuality and interpretation. And those nonfictional texts of which I am particularly critical are disparaged because they attempt to look only outward, holding the world responsible for the forms of imagination they enact or reproduce.

The coherence of what follows, therefore, is informed by two commitments. The first is that social theory is primarily a literature, and it tends, when critical, to recognize that its textual practice is constitutive of its contribution. The second is that writing as a form of political action functions within an imaginative geography that preorganizes the world toward which it is aimed and within which it functions as a critical intervention.

CHAPTER 2

Politicizing Ulysses
Rationalistic, Critical, and
Genealogical Commentaries

Representing the Self

Read with the appropriate discernment, the history of autobiography reveals how the structural features of an age are reflected in the modes of representation through which persons or selves are identified. For example, in
the Middle Ages the individual was typecast and not, as in today's autobi-
ographies, represented "through the organizational center of his own individual inner life."[1] The medieval self was situated in a spiritual Odyssey
with stereotypes the writer drew from the morality of the day, and, in general, the medieval individual was represented in ways that valorized the then
dominant institutions, the nobility and the church. Although in every age
some writers have employed textual practices subversive of the approved or
authorized models of the self—Rabelais is exemplary here[2]—for the most
part, the various genres of writing participated within the discursive economies that lent capital to prevailing institutions.

Consider the reworking of classic stories, what Michel Foucault calls the
"commentary" and Hans Blumenberg refers to as "work on myth,"[3] a
genre of writing that has persisted since antiquity. Although Foucault places
the various retellings of epics such as the *Odyssey* in the context of the procedures through which discourse aids and abets power and Blumenberg
takes a more benign view, emphasizing work on myth as humanity's attempt to exact a greater measure of control over nature, both encourage us
to read each reworking of a classic story as an expression of the political
problematics of the period of the writer rather than as evidence of the pe-
rennial relevance of the tales themselves.

The *Odyssey* is a classic that has continued to attract commentators, most
of whom have appropriated it as a vehicle for thinking about problems of

the contemporary self and order. For example, the medieval authority questions are evident in Dante's reworking, for his version amounts to a reassertion of the importance of divine will and the human quest for salvation.[4] Dante's Ulysses does not, as in Homer's version, pass through the perils of the Sirens and other dangers to close the circle and return home strengthened and rendered wiser by his success at overcoming outer dangers and inner temptations. While Homer's Ulysses is a tested self who returns home to reassert the value of certain structures of domesticity, Dante's is headed for destruction because he represents an old form of wickedness, the unredeemed, willful individual who fails to subordinate his curiosity to God's plan. Driven by his uncontrolled appetite for experimentation, he crosses the boundaries of the known world and ends up wrecked against the mountain of Eden, a victim of desires that fail to subordinate themselves to a higher power.[5]

Dante's commentary exemplifies the legitimation tendencies described above in connection with the genre of autobiography. The unsuccessful Ulysses in Dante's retelling helps to reassert the primacy of a self subordinated to a divine order. Dante's textual practice, the epic written as religious allegory, aligns itself with other practices of his age that script a self consistent with the prevailing ecclesiastical structure of power and authority. His commentary is thus a mythification, for, in general, myth is a form of cultural production designed to produce individual and collective identifications and actions that are authoritative in the ages and social contexts to which they are addressed.

However, not all reworkings have been mythological and legitimation oriented. For example, Joyce opened up the circle Homer had closed and resisted the appeal to domesticity operative in the Homeric temporal structure. His kaleidoscope of separate adventures exemplifies a different temporal trope, which renders his story antimythological. Rather than the narrative of a person, each event in Joyce's Ulysses is "a space-time block of words."[6] And most of Joyce's style in the novel takes its force through ironic contrasts with Dante's as well as Homer's story. It is therefore reflective about literature and myth and does not attempt to appropriate aspects of the Ulysses story to lend support for contemporary systems of authority.

Homer's Odyssey continues to attract reworkings, and a recent one by political theorist Jon Elster is particularly interesting because it exemplifies both a major genre of social and political thought and one of modernity's dominant modes for constructing the problematic of the self and the order. Elster's analysis in his Ulysses and the Sirens treats Ulysses as a rational decision maker. Although Elster's commentary is aimed at providing a political pedagogy, the approach is ultimately depoliticizing, for, as I shall argue, the rationality problematic, as a mode for thinking the self and the order, fails to raise questions about the distributions of those spaces that are deemed ac cessible and problematic enough to call for "decisions, policymaking," and so forth, and it also fails to raise questions about the identities of the selves given eligibility to operate in these spaces. These questions are foregrounded within the critical and genealogical perspectives, which I shall elaborate after analyzing the rationalistic mode.

The Rationalistic Imagination

There is an irony in Jon Elster's addressing himself to the myth of Ulysses and the Sirens. Here we have a theorist strongly identified with privileging reason over myth turning to myth to exemplify an aspect of rationality. And, as I shall suggest below, the irony deepens. But at the outset it should be noted that of all the reworkings of this part of the Homeric epic, Elster's commentary is undoubtedly the most economical. This is because his treatment is not an attempt to appropriate the story to reflect on the meaning and value of various boundary crossings–the issue that has attracted most commentators—but to explore an issue in the problem of individual rationality. In this respect, Elster's preoccupation mirrors that of his age, which has produced a human science complicit with its concern with the measurement and calculation of individual conduct.

Beginning with the immediate problem that Homer gives Ulysses in the Sirens episode, satisfying his curiosity about the allure of the Sirens while avoiding destruction lest he be unable to resist their beckoning, Elster attends to Ulysses having himself bound to the mast. This "binding," which has immense allegorical significance in other commentaries, becomes in Elster's treatment an example of "precommitment," a decision taken at one stage in order to restrict the decisions one can make at a later stage. Summarizing the strategy of precommitment or binding, he states:

> To bind oneself is to carry out a certain decision at time t_1 in order to increase the probability that one will carry out another decision at time t_2.[7]

Here is, among other things, a demythification of the story, for Homer's epic depends on a narrative sequence in which an ancient (and subsequently medieval) temporal trope is integral to the story. Ulysses begins at home in the *Iliad* and returns home in the *Odyssey,* and his movement through time and space is fraught with significance. This is not the linear time of modernity but the cyclical and pregnant-with-meaning time of ancient and medieval cultures, where the movement from event to event is thought to reproduce a preexisting pattern of significance.

Elster's substitution of the Ulysses and the Sirens episode as an "indirect means for achieving rationality," in which Homer's temporal trope becomes reduced not only to a linear time perspective, but even further to a discrete linear model (with only time t_1 and t_2) revalues the story. The original mythic dimension disappears in favor of an almost purely logical grammar and temporality adequate to issues in the rationality of individual decision making. However, while this is an exemplary demythification in one respect, there is the perpetuation of another kind of mythology, for the rationalistic construction of the self and the order carries its own mythifications. These operate at two levels, both of which are connected with the problem of writing.

While Elster's impoverishment of Homer's story—neglecting the genre of an epic and of the related temporal strategy—is excusable given the purpose to which he appropriates the episode, his impoverishment of political theory in general (of which his treatment of the episode is a symptom) is what I want to explore. The relevant issues come into focus initially in a passage in which Elster develops his theory of action, conceiving of the "set of abstractly possible actions" as something the individual evokes in consciousness.[8] Here Elster perpetuates the same myth that belongs to behavioristic accounts of the self and the order: the idea that selves and orders develop independently and that human agency operates within a meaning situation that is self-generated and wholly available to the active consciousness of the actors. It is also the same myth that Elster elaborated in his *Logic and Society,* where he mentalizes the standing of actors by construing political power within the assumption that a person's control over value requires that he or she be able to engage in the intelligent production of desired states.[9]

Here, as in his Ulysses and the Sirens essay, Elster reproduces the myth of individual meaning production. Such a story is insensitive to sources of meaning production that extend temporally and spatially beyond the activities of the individual. Without an imagination that includes the historical production of meaning and value, which reside in the discursive economies through which persons, situations, and "desired states" are represented, one cannot discern how power partakes of relations among persons whose "ability" to act is partly dependent on the historical and structural preconditions of their *eligibility* to act. For example, a person may desire to be rich, but it is misleading to reduce, as Elster does, the power to become rich to an "ability."[10] A person's being rich is not merely an attribute of that person. It assumes, first of all, an institutionalized interpretive frame that lends value to the person's holdings and second, a relationship with others. X's being rich is a relation in which Y (or a multiple of others) is poor.

Ironically, it was Marx, a thinker on whose writings Elster has labored extensively, who contributed to an interpretive frame within which relations of inequality and dominance can be recovered out of descriptions that seem to pertain only to individuals. The development of such a frame involved a recoding of relations represented in classical political economy as relations between persons and things. But this kind of recoding is lost in Elster's version of Marx, for he evaluates Marx's writings within a mechanistic model of causal explanation and a conception of language that restricts the meaning of statements to their referential dimension.

Within such a view of language, Elster has to ignore a thinker's interpretive contributions. Thus, for example, his Marx hovers ambiguously between modes of explanation (functional versus intentional, according to Elster),[11] and we learn nothing about the Marx involved in critique of ideology, the Marx who textualized the discourses of his age, showing that power is entrenched in modes of expression that purport to be scientific and apolitical.

The limitations of reading a thinker in general and Marx in particular within a mechanistic model of causal explanation (or intentional explanation, another of Elster's theoretical templates) are evident in Elster's treatment of what he calls "Marx's explanation of the coup d'etat of Louis Bonaparte," an event he addressed himself to initially in his essay on Ulysses and the Sirens and later in his treatment of Marx. Referring to Marx's discussion of the French bourgeoisie's abdication from power in favor of Louis Bonaparte, Elster quotes the following passage from *The Eighteenth Brumaire*:

> Thus by treating as 'socialistic' what it has previously extolled as 'liberal,' the bourgeoisie confesses that its own interests dictate that it should be delivered from the danger of its *own rule;* that in order to restore tranquillity in the country its bourgeois Parliament must, first of all, be given its quietus; that in order to preserve its social power intact its political power must be broken; that the individual bourgeois can continue to exploit the other classes and to enjoy undisturbed property, family, religion, and order only on the condition that his class be condemned along with the other classes to like political nullity; that in order to save its purse it must forfeit the crown, and the sword that is to safeguard it must at the same time be hung over its own head as a sword of Damocles.[12]

Elster refers to Marx's statement here as "rhetoric . . . rather than analysis," because it does not *explain* "the emergence and maintenance" of the Louis Bonaparte regime. And in his later elaboration on Marx's explanatory inadequacy, he states that Marx, in offering an explanation of the rise of Louis Bonaparte, is offering something that "sounds very much like an intentional explanation. Yet Marx offers no evidence that the united Bourgeoisie actually deliberated in this way, nor that they welcomed Louis Napoleon's rise to power."[13]

But is Marx not speaking in an ironic way and with very effective rhetorical figures (crowns, purses, swords, etc.), not of a causal process of ascension to leadership but of an irony built into the structure of power relations spawned by the class system? If we step outside of the boundaries enforced by the notion that all theoretical thinking of worth produces assertions about causation, we see Marx offering not an explanatory account of Louis Napoleon's rise to power but a critical *interpretation* of the relationship between state control and class power. And, because the irony in his style replicates and reveals the irony in the situation, he *demonstrates* the disabling understanding one gets of political phenomena if one assumes that control over value is entirely a function of directly holding state power. Contrary to Elster's demand for evidence of bourgeois conniving, the import of Marx's analysis is that structural dynamics are such that direct control by the class who reaps the rewards is unnecessary. There are structural encouragements to the irony of the powerful class condemning itself; showing this is a far more effective mode of analysis than the depositing of documents showing a cabal consciously directed by most of the bourgeois members of the society.

The demonstration is, put simply, that, ironically, a state can serve class interests even when it derives much of its legitimacy from a public condemnation of that class. In a sense, Marx's highly rhetorical passage is a passage about rhetoric, not about the causal efficacy of intentions, for it shows that we cannot appreciate the irony of public expressions if we assume that the power of the state (in terms of the economic benefits it helps deploy) can be understood on the basis of a model of who is holding the reins.

In some ways, more interesting than Elster's restrictive reading of Marx with explanatory imagery is his condemnation of rhetoric. This is the second level of the mythification noted above. Immanent in Elster's rationalistic construction of selves and orders is a commitment to language as a mirror of the world of referents.

Marx was a polemical writer, and the performative dimensions of his statements are very much a part of the value of his interpretations. His "rhetoric," as Elster calls it, was not an abdication of analysis but integral to it. Andrew Parker has pointed this out, in a passage that effectively addresses attempts to dismiss the rhetorical dimension of Marx's analyses.

> To reduce Marx's writing simply to its explicit argument is to betray the spirit of the eleventh thesis on Feuerbach, to situate Marxism itself as a branch of the very discipline from which Marx attempted to distance himself: philosophy. For if philosophy constitutively suppresses its own status as discourse, comprehending its work of reading as the simple transference of a discrete semantic content across a passive transparent medium, Marx by contrast would challenge this philosophical tendency to *interpret* the world from a position of mutual exteriority, stressing instead the performative dimension of discourse that puts its own integrity at risk in acting on the world, in attempting to *change* it, in acknowledging the possibility (as in the *Eighteenth Brumaire*) that success may not always be achieved. Such a risk is evaded, once again, by those "orthodox" readers

who restrict themselves entirely to an analysis of Marx's concepts without examining the manner in which these concepts find articulation—who content themselves, in other words, merely with what Marx has to say while failing to consider what the texts actually do.[14]

Here, then, is the way to make sense of Marx. Marx recognized that the political structure to which his writing was addressed was supported by modes of representation and thus wrote in a way designed both to reveal the value and meaning effects of the dominant modes of representation and to offer a discourse with which an alternative mode of making meaning and value could be realized. Now there may very well have been a gap between Marx's self-understanding and his method, for he tended to privilege a direct understanding of the "real" over what he regarded as mystifying representations (which are ideological). Without elaborating the deconstructive potential that this self understanding of Marx makes possible, it should nevertheless direct our attention to Marx's objects of analysis as texts or modes of representation, and thus his writing/rhetoric as attempts to disarticulate the structures of the scripted modes of reality whose density sequestered relations of power.

Despite Elster's inattention to textual practices, a consistent style or rhetoric can be discerned in *his* work. It is a style that, as I have suggested, detextualizes as it demystifies an ancient myth (Ulysses and the Sirens) and a thinker (Marx). It is also a style that decontextualizes (and thus depoliticizes) the self and the order. Elster's self is, first of all, a mentality, a person situated not in a domain of practices lending the self an identity, as politically perspicacious positions would construct it, but in a wholly mentalized world of intentions or plans. To the extent that there is a hint that the self is connected with others, it is expressed in the attribute that Elster refers to as an "ability." The self, he asserts, has power to the extent that it is able intentionally to bring about desired states.[15] But all of the meanings that authority and power constitute as "desired states" are conjured away with Elster's logically oriented rhetoric and traditional epistemological grammar. Grammatically, Elster has isolated selves contemplating possible objects, and rhetorically, he generates contentless "desired states" by focusing his analysis on the probability of individuals achieving such states. The social dynamic for Elster thus involves individuals producing events.

What this mythology of individual efficacy suppresses is a more politicized and substantial historical narrative within which the structural constraints and institutionalized identities confronting persons can be discerned. There are many frames within which the silences administered by Elster's logically oriented tropes can be made voluble. What is required, first of all, is a model of temporality that can register historical/social *process*. Then, one needs to connect that process with the production of meaning and value that leads to things being constituted as "states," "actions," "events," and the like.

Part of what is required becomes evident when, for example, one heeds Norbert Elias's conception of the sociogenesis of institutions. Recognizing that individuals do not, themselves, bring about states of affairs, but rather that the social configuration constituted by the order tends to structure meanings as well as parcel out "desired states," he says:

> This order is neither rational—if by "rational" we mean that it has resulted intentionally from the purposive deliberation of individual people; nor irrational—if by "irrational" we mean that it has arisen in an incomprehensible way.[16]

For Elias, the individual functions within a preconstituted reality that exceeds "mental habits." What one regards as rationality in a given age has to do with what are regarded as legitimate performances within the strictures of prevailing institutions that control the meanings, which have a historically specific and local character. All of this cannot be accessed or read with the discrete temporal tropes and logically oriented rhetoric with which Elster constructs the self and the order. His ahistorical, depoliticized rhetoric has selves, on which one cannot discern the scripting of historical, institutionalized meaning and value, for they operate in neutral space that is objectified, bearing no trace of historical and current struggles, complexities, and possible differences. It is a pacified social space, which Elster's rhetoric further pacifies. Elster's rationalistic textual practice amounts to what Habermas, in his meditation on decisionist models of the self and the order, has called "instruction in control over objective or objectified processes."[17]

Toward a Politicized Textual Practice: The Critical Imagination

Shifting one's focus to the political sensibilities of modes of analysis, one's attention is necessarily turned both to the complicity that some textual practices have with an order's way of producing subjectivities and the distance that others manage to achieve as they create a space for the self to think itself outside of those constraining subjectivities. Within such a sensibility, moreover, one can investigate the politics of the self and the order as they are represented in alternative theoretical paradigms.

One of the more politicizing textual practices was developed by Theodor Adorno who, conveniently, has also addressed himself (along with Max Horkheimer) to the Ulysses and the Sirens story. It is striking how sensitive Horkheimer and Adorno are to all that is flattened and ignored in Elster's treatment, and, as if they had anticipated this comparison, they introduce

their analysis with a discussion addressed directly to the mythifying qualities in Elster's mode of analysis. Noting that "false clarity is only another
name for myth," they go on to show how neo–Baconian or scientistic models of science remythologize by failing to reflect on their own practices.[18]

For Elster, the problem of meaning is part of one's analytic language, not
part of the social order that the language of analysis is designed to penetrate.
Meaning thus reduces to a requirement for definitions that are clear enough
to be falsifiable, and the order, which is the object of analysis, is seen as a
domain of individuals struggling over ends rather than as a struggle over
meanings. In addition, Elster, in his reaction to dialectic thinking, which is
designed to treat the problem of the embeddedness *in* the order of modes of
thought that try to think *about* the order, reduces dialectics to social psychology.[19]

Horkheimer and Adorno, by contrast, recognize that "reality" is a textual phenomenon, not something available to a transparent mode of perception. Contrasting this dialectical imagination with Baconian models of science, they assert, "Dialectic . . . interprets every image as writing,"[20] and
their sensitivity to writing is reflected, among other things, in their attention to genre, to the fact that Homer's treatment is in the epic style. This
recognition renarrativizes what Elster's discrete temporal model (Ulysses at
time t_1 and t_2) denarrativizes. It permits an encounter with a Ulysses who
is not simply someone *wanting* a simple goal (hearing the Sirens) and also
wanting to move on after hearing them and *knowing* that there are risks, but
is also someone *representing* an ontological condition. It is shown that there
are monumental tensions between being governed by desire and being a
home–oriented social being. Desiring is thus situated as a problematic in the
constitution of the order.

Horkheimer and Adorno locate the self as something that cannot be
clearly separated from the practices that constitute an order. Recognizing
the interdependence of the self and the order, they give us a Ulysses who is
not simply a mentality trying to reduce risk in the attempt to achieve ends
or states that are wholly detached from social, institutionalized forms of valuing; rather, they place Ulysses in an order as a property owner witnessing
the end of some of the nomadic forms of existence. Ulysses is thus a self
constituted in part by his real estate holdings.[21] Placing Ulysses in this
frame produces a reading of his adventure in terms of the self-preservation
of a situated self, one with a connection with others in a subordinated structure of a division of labor delegated in large measure by property ownership.

It is *this* self-preservation, not of an isolated mentalistic self but of an order that privileges a particular kind of selfhood, that is allegorically at risk in
Ulysses' adventures. This kind of reading, moreover, requires the recognition that Homer wrote an epic, a story with a message based on the move-

ment of the characters through a time fraught with significance. Homer, according to Horkheimer and Adorno, begins with myth, a celebration of the gods and their role in delegating fateful events, but ends in antimyth as Ulysses takes control as a bourgeois individual. Accordingly, Homer's narrative constructs the early adventuring Odysseus as a type that can no longer be countenanced. As the story progresses, the mythic style of the epic itself becomes impugned, for ultimately the epic is a genre that is alien to a story that ends up heralding the emerging political economy of Homeric Greece. As Horkheimer and Adorno state it, the epic moves, through its changing representation of Ulysses, away from the ancient, mythic cosmos of the gods. "The cosmos of the meaningful Homeric world is shown to be the achievement of regulative reason."[22]

Once this epic structure is disclosed, the meaning of the episodes becomes intelligible as part of the narrative structure. For example, the narrative of Ulysses' cheating of the natural deities becomes the cheating of "the civilized traveler." The bartering and conniving through which Ulysses manages to move successfully through his adventures represents a pattern of rational exchange, "a device of men by which the gods may be mastered."[23] The epic is thus a demythologizing genre because it has the effect of celebrating the gods within a narrative structure that ultimately overturns them; they are destroyed by the very system (mode of writing) by which they are honored.

Horkheimer and Adorno disclose a Homeric text that celebrates a form of collective, not individual, rationality, a process by which the self is rationalized with respect to an emerging order. What makes the story epic is indeed its level of focus, not on the story of a self engaged in rational strategies but on the story of the making of a kind of self that can be rationally situated in an order (Ulysses ending his life as a family man and proprietor, etc. — the lamenting Ulysses of the Tennyson poem). Within this focus the various adventures represent the difficulty involved in molding a self. Indeed, what this critical reading does, among other things, is demonstrate the weakness of mentalistic, decisionist approaches to rationality. Selves are not isolated entities engaged in meaning-production and value-achieving practices that they deploy on the order. The coherent self that Ulysses becomes is one related to the systematization of reproduction in the family and the system of proprietorship related to managing one's affairs in a hierarchical, landholding structure. The achievement of an appropriate, situated self is not a strategy of Ulysses but a textual strategy in the epic; it is Homer's representation of a historical judgment to which Ulysses succumbs. It is less the case, therefore, that Ulysses desires certain states than it is that desire itself becomes domesticated. To pluck Ulysses out of this narrative of the sacrifices the self must endure to achieve coherence in an order is to detextualize and thus depoliticize one's understanding of selves and orders.

Adorno's critical method, reflected in this reading of the Ulysses episode, is tied to his self-consciousness as a writer. The writing problem is exemplified in Adorno's treatment of "reification," which his dialectical style was designed to overcome. For Adorno, "dialectics means intransigence towards all reification."[24] The reification or objectifying of aspects of the self and the order is created by "identity thinking," which is the illusion that one's concepts are identical with their objects.[25] Arguing that "identity is the primal form of ideology," Adorno adopted conceptual and writing practices designed to resist the static picture of a neat fit between the self and the order that is encouraged by a grammar of descriptions that separates the subject as an individual psychologized entity surrounded by an objectively given structure.

For Adorno, the individual is a social text with identities inscribed dynamically by the operation of structural imperatives. Conveying this individual-society relationship with his style, Adorno used a variety of rhetorical gestures, including chiasmus, a grammatical trope in which the order of words in one clause is inverted in the second to convey the complex entanglement between the self/order and the methods used to apprehend that self or order. For example, writing about the misleading ideas associated with a "science of society," he structures his discussion with several grammatical shifts between the order of presentation of "science" and "society" to show that positivist science represents society as a static structure and that it is the social structure itself that produces the entities described in scientific discourses.[26]

Insofar as science fails to capture this dynamic interrelationship, it is complicit in the operating social ideologies that reify both structure and the human identities or subjectivities resident within it. To the extent that an approach hypostatizes a radical separation of the meaning-constituting force of both the self and the order, asserts Adorno, it takes "the individual state of mind, itself the ephemeral product of an individualistic society, literally."[27]

While Elster's construction of the social structure is a series of isolated purposive behaviors, Adorno constructs it as a meaning-production process. Recognizing, with Nietzsche, that the only concepts that can be defined are those without a history,[28] Adorno views society as a dynamic mediating phenomenon. Moreover, he resists giving the idea of the order the kind of immediacy or presence of one who tends, as he puts it, to "transform chronic social antagonisms into *quaestiones facti*."[29] Adorno, by dint of his critical theory/writing style, represents society in a way that opposes a depoliticizing rhetoric of reassurance within which, a la Elster, individuals formulate intentions to pursue detextualized objects. For example, to understand persons engaged in consumption ("consumer behavior"), Adorno gives us an image, not of isolated acts of rationality — persons' logically consistent plans to acquire the objects to satisfy their needs — but of a process in which persons take on the identity of consumers within an order that imposes value on objects. The process of imposition structures both the desiring persons and the objects of desire as people are "fashioned into a vast network of consumers."[30]

A social theory that adopts the same means-ends individualistic rationality that the modern political economy imposes helps that structure operate rather than effecting a theoretical distance from it. Adorno's critical theory of society, by contrast, avoids using the entrenched language of power and authority. His critical essays constitute dialectical encounters with the prevailing modes of thought, for Adorno was first and foremost a linguistic tactician who set up positions from which it becomes apparent that selves and orders are interrelated dynamics that cannot be contained within the naturalized, static categories that purport to represent, scientifically, selves, actions, and structural patterns.

The Genealogical Imagination

Like critical theory, genealogy is a disruptive, critical practice, but unlike the critical raids conducted by Adorno, which were designed to overcome inadequacies of representation (where adequacy is a structure of representation that enables social actors to understand the structure of causation or effectivity within which they function), genealogy is, in Foucault's words, "gray, meticulous, and patiently documentary."[31] Committed to inquiry, it seeks endlessly to dissolve the coherences of systems of intelligibility that give individual and collective identities to persons/peoples and to the orders that house them by recreating the process of descent within which subjectivities and objectivities are produced. The standard or quest thus bears a strong resemblance to one of Adorno's versions of dialectics, the opposition to all reification. But genealogy does not locate that quest in behalf of a particular model of the self's relation to the order, one in which the self is able to control nature without losing itself within ideologies of the subject, as some critical theorists would have it. While critical theory in general and Adorno, to some extent (although his position is ambiguous here), base their readings of the reification of the self on a model of an authentic model of intelligibility, within the genealogical perspective, all modes of intelligibility are appropriations, the momentary fixing of the resultants of contending forces that could have spawned an endless variety of coherences within which the "real" can be identified.

Genealogical theory is thus "patient" in the sense that its mode of questioning operates within a different ontology than that of critical models based on a dialectic. It is not that the self is a form of life that is alienated from itself in a system of intelligibility that mystifies the self's more basic identity or social and political standing. The Nietzsche-inspired, genealogical question is not, Who is man? but, Which one?, which possible life or self is being imposed? Genealogy views every form of life as producing its human identities and systems of value in a struggle with other possible forms of life.[32]

Its ontology, in which any self and order is an arbitrary imposition of meaning and value, emerges in the very grammar of genealogical writing. If Adorno's critical theory and the textual practice through which it is thought serves as a resistance to depoliticizing, rationalistic modes of constructing the self and the order, the genealogical imagination serves as a thoroughgoing affront to rationalism. One of its most powerful pieces of imagery is Foucault's metaphor for reading the history of the body.

> The body is the inscribed surface of events (traced by language and dissolved by ideas), the locus of a dissociated Self (adopting the illusion of a substantial unity), and a volume in perpetual disintegration. Genealogy, as an analysis of descent, is thus situated within the articulation of the body and history. Its task is to expose a body totally imprinted by history and the process of history's destruction of the body.[33]

In this passage the textual practice and the politicizing mode of genealogical analysis are inseparable. The argument is about the historical constitution of human subjects, whose identities are imposed. Thus a genealogical history will "expose a body totally imprinted." The explicit case made for this kind of history is supplemented by the grammar and rhetoric of the passage. Foucault's grammar displaces the subject of consciousness so that the subject as actor or producer of meaning is replaced by a recipient of social meanings. Supplementing this Kafkaesque grammar of the subject as object of disciplinary practices is a figuration that changes static conceptions into historical process. For example, by representing the body as "a volume in disintegration," Foucault supplies an impertinent metaphor that dissolves the unity and coherence of the person familiar in administrative, legal, and everyday discourses.

Foucault does not here argue that persons do not have the potential to create meaning and value. He is presuming, rather, that what is to be resisted is what Nietzsche regarded as Western metaphysics' model of subjectivity, the assumption that there is a "stiff, steadfast, *single* individual,"[34] a natural, universal form of selfhood that must attract all individual self-making efforts. Accordingly, his style writes against modes of theorizing that represent the prevailing structure of human identities as natural and thus exhaustive of the possibilities. Foucault writes not within an imagery designed to overcome an estrangement between an adequate self and a mystified one constructed within expropriated discourses of meaning and value—the background assumption of the critical theory textual practice. Rather, his writing conveys the process of self-making, a dynamic that belongs to the history of power over individuals. Foucault assumes that there is an indeterminant range of possible selves and that every particular form of self emerges from a restrictive practice. In keeping with the genealogical commitment to patient inquiry, he resists exhortation and maintains a documentary approach. He produces histories of the subject reflecting histories of power and authority. This is not the form of power encoded within traditional political theory, which focuses on a history of the limitation of sovereign power possessed by the head of state, but a power represented in the positive, identity-producing impetus of the proliferating forms of new knowledge that have normalized the human subject from the classical age to modernity.[35]

This analysis of power, connected to a genealogical analytic, is perhaps the most radical departure from a rationalistic analytic within which the order is a container for individuals who pursue objectives and have power to the extent that they are able to achieve desired states. Like Adorno, Foucault offers a more politically acute understanding of the order by focusing on systems of meaning rather than patterns of activity, described in a detached language of behavior, intentional or otherwise.

In the rationalistic approach of Elster, society is constructed as a vast container whose individuals have mentalistic standing with respect to value and varying degrees of ability to act. This perspective cannot register the extent to which one's "ability" to act is constrained by the structurally induced valuing of acting locations. By contrast, Foucault emphasizes the meaning and value of the differing locations in social space as its configuration shifts from age to age. The Middle Ages, for example, was a "hierarchic assemblage of places: sacred places and profane places; protected places and open, exposed places; urban places and rural places."[36] And all of these places, along with the privileges of those given the identity credentials to operate effectively within them, were legitimated within a cosmology that naturalized this ordering of places. In this context, Galileo's "scientific discovery" had an important impact on policy, for as Foucault notes, the "real scandal" was Galileo's creation of "an infinite and infinitely open space,"[37] which had the effect of desanctifying the medieval arrangement. After tracing the creation of various spaces after the breakup of the medieval cosmology in which new individual differences are created and administratively handled in new types of locations (the development of "heterotopias" or places outside of the normal and regular social spaces), Foucault turns to an analysis of modernity. The modern age is characterized, he suggests, by the production of "heterotopias of deviation" — the rest home, psychiatric hospital, prison, and the like, and he wonders about the price for containing the possibilities of the self within an administration of space that proliferates such heterotopias.

Evoking the theme connected with Galileo's contribution to the opening of the space of the medieval period, Foucault romanticizes the ship as the heterotopia that is the "greatest reserve of the imagination," because it moves between and beyond rather than within modes of confinement constituted by modernity's tightly administered "heterotopias of deviation." Shipping, according to Foucault, is a kind of identity commerce that is being lost, and he offers a lament that evokes images of Ulysses' travels: "In civilizations without boats, dreams dry up, espionage takes the place of adventure, and the police take the place of pirates."[38]

Ulysses and the Sirens: A Genealogical Gloss

For the genealogist, the prevailing social noises with meaning are not to be evaluated on the basis of their truth value—the extent to which they faithfully describe objects or anticipate events. The discursive practices of a society are not to be understood as a series of relatively accurate or inaccurate, coherent or incoherent assertions about something, but as a historically produced economy of meaning and value. Statements have a currency insofar as they enable kinds of persons to act and allow various patterns of life to emerge. The domain of the nondiscursive is not the field of objects or referents of statements, but the domain of the possible, all of the life forces, possible human identities and activities, that are silenced in the prescribed system of volubility and intelligibility.

A given institutional arrangement, for genealogists, is thus an outcome based on differential force. To translate this into a specific historical example, the codes through which institutions in modern nation-states constitute persons, actions, and events are the codes supporting the activities and interests of land-tenure-oriented groups. In most cases, these codes have prevailed over alternative ones expressing ways of life of formerly nomadic peoples, whose present, marginalized material status is reflected in the failure of their meaning and value systems to achieve articulation in official, policy-relevant discourse. In this respect, then, modern institutions administer zones of silence.

Operating within this kind of understanding of the history of modernity's audible codes, Nietzsche made frequent reference both to noise, an image he used to characterize official talk—the talk of the state that masquerades as if it describes reality rather than its own inventions—and to silence. Seeing the institutionalized system of official utterances as an arbitrary imposition of meaning and value, Nietzsche privileged silence over noise, because noise represented for him the sounds of old reactive values promoted in the talk of the state. Silence is a counterpoise to the noisiness of reactive values; it is the vehicle of new values. Thus Zarathustra, conversing with the "fire hound," one of the earthly diseases, chides him for his noisiness:

> "Believe me friend Hellishnoise: the greatest events — they are not our loudest but our stillest hours. Not around the inventions of new noise, but around the inventions of new values does the world revolve; it revolves inaudibly."[39]

Nietzsche left no doubt that his disparagement of noise was aimed at the official discourse, the talk of the state, when later in the conversation Zarathustra responds to a query about the church, telling the fire hound that it is "a kind of state — a most mendacious kind." Zarathustra goes on, "But be still, you hypocritical hound! You know your own kind best! Like you, the state is a hypocritical hound; like you, it likes to talk with smoke and bellowing — to make himself believe like you, that he is talking out of the belly of reality."[40]

Complementing his treatment of noise is Nietzsche's allegorical use of the ear, the receptor of the noise. Characters who are disparaged in Zarathustra have long or large ears and are thus open and receptive to state talk. He represents the state as a "new idol" operating in an era heralding the death of "peoples." The state "coldly . . . tells lies," such as "I, the state, am the people,"[41] and those most receptive to the lies are "the long eared and shortsighted."[42] And in one of his most powerful pieces of imagery, Nietzsche introduces the "inverted cripples — human beings who are nothing but a big eye or a big mouth or a big belly or anything at all that is big."[43] The creature with the big ear is dramatically presented as Zarathustra comes upon it:

> And when I came out of my solitude and crossed over the bridge for the first time I did not trust my eyes and looked and looked again, and said at last, "An ear! An ear as big as a man!" I looked still more closely — and indeed, underneath the ear something was moving, something pitifully small and wretched and slender. And no doubt of it, the tremendous ear was attached to a small, thin stalk — but this stalk was a human being![44]

Insofar as we are unreflective subjects of state talk, then, we are all ears to the official discourse. Accordingly, to be a free person, a self that resists being subjected, you have to be either deaf to such talk or, as Derrida has put it in his meditation on Nietzsche's ear imagery, have "finely tuned ears" instead of opening "wide the portals of your ears to admit the state."[45]

It is ear/noise/hearing imagery and the kind of connection it has with official talk that animates Kafka's dramatic reversals in his brief story/ commentary on the Sirens episode of the *Odyssey*. Kafka's Ulysses puts the wax in *his* ears and has himself bound to the mast of his ship. And the Sirens are silent.

> To protect himself from the Sirens Ulysses stopped his ears with wax and had himself bound to the mast of the ship. Naturally any and every traveler before him could have done the same, except those whom the Sirens allured even from a great distance; but it was known to all the world that such things were of no help whatsoever. The song of the Sirens could pierce through everything, and the longing of those they seduced would have broken far stronger bonds than chains and masts. But Ulysses did not think of that, although he probably heard of it. He trusted absolutely to his handful of wax and his fathom of chain, and in innocent elation over his little stratagem sailed out to meet the Sirens.[46]

Like Elster, Kafka evokes the concept of strategy here, but in this case it is not done in pursuit of a pedagogy about rational decision making. Kafka's world is not one in which values are isolated moments or holdings in the consciousness of individuals who to the extent that they have power have the ability to achieve them and to the extent they are rational can organize episodes of their behavior over time to avoid letting desire foul up their goal-directed planning. Rather, Kafka sides with the genealogists in that he sees ordinary consciousness as a burden that subjugates instead of as an instrument of rational planning (hence the piercing of the Siren's song, assisted by conscious imaginings that amplify it!). And Kafka sides with genealogists stylistically as well as conceptually. First, he reads the order as a series of inscribed texts—power/authority writing on the body (the "penal colony")—and second, his analytic takes the form of *writing,* of subverting the "process" of inscription by exposing its mechanisms as scriptural practice rather than natural order with an insurrectional style of writing, such as stories whose vehicles are impertinent metaphors, which have the effect of challenging ordinary notions of pertinence (e.g., "The Burrow").

Kafka's stories are often aimed at casting suspicion on the functioning of ordinary consciousness, to demonstrate the radical ambiguity as to whether consciousness is a defense against meaning and value imposed from the outside or rather its unwitting ally, whether it is a mechanism for simply reinforcing a system of meaning. Interpretation of the "outside," which ordinarily is one's mode of rationally planning and organizing, founders on the dilemma of not knowing what is intelligible in itself and what is made intelligible by the very act of interpretation.

In Kafka's "Silence of the Sirens," the encounter with this radical ambiguity—the difficulty of discerning whether one is merely susceptible to summonses from the "outside" or whether one simply creates or recreates that summons with one's consciousness—is central. Insofar as consciousness is an ally of the outside forces imposing a system of intelligibility, even silence from without is powerful (perhaps more powerful than noise). As Kafka puts it, "Now the Sirens have a still more fatal weapon than their song, namely their silence."[47]

As the brief story continues, it becomes ambiguous as to whether Ulysses has lent his consciousness to outside forces, for he fails even to hear their silence:

> Ulysses, if one may so express it, did not hear their silence; he thought that they were singing and that he alone did not hear them. For a fleeting moment he saw their throats rising and falling, their breasts lifting, their eyes filled with tears, their lips half-parted, but believed that these were accompaniments to the airs which died unheard around him.[48]

But their silence fails to overcome him, for he manages to seize control by fixing his gaze on the distance (the next part of the narrative in which he is caught).

> Soon, however, all this faded from sight as he fixed his gaze on the distance, the Sirens literally vanished before his resolution, and at the very moment when they were nearest to him he knew of them no longer.[49]

Has Ulysses escaped by being distracted by thoughts of his mission? It seems to have been cunning rather than inattention, for Kafka adds a codicil:

> A codicil to the foregoing has been handed down. Ulysses, it is said, was so full of guile, was such a fox, that not even the goddess of fate could pierce his armor. Perhaps he had really noticed, although here the human understanding is beyond its depths, that the Sirens were silent, and held up to them and to the gods the aforementioned pretense as a sort of shield.[50]

Ulysses proves to be wily after all. He breaks out of the noise/silence circuit by resorting to fiction. He, like Kafka, is a writer, one engaged in imaginative enactments that provide an escape route, taking him outside and beyond the threats of capture by either the noise or the silence—outside of both the audible systems of intelligibility and the reproductions of them staged by subservient forms of consciousness. Ulysses thus ends this brief story as a representative of Kafka himself.

For Kafka, writing was indeed a form of duplicity and an avenue of escape. He saw the writer as one always caught in a struggle to resist the articulations that come from outside. Kafka carried on his struggle metaphorically, resisting both noise and its interpretive allies through a figuration nested in his seemingly simple stories. The stories and novels evoke, not a simple juxtaposition of freedom versus entrapment, but the need to find routes in and out of the maze of vociferations that represent society's meaning system.[51] Kafka the writer places himself in the kind of place in which he locates the characters and creatures in his stories, in the margins of the social world. In accord with this kind of writing problematic, how the writer is situated vis-à-vis other voices, his "Josephine the Singer" is exemplary because she occupies an ambiguous position with respect to the normal noises of her society. Everyone "pipes," and it is difficult to tell if Josephine's singing, which is acknowledged as somehow (but not clearly how) a contribution, is different from the ordinary piping that everyone does all the time. In any case, Kafka's piping imagery is an appropriate way to conclude the critique of the rationalistic mode of reading/writing, a mode of analysis unaware of whose noises are being passed on, a mode that is mere piping:

> Is it in fact singing at all? Although we are unmusical we have a tradition of singing; in the old days our people did sing; this is mentioned in legends and some songs have actually survived, which, it is true, no one can now sing. Thus we have an inkling of what singing is, and Josephine's art does not really correspond to it. So is it singing at all? Is it perhaps just a piping? And piping is something we all know about, it is the real artistic accomplishment of our people, or rather no mere accomplishment but a characteristic expression of life. We all pipe, but of course no one dreams of making out that our piping is an art, we pipe without thinking of it, indeed without noticing it, and there are even those among us who are quite unaware that piping is one of our characteristics.[52]

CHAPTER 3

Weighing Anchor
Postmodern Journeys from
the Life-World

The Terms of the Debate

For some time, the debates over the politics of postmodernism have tended
to be debates over the way to treat representation. The more conservative
postmodernists, reacting against radical modernist styles, have preached a
return to "representation," which they understand as a close connection between what "is" and the way of expressing it. The more radical forms of
postmodernism, such as the poststructuralist version, have advocated a different view. Critical of an exclusive emphasis on an epistemological, truth-
falsity axis for treating representations, they have focused on the domains of
power and authority with which various modes of representation are complicit.[1]

This latter focus, central to the contributions of the more radical forms of
postmodernism to political insight, cannot be articulated within traditional
epistemological discourses. Even the more recent epistemological positions
developed by critical theorists, who have abandoned correspondence theories of truth in favor of more dialectical or conversational models, fail to
come to terms with the political impetus of this kind of postmodernism. For
example, reading Lyotard's influential treatise on postmodernism, Seyla
Benhabib, in a charge characteristic of the critical theorist's reaction to radical postmodernism, asserts that he conflates power and validity.[2]

Central to Benhabib's reading is her attack on Lyotard's position that language moves are power moves. However, her treatment of "language
moves" constructs discourse as primarily a face-to-face, conversational exchange of intentionally controlled meanings. For example, she refers to the
effects a speaker "wants to generate."[3] Because she treats language as conversational communication, she infers that Lyotard is equating the persua-

sive effects of a statement (what Austin calls the perlocutionary level of meaning) with the illocutionary or meaning force of the statement, the speech act or what is done *in* saying something.[4]

But Lyotard recognizes, as indeed Austin did, that what gives a statement its force is not its psychological correlates but the institutional context in which it is uttered. Like other postmodernist thinkers, Lyotard recognizes that statements are situated in structured interpersonal relations. The power and authority resident in statutes, boundaries, spatial allocations, and sociocultural norms in all modes regulate their circulation and contextualize their meaning and value. At present, therefore, their use value cannot be separated from the power configurations that characterize modernity. Moreover, because meanings exceed what speakers may want to do with statements, persuasion is as much a function of who is speaking and under what circumstances as it is of whatever personally motivated markers may exist in the statement.

Intelligible exchanges are always situated. This claim is much more than the banal assertion that there are rules for language use which are dependent on the immediate context of the utterance, for the context-meaning relation subsumes a complex history of struggle in which one or more ways of establishing contexts and their related utterances has vanquished other competing possibilities. Therefore, to erect the conversational genre as the context in which to apprehend the postmodernist treatment of discourse is to create a dehistoricized frame that cannot adequately encode the politics of postmodernist analyses, which depend in part on an appreciation of the trace of losses associated with the victories of given, institutionalized systems of intelligibility. Thus an appreciation of the politics of postmodernism comes with attention to the politics of linguistic forms, to their historical depth and the economies within which they have displaced competitors rather than to their intentional or more immediate strategic usage.

The Politics of Linguistic Forms

There is a tension between participation in a collectivity and analyzing it, between the linguistic competence one needs to join in intelligible conversations and the linguistic resources one needs to create discursive practices productive of political insight. In everyday life this tension tends to be suppressed because the achieving or exercising of a competence in the dominant social forms of intelligibility is a major social problematic. In the case of children or others in marginal positions (e.g., recent immigrants), the phenomenology of everyday life is organized around showing one's eligibility for full participation within the institutionalized forms of intelligibility. The objects and events that dominate their mental lives are produced within the motivated conceptual space of seeking full membership. Even those with full-fledged social credentials often remain in a membership-oriented praxis because negotiating one's way through a complicated public space requires an energetic exercise of acquired interpretive and conversational skills.

To the extent that a culture is well articulated, that mutual expectations are readily discernible, and that people's situations and tasks are represented unambiguously, the tensions associated with resistant, insurrectional, or merely questioning modes of interpretation remain suppressed. There are few day-to-day occasions in which the tensions are revealed, for most linguistic genres, whether presentational or interactive in form, are merely communication oriented; they emphasize joint task achievement rather than rendering problematic the society's systems of meaning and value. And, thanks to Gramsci, we can appreciate that even though the dominant ("hegemonic") systems of intelligibility are disadvantageous to many, they usually fail to produce or master resistant discursive assets and thus end up treating as natural discursive frames in which their oppression is legitimated.

This issue of the extent to which a given discourse is resistant or complicit with the predominant forms of intelligibility (and their distributive effects) bears on the various discourses of intellectual inquiry as much as on those of everyday life. For present purposes, it is useful to distinguish the interpretive practices of those who aim their inquiries primarily at ongoing sociopolitical conversations and those who seek to make such conversations problematic. Like the choices involved in everyday life, one can seek participation in an extant conversation or produce a mode of analysis resistant to it.

The Problem of Conversation

In the midst of a discussion about poststructuralism, Michel Foucault's interviewer from the journal *Telos* evoked the concept of "post-modernity." In response Foucault remarked, "What are we calling post-modernity? I'm not up to date."[5] To grasp the ironic turn of Foucault's remark we must recognize its different levels. At one level, it is a remark about himself. He seems to be saying that because he is not au courant, he is unprepared to discuss the issue. Seizing on this simple level, his interviewer produced a long soliloquy on the concept of postmodernity. At another level, however, the remark is not an observation about personal knowledge but a more general, epistemological point. Foucault can be read as saying that "we," those of us situated in this historical period, cannot understand our age if we remain within contemporary conversations.

Foucault's playful response is therefore more than merely dismissive. It becomes significant and theoretically provocative when considered in the context of the different genres in which he expressed himself in his last years. On the one hand, there were his writings, historical analyses that both situate and defamiliarize, or make remarkable, contemporary conversations. These investigations were aimed not at deepening contemporary forms of intelligibility but at imperiling or at least ambiguating them. On the other, there were his public conversations, the increasingly frequent interviews on his work and its relationship to contemporary intellectual/ political positions. In these he was being called upon to contribute to *an* understanding, to build a conversational bridge between the depth politics of his genealogical work, which imperils intelligibility, and an already-practiced form of intelligibility.

Foucault's remark thus has the effect of announcing that there is an ironic dimension to such interviews. Since his work is, among other things, a concerted effort to distance us from contemporary conversations, its logic cannot be elaborated easily in a conversational mode. Because the conversational mode necessarily treats the present situation as a shared and unproblematic background, which facilitates conversation, rather than as part of the problem for investigation, demands that Foucault enter such conversations were effectively demands that he stand still and momentarily inhibit his continually restless penchant for inquiry.

Foucault's unusual perspective on the conversation is addressed obliquely in several of his well-known historical works, but it achieves optimal lucidity in a brief and rarely noted essay on the origin of contemporary preoccupations with "criminal danger."[6] There his initial object of analysis was a 1975 conversation in a Paris criminal court, the interrogation of a defendant accused of several rapes and attempted rapes. When questioned by the presiding judge—"Have you tried to reflect upon your case?"; "Why at twenty-two do such violent urges overtake you?"; "Why would you do it again?"; and so on—the accused remained silent, and his silence impeded a judicial process, which in the modern period registers its interest in "the criminal" by asking the accused to elaborate his or her self-understanding. Summarizing the import of the judge's question as "Who are you?," Foucault pointed out that this kind of question, which is perfectly intelligible and appropriate in modern tribunals, "would have a strange ring to it 150 years ago."[7]

Prior to the nineteenth century, criminal law paid attention only to the offense and the penalty, while the contemporary juridical gaze peers through the crime, which has become "but a shadow hovering about the criminal, a shadow which must be drawn aside in order to reveal the only thing which is now of importance, the criminal."[8] In showing, with this exemplary conversation, that legal justice today is focused more on crimi-

nals than on crimes, Foucault is distancing us from the conversation in order
to show that what we have come to regard as perfectly normal and intelligible is remarkable, for it is the product of some fairly recent and dramatic
historical changes. Taking us back to the early nineteenth century, he elaborates some stages in "the psychiatrization of criminal danger," which created and legitimated "discussions between doctors and jurists." This brief
account shows that this new field of "knowledge of criminals" was correlated with other developments, for example, "the intensive development of
the police networks, which led to a new mapping and closer surveillance of
urban space and also to a much more systematized and efficient prosecution
of minor delinquency.[9]

Without looking closely at aspects of the political context of crime,
which Foucault's analysis helps to disclose, it is already evident that his analysis situates the courtroom conversation in a highly politicized field of
power relations and, further, that such a field is not easily recoverable
within the confines of contemporary conversations. Becoming involved *in*
the conversation would make it difficult to resist being drawn into the issue
bothering the court during this 1975 case, whether it would be appropriate
to invoke the death penalty without a more elaborate understanding of the
accused. But Foucault's approach to conversations counsels resistance to being drawn into the problematic governing communicative interaction. Instead it makes remarkable the conversation as a whole, allowing one
thereby to perceive the emerging power and authority configurations that
the identities of the conversation partners represent. It becomes evident that
insofar as one remains within the conversation in the courtroom, it is difficult not to accept the policy terrain already implicated in the intersection of
psychiatric and penal discourses and to be led to ponder the proprieties of
the issue of capital punishment. Encouraged, under the direction of Foucault's brief genealogy of criminal danger, to resituate the conversation
within the more politicized space of modernity's novel approach to crime
and the correlation of that approach with emerging structures of power and
authority, one encounters a range of political insights unavailable within the
confines of contemporary conversations.

The Hermeneutic Anchor

Foucault's treatment of conversations, the strategic distance he maintains
from them, represents a fundamental rift between his mode of analysis and
that which is generally referred to as hermeneutic. Whereas those involved
in a hermeneutic approach, for example, various contemporary ethnographic investigators, seek to deepen understanding or mutual intelligibility, a Foucauldian analysis destabilizes interpretations and understandings,

disclosing the economies within which they operate. For every understanding or field of consciousness achieved there is, as Foucault puts it, a positive unconscious, a silence positively administered.

In figuring the process of understanding as a kind of conversation, a hermeneutic approach is aimed at reaching understanding (conversational agreement) between the self-understanding or ground of the investigator and the self-understanding of the society or polity under investigation. By contrast, the Nietzsche-inspired genealogical (as well as the deconstructive) mode of analysis opens gaps by disclosing a kind of delusion that those with faith in the process of conversation manifest. The deconstructive contribution to disclosing this delusion is, of course, best exemplified in Jacques Derrida's attacks on "phonocentrism," the thought, encouraged by seeing ourselves as involved *in* conversations, that the meanings conveyed are wholly present to the speaker. As he put it in one of his earliest works:

> The subject can hear or speak to himself and be affected by the signifier he produces without passing through an external detour, the world, the sphere of what is not "his own."[10]

Much of Derrida's subsequent philosophical work is dedicated to demonstrating the delusion of the ownership of the meaning of one's utterances. Meaning, according to Derrida, is controlled instead by a prescripted structure of signification, which precedes individual speakers or writers. For example, in an exemplary deconstructive reading, he shows that the linguist Emile Benvenist's inquiry into whether thought and language can be regarded as distinct is already determined by the inherited philosophical vocabulary within which he has represented the issue. His unreflective acceptance of the notion of the "category" had amounted to the acceptance of a linguistic frame that already holds thought and language to be distinct.[11]

The strategy involved in a Foucauldian genealogy treats the same delusion of control over meaning within conversations but from a different, less purely linguistic perspective. Foucault's emphasis on spatiality or domains of practice has had the effect of denaturalizing the arenas within which conversations take place. For example, by showing how prisons were invented as part of a series of strategic knowledge practices committed to a surveillant form of normalizing power, he indicates that such modern domains are, in effect, protoconversations that already determine the power relations within which subsequent conversations take place.

However, there is an additional, politicizing move involved in a Foucauldian genealogy. Foucault's genealogical disclosure of such protoconversations is supplemented with an impertinent textuality. In addition to the historicizing move that denaturalizes the practiced domains of modernity, there is a stylistic move that recodes and thereby reframes present arrangements. For example, while he represents the present as a stage in the process of increased surveillance, he expands the notion of incarceration to include such "services" as social work, education, caring, and curing as part of the "carceral apparatus."[12] This recoding takes what has been understood as an unproblematic set of benign practices and locates them in a more political frame within which they can be seen as contention forms of social control.

Although the genealogical approach to the conversation is distancing in comparison with the hermeneutic approach, which generally seeks to improve conversations, hermeneutics has had its distancing effects. While its orientation to interpretation is primarily aimed at deepening intelligibility and closing the distance between disparate self-understandings, much of its initial impetus stemmed from attempts to gain a critical distance from traditional, empiricist concepts of knowledge.

It should be recalled that a founding gesture of the hermeneutic tradition, as it is represented by Hans-Georg Gadamer, is an attempt to distance us from a history of social thinking based on epistemology.[13] A major dimension of Gadamer's contribution to social theory is a dramatic shift from the problem of knowledge, on which explanatory social science is predicated, to the problem of understanding, which supports interpretive analyses. While the epistemological tradition constructs knowledge as a problem of method for allowing subjects to attain truth about the natural or social world of objects and relations, Gadamer's focus is on the situating of subjects in a background of practices—scientific, artistic, legal, and so forth— that express fundamental aspects of human identities and can only be discerned through reflection. Such reflection is engendered through events, through concrete attempts to become familiar with what is initially unfamiliar. These episodes of understanding have the effect of enriching people's conversations about themselves as much as they create broader spheres of mutual intelligibility.

It is here that genealogists depart markedly from hermeneuticists. Most significant in the comparison are the different models of subjectivity the two approaches entertain. To achieve "mutual intelligibility" from the point of view of the inquiring subject (e.g., an ethnographer), one must assume that both subjects are unitary and coherent selves. Sophisticated ethnographers like Clifford Geertz have recognized that the self-understanding of the ethnographer can change as a result of a confrontation with an exotic other, but for Geertz, that change results in a better self-interpretation. Thus, for example, Geertz's analysis of the nineteenth-century Balinese state, the Negara, is aimed not simply at showing how cultural systems dominate political relations *there* but more generally at showing how any polity is misunderstood by those who are overly "impressed with command" and thus neglect various cultural systems involved with symbolic exchange.[14]

The dialogic element of Geertz's argument is a tacit conversation with both Marxist and liberal-capitalist modes of political interpretation, both of which, according to Geertz, fail to appreciate the "design" of the cultures within which power and authority function.[15]

Adequacy of understanding is ultimately the guiding aim of Geertz's investigations, and the frame within which he functions is paradigmatically hermeneutic; he sees himself overcoming a poverty of meaning in political understandings that has arisen from a neglect of the cultural context or whole within which acts and institutions are assessed.

Foucault, by contrast, is not after adequacy, especially since he refuses the idea of the stable subjectivity necessary to anchor understandings. Subjectivity is not a basis from which and for which interpretation is to be achieved. It is not a not–yet–self–sufficient entity in need of more self–understanding. Rather, subjectivities are arbitrary, unstable interpretations. If at any moment a model of the self is enjoying a measure of institutionalized acceptance and general recognition, this is the result of some self–making forces enjoying a temporary victory.

Accordingly, Foucault's genealogical analyses are aimed at overcoming any pretense that given views of the self are timeless, universal, or natural.

> Where the soul pretends unification or the self fabricates a coherent identity,
> the genealogist sets out to study the beginning—numberless beginnings
> whose faint traces and hints of color are easily seen by an historical eye.[16]

By revealing the events surrounding the fragile victories of various modes of subjectivity, a Foucauldian genealogy discloses the interpretive economy within which there emerges the production and maintenance of various versions of the subject. This opens the way to a political analysis of the consequences of the victories of those interpretations and their correlative structures that constitute and dominate various fields of knowledge.

Within such a historically sensitive, politicized understanding, it becomes possible to point out, for example, that the production of the juridical subject—the person with rights—is not simply a culmination of an inevitable developmental sequence but is as much a modern form of subjugation (a temporary fixing of a form of self–producing interpretation) as it is a desubjugating or liberating development.[17]

Therefore, whereas hermeneutically oriented ethnographic investigators, influenced by the phenomenological privileging of subjectivity, try to disclose more abiding and stable modes of subjectivity by confronting one manifestation that is familiar with one that is exotic, the genealogist takes a familiar interpretation and confronts it with another interpretation from a different historical period. This has the effect of rereading the present forms of subjectivity in a way that denaturalizes them and produces, thereby, a distancing or, in Foucault's terms, a "dissociating view . . . capable of . . . shattering the unity of man's being."[18]

Foucault is not, like a hermeneutic ethnographer, seeking a frame of analysis that shows how the behavior of various actors can be recovered if we know their cultures or background fields of meaning and use a more informed view of culture. To interpret, according to Foucault, is to unreflectingly accept the "rarity" of sets of statements; it is to seek to find their underlying meaning rather than to undertake a more politicized inquiry into the discursive economies they represent. Accordingly, Foucault has sought not to improve extant political conversations by making them more comprehensive, but to distance us from the various linguistic practices that give us objects, subjects, *and* the more general valuing practices within which they function, the discursive economies of meaning and value in given historical periods.

Nevertheless, despite the antihermeneutic impetus in genealogical analyses, they are stabilized by a number of hermeneutic anchors. One of the main ones in Foucault's investigations is a political orientation. He is an incessant politicizer; he wants to insinuate his analyses into conversations about politics and power. This much is clear from the very fact that Foucault is intelligible. While his analyses depart in many ways from ordinary discursive modes and thus create discomfort with the prevailing fields of analysis, they still communicate; they engage at least part of the ways of thinking/speaking already in circulation. He has stated quite explicitly that in the modern age, there has been a failure to incorporate the workings of power into the predominant political discourse because of a neglect of the normalizing power of disciplinary agencies and systems of "knowledge." What is not encoded in contemporary political talk is the way that modernity has experienced a structure of domination elaborated through the various mechanisms of power. These mechanisms are not to be understood as things operating from a distance in the control of the willed forces of individuals. Power is incorporated into individual and collective identities such as the "criminal" or the "population"; it functions through what is "known" about people.

Foucault's main hermeneutic anchor is therefore his commitment to an ongoing discussion of politics and power. In arguing that the terms of the discussion have been disabling, he lines himself up with others, like Geertz, who are also trying to improve our political conversation. Foucault's hermeneutic anchor is tossed out explicitly in several places, but one general characterization he has offered should suffice for purposes of this discussion.

> The question I asked myself was this: how is it that the human subject
> took itself as an object of possible knowledge? Through what forms of
> rationality and historical conditions? And finally at what price? This is my
> question: at what price can subjects speak the truth about themselves?[19]

Insofar as the statement is primarily a description of the genealogical mode of analysis, Foucault's treatment of knowledge as a power-related practice puts pressure on customary discursive distinctions. But the "at what price" portion of the remark invokes the hermeneutic dimension of Foucault's project. It is an encouragement to recalculate the economies of the exercise of power within this altered way of representing the locus of power.

The genealogical and hermeneutic strategies thus work together. First, against naturalizing views of the intrinsic value of things, genealogy reveals the process by which humans invest the world with value as part of the process through which meanings are produced. But, second, once a world of significance is formed and continuously reproduced within the use of such established systems of meaning, one can ask value questions *about* it, and this kind of question *about* value is a hermeneutically not a genealogically inspired kind of question. Within the hermeneutics of value questions, Foucault is asking about the political costs of a disciplinary society in which that discipline, which is a form of power, is disguised within depoliticizing forms of discourse. He is issuing an invitation to weigh the costs of this modern, masked form of power that represents itself as something else.

The genealogical part of his analysis is taken up with a figuration—the politics of the body—designed to overturn more pacifying rhetorics and disclose the events surrounding meaning production. However, it operates within an already achieved system of meaning that makes intelligible the price moderns pay for this system. What does it cost, he is saying, to be dominated and subjugated in the names of healing, curing, nurturing, and educating?

An appreciation of how the different modes of analysis, the hermeneutic and radical forms of postmodernism, position themselves in relation to problems of intelligibility, makes it possible to locate the different aspects of politics to which they are addressed. Certainly there is a readily available "politics" in every society, the politics that exist in what are recognized as political conversations and are part of the reigning system of intelligibility. And any mode of social analysis tries to connect the intelligibility of these aspects of politics to a more distanced view, to connect, as it were, the life-world to a less hectic conceptual world of analysis. The politics of the life-world contains recognized forms of partisanship, cleavages that can threaten social solidarity but that are, for the most part, constitutive of that solidarity.

With this as background, a hermeneutically oriented politics emerges as a politics of reconciliation. Richard Rorty, for example, tends to endorse the hermeneutic view, using the conversation as his justification for moving away from the epistemological tradition. And Rorty wants an engaged hermeneutics, one that helps to resolve extant forms of partisanship, one that makes a connection with "the daily problems of one's community," that "enhances communication and harmonious solidarity."[20] He chides Foucault for maintaining his distance from existing forms of partisanship, referring to his as a stoic:

> It takes no more than a squint of the inner eye to read Foucault as a stoic, a dispassionate observer of the present social order, rather than a concerned critic.[21]

He goes on to complain of Foucault's "dryness," which he sees as produced by a "lack of identification with any social context, any communication." Rorty also complains that Foucault affects to write "from a point of view light-years away from the problems of contemporary society."[22] Finally, he states that there is no "we" to be found in Foucault's writings, nor in those of many of his French contemporaries.[23]

The View from Offshore

There are several misapprehensions in Rorty's plaints against Foucault, each of which joins with issues others (e.g., Habermas and Lyotard) have raised in debates over the politics of postmodernism. To begin with, Rorty is insensitive to the politics of radical postmodernism's grammar. He is indeed on to something when he looks unsuccessfully for a familiar "we" in the writings of Foucault and "in those of his French contemporaries," for what radical postmodernists are doing in questioning the familiar theoretical constructions of the life-world that fail to situate actors in contentious terrains of meaning. Like Habermas, Rorty sees the life-world as a set of conversations about contemporary problems, and also like Habermas, Rorty cannot see the relevance to social criticism of thinkers who challenge the grounds of those conversations rather than entering them within the terms of the contemporary debates.[24]

While Rorty (and Habermas) emphasize one aspect of language, communication, and one aspect of a social formation, the shared background of practices that support conversations, Foucault and others emphasize the discursive economies of language, its effects in constituting privileged actors and locations for the exercise of control over meaning and value. And rather than seeing the life-world as a relatively uncontentious sphere within which "problems" are approached, they see it as a potentially contentious domain of *problematization*. The grammar here is significant, for Foucault shows how a particular range of recognized social problems, those that have achieved recognition within dominant modes of policy discourse, is only one set or kind of problem among a vast variety of possibilities. It is one thing, for example, to ask what is the appropriate policy with which to respond to "crime" and "sexual deviance," and another to show how contemporary modes for problematizing crime and sexual deviance are peculiar when seen in a particular kind of historical context.

The life-world in which Rorty and Habermas valorize communicative competence and solidarity is quite different in Foucault's construction of it. For Foucault, it is a pattern of volubilities and silences, of problems about which some communicate and nonproblems, alternative possible modes of problematization. Moreover, what constitutes competence—knowledge, expertise, eligibility—is a product of the way a given social formation in a given age carves up its spaces. To go back to the example introduced above, psychiatric discourse has juridically relevant meaning *now;* it helps to constitute knowledge of "criminals" in the present age because of the way in which modernity problematizes crime. It is therefore politically vacuous to speak about an intersubjectivity as the ground of communication without situating subjects in the distribution of spaces—professional, delinquent, administrative, marginal, and so on—that direct the meaning, value, and authority of their utterances.

This sheds a different light on the problem of the "we." We, in radical postmodernist terms, are not all the same. The meaning of an utterance is not controlled by the intentions of the speaker. Rorty, in his emphasis on conversations among nonsituated speakers, appears to adopt, with Habermas, a grammar of subjectivity in which subjects intentionally produce meanings. Despite his attempts to transcend a subject-centered version of reason by resort to the idea of communicative action, which presupposes an intersubjective meaning context, Habermas' grammar remains relentlessly subjectivist. Even his recent call for a "paradigm of mutual understanding" is constructed with an intentionalist rendering of the subject-meaning relationship.[25] But Austin's speech act theory, heavily relied on by Habermas, does not lend itself to an intentionalist, communication-oriented gloss. While Habermas speaks of communicating actors who "pursue illocutionary aims,"[26] what gives an utterance an illocutionary emphasis is not the intention of the speaker but (as pointed out above) the context of the utterance. An utterance for Austin becomes illocutionary as a result of the rule-governed context in which it is made. Although Austin never got around to historicizing those "rules" and problematizing or making contentious those contexts, his approach to language does not license an intentionalist grammar of subjectivity. That grammar, as it emerges in the analyses of postmodernists, is further radicalized to construe subjectivity as a historically specific practice, as something epiphenomenal to meanings, not as a function of the intentional actions of subjects.

There is indeed a "we" in Foucault's approach, which assumes that meanings make subjects. It is not a unitary, univocal we but a fragile series of produced we's that are resident in the institutionalized forms of utterance, and hovering in the background are alternative possible we's. The politics of

Foucauldian grammar thus rests on a Nietzschean way of posing questions about subjectivity; the question is never "who" but "which one," which of the multitude of possible selves is being brought into recognition by a particular institutionalized form of intelligibility and the practices it encompasses.

Rorty is also on to something when he notes that Foucault is operating from "a point of view light-years away from the problems of contemporary society."[27] Distance is indeed what Foucault's analyses achieve. In disclosing the present as remarkable, as a peculiar set of practices for problematizing some things and naturalizing others, for allowing some things into discourse and silencing others, Foucault provides a critical distance from it. He turns current "truths" into power-related practices by situating them in relation to alternative past practices and tracing the correlated economies of their emergence.[28]

This is not, moreover, the dispassionate observation of a stoic but a textual practice oriented by a commitment to freedom, a freedom that is not the traditional, liberal individualist model of minimizing the domain of controlled public space but the freedom that allows one to see the possibility of change. Foucault argues that "by following the lines of fragility in the present—in managing to grasp why and how that-which-is might no longer be that-which-is," it is possible to "open up the space of freedom understood as a space of concrete freedom, i.e. of possible transformation."[29]

In short, Foucault's analyses politicizes what passes for the uncontentious; they operate outside the politics resident in contemporary conversations in a frame that makes them peculiar. In so doing the writing does not consort with the distribution of conversations locked within the all-too-familiar present set of recognized problems.

> The problem is not so much that of defining a political "position" (which is to choose from a pre-existing set of possibilities) but to imagine and to bring into being new schemas of politicization.[30]

Conclusion: Weighing Anchor

It was suggested that Foucault operates from a position offshore, that he was anchored in a strategic position that gave him distance but at the same time a strategic view of modernity's present. It is now time to weigh anchor and sail to another distancing location, to Robinson Crusoe's island, which will allow for an exemplary demythologizing that will articulate with the political impetus of postmodernist analysis. The focus here is on Michel Tournier's version of the Crusoe myth, a version that makes Friday one who chooses to subvert rather than aid and abet Robinson Crusoe's rationalization of the island terrain within the understandings afforded by political economy.

At its origin, myth is designed to legitimate an order by either rationalizing the origin of its construction or providing a view that naturalizes it. Subsequent retellings or commentaries also tend to have a legitimating function, for they are retellings complicit with the various discursive procedures through which prevailing structures of power and authority are implemented.[31] However, some "work on myth" is demythologizing, putting pressure on institutionalized sources of authority and value rather than encouraging allegiance to them. Such is Tournier's, which seems to operate within the postmodernist assumption that much of the thinking under the rubric of "political economy" has mythological rather than foundational legitimacy.[32]

Recent analysis is convincing on the issue of the mythologizing impetus of Defoe's original treatment. Rather than creating distance from the dominant conversations of his age, Defoe was valorizing them. His Robinson Crusoe is at a distance only geographically, for he reproduces and rationalizes the political/economic practices of his age. Despite the popular assumption that the original Robinson Crusoe was designed to celebrate a concept of a nature free of the busy commercial behavior of England, Defoe identified the domain of commerce *as* natural: "Nothing follows the course of Nature more than trade. There Causes and Consequences follow as directly as day and night."[33] And there is little doubt as to what model of trade Defoe's story is meant to exemplify. As one critical reader has pointed out:

> Defoe's hero—unlike most of us—has been endowed with the basic
> necessities for the successful exercise of free enterprise. He is not actually a
> primitive or a proletarian or even a professional man, but a capitalist. He
> owns freehold, an estate which is rich but unimproved. It is not a desert
> island in the geographical sense—it is merely barren of owners or
> competitors.[34]

As is well known, many subsequent commentaries on Robinson Crusoe enlist the story as material for the historical conversation about alternative models of political economy. The classical political economists simply explicate their systems through Crusoe, while, of course, Marx uses him in his critique of these political economists to attack the mystifications involved in their theorizing of the commodity. For Marx, Robinson Crusoe was a exemplar of clarity, the meeting of a man and his labor capacity with a nature filled with abundance. The result is the unambiguous transformation of nature into need-satisfying goods, "useful objects for himself alone."[35]

Marx's approach to value remains very much within the classical tradition, and, as Foucault has noted, despite Marx's opposition to bourgeois theories of economics, the struggle with the political economists takes place within the confines of the same discursive space.[36] Jean Baudrillard has also argued that Marx failed to achieve the distance from the bourgeois discourse of political economy he thought he had, for insofar as he assumed that there can be a transparency in "man's relation to the instruments and products of his labor," he accepted that part of "bourgeois thought" that fails to register the politics of representation.[37] This shows itself in Marx's treatment of Crusoe, which is parasitic on the discourse of political economy that he scorns. Marx wrote within a discourse that represents the production and exchange of value within a society wholly within the terrain of the economic.[38] It is a discourse which, in Baudrillard's terms, continues "the apotheosis of the economic."[39] Marx, like the political economists whose commentaries on Crusoe are his object, thus accepts the two major determinants of their argumentation: (1) the idea that one's relation to value is transparent or unmediated by representational practices, and (2) the quarantining of social value within the imagery of economic, productive relations.

By contrast, the radical forms of postmodernist writing are highly attuned to representational practices. Showing this level of attention, Tournier gives us a Robinson Crusoe story that achieves a significant distance from the perspectives on political economy that have marked the capitalist and Marxist discourses, which, in Baudrillard's terms, "were born together, in the historic phase that saw the systematization of both political economy and the ideology that sanctions it."[40] What Tournier's novel *Vendredi ou les limbes du Pacifique* does is offer a parody that shows the limitations and self-defeating difficulties of a view in which traditional political economy is the only way to represent value.

The subtitle of Tournier's novelistic parody is important because "the limbo of the Pacific" expression locates Robinson Crusoe's island both spatially and temporally in a place remote from Crusoe's home, the English society of the eighteenth century. While there are a number of significant implications involved with Tournier's changes in the frame — for example, moving the story from the seventeenth to the eighteenth century — what is most significant here is the way that the limbo in which the island is placed allows Tournier to subvert the Robinson Crusoe myth.[41] The beginning problematic in the novel is Robinson Crusoe's solitude, but rather than reinforcing the myth of the natural autonomy of the individual, Tournier's Crusoe becomes disoriented by his solitude once he fails in his initial attempt to build a boat to escape the island. Deprived for a while of a social context, Crusoe degenerates into a nonhuman creature, finally hitting "bottom" (if one takes an anthropocentric view) when he wallows in a mud hole. Then deploring his state of degeneration from the familiar human condition, Crusoe attempts redemption through administrative organization. He begins ordering and administering his island, having decided that his choices consist of returning to the mire or reproducing, as governor and architect, a wholly "humanized estate."[42]

In the process of constructing this estate, Crusoe lives out a mythical human historical narrative, starting as a hunter-gatherer and proceeding to the role of cultivator and herdsman, not because this sequence is demanded by the necessity for food and shelter but seemingly out of a symbolic necessity. Insofar as he constructs what constitutes humanity on the basis of the political economy of eighteenth-century England, he is led to reproduce the up-to-date conditions of production and the narrative of human progress that legitimates those conditions in order to affirm his humanity and achieve modernity. Tournier's Crusoe is thus laboriously involved not only in surviving in a remote place but also in naturalizing the political economy of his homeland, thereby bringing home what is spatially and temporally remote. He even goes so far as to "humanize" plant life, taking as a sexual partner a "quillac-tree" that has been blown over by the wind, whose bark is "smooth and warm, even downy" and which has "two branches thrusting out of the grass" that appear to him to be "huge, black, parted thighs."[43] Among other things, Crusoe's conjugal relations with the island represent another aspect of his attempt to reproduce a familiar self. He makes of the island a feminized other in order to regain his purchase on himself as a "man."[44]

It becomes evident that the man-woman relations that Crusoe establishes are just as entangled with notions of proprietorship on the island as they were in eighteenth-century England. His "vegetable way," as he puts it in his reference to his relationship with the plant, is not confined to the sexual act itself. He takes a proprietary attitude to "his tree," referring later to sprouting plants nearby as "his children," and subsequently administering a severe beating to Friday when he catches him copulating with "his tree."[45]

This is but one of Friday's many transgressions of the island administration. His arrival and subsequent playful disregard for Crusoe's administered spaces provides Tournier with the parodic material he needs and Crusoe with the reductio ad absurdum he needs to think his way out of the confining, political/economic frame within which he has constructed his understanding of humanity and his administration of the island. After Friday's arrival, Crusoe reproduces the conditions of a capitalist system, using the money he saved from the wreckage of his ship to make Friday a wage earner. But although Friday is initially docile and seems to accept his status in Crusoe's strictly administered island, complete with a money system and a penal code, he becomes increasingly resistant and ends up subverting the system, destroying almost every aspect of Crusoe's rationally administered island, while, at the same time, creating another kind of island, one dedicated to play rather than the duties of administrator and wage earner. It takes some time for Robinson Crusoe to discover this other island. In the transition from stern island administrator to Friday's student, he evinces strong ambivalence before finally succumbing to "Friday's devotion and calm logic," which allows him to rid himself of his administrator's consciousness.

> [T]here were times when the Governor, the General, and the Pastor gained the upper hand in Robinson. His mind dwelt on the ravages caused by Friday in the meticulous ordering of the island, the ruined crops, the wasted stores and scattered herds; the vermin that multiplied and prospered, the tools that were broken or mislaid. All this might have been endurable had it not been for the *spirit* manifested by Friday, the tricks and devices, the diabolical or impish notions that entered his head, setting up a confusion by which Robinson himself was infected.[46]

When eventually Crusoe's bafflement and ambivalence are replaced with recognition, what he is able to discern through Friday's subversion is that his administered island is but one among other possible islands. Friday has existed on such an other island all along, dedicated not to a system of rational exchange but to an order based on expressivity or play, demonstrated by such acts as taking objects that have a high exchange value in eighteenth-century England and using them to decorate plants and then enlisting them in elaborate rituals of imagination. Once, with Friday's help, Robinson Crusoe discovers this other island and is thereby able to denaturalize his former home, England, he is able to see that political economy is but one possible model for representing value. Finally extricated from the confines of his old domestic conversation, he elects to remain at a distance. When a ship arrives and he is offered passage home, he decides to stay offshore, living in a world that had, before his tutelage under Friday, existed in the shadows of England's mythic discourse on political economy. For "us" (those involved in theorizing the issue of choosing modes of analysis) it is not a question of choosing a permanent venue, either on- or offshore; it is a question of seeking distant terrains that are exotic to the extent that every homecoming (every subsequent conversation) takes on its meaning and value in a broader context of possibilities. It is necessary, moreover, to recognize that each homecoming is a temporary concord, not a peaceful anchorage that should end the desire for exploration but an interval of communicative exchange to be succeeded by a subsequent restlessness and discontent with available utterances and understandings.

CHAPTER 4

Political Economy and Mimetic Desire in *Babette's Feast*

"What does one do at a feast if not exchange?"

Michel Serres

Culture and Economy

There are repressed "economies" (systems of value production, interpretation, and exchange) immanent in cultural practices and texts, but these economies and the systems of authority and power to which they are related tend to remain fugitive. They usually achieve oblique expression and do not receive explicit recognition as part of discourses that are understood to be economic in orientation. Part of the problem inheres in the traditional practice of putting narrow boundaries around "economy" and restricting its recognition to more familiar systems of exchange involving money payments. Pierre Bourdieu has characterized this tendency as "economism," a way of treating economy that fails to acknowledge the "socially repressed" dimensions.[1] In both everyday life and academic discourses, the value involved in systems of circulation and exchange is represented as radically distinct from both systems of meaning involved in cultural practices and institutionalized systems of power and authority. This tendency in representational practices tends to assume that the value of objects owes virtually nothing to cultural practices involving the exchange of recognition and political practices determining distributions of authority and eligibility.

The modernist tradition represented in Marxist and neo-Marxist political economy has attempted to resist this latter form of economism. We owe to Marx and subsequent Marxist thinkers a recoding of exchange relations to provide a discursive space within which structures of domination and subjugation can be discerned within the ambit of "economic" relations. But at the same time that Marxist insights unlock the gate between the traditional notion of economy and the domain of political relations, thereby politicizing "economy," they erect barriers that also depoliticize aspects of economy.

It is certainly the case that Marxian political economy is critical compared with liberal/capitalist formulations. Among other things, the liberal/capitalist model constructs culture as a benign arena of consensual normativity, a relatively unstructured domain of valuing that serves as a support system for both political and economic institutions. In contrast, Marxist political economists and cultural theorists view culture as an obfuscating ideational system designed to reproduce allegiances to the institutions that maintain or help reproduce an oppressive system of exchange.

But this aspect of Marxist thinking has the effect of radically separating culture from economy by treating culture as a separate domain of ideation that plays no role in constituting the value of objects. A contrary view is available in many domains of contemporary social thought in which culture is seen as contributing to "value" as it mediates the relationships between persons and things (as well as providing norms that contribute to the constitution of "things").

The structure of Marxian anthropology, as it emerges from *Capital,* is parallel to the epistemological structure of traditional empiricism. Eschewing socially mediating frames for the production of meaning and, therefore, what is valued, it posits a simple causal theory of meaning. "Real" or authentic value, for Marx, involves a meeting of objects and persons. The physical properties of the object confront the "needs" of the user. There is no individually or sociosymbolically motivated interpretative work shaping the object. The person is simply ready for the thing inasmuch as persons are a collection of needs, and desire is involved only to the extent that it is seen as desire to fulfill needs.

Within such a model, objects or "commodities" must be more or less useful, and "usefulness" inheres in the commodity. As Marx put it, "The usefulness of a thing makes it a use value. But this usefulness is conditioned by the physical properties of the commodity, and has no existence apart from the latter."[2]

As is well known, Marx contrasts this unmediated, need-fulfilling aspect of a thing with its exchange value, which exists in the domain of appearances, in the alienating social discourses where things are transformed into a "social hieroglyphic." Marxian political economy is thus modernist in that it opposes representation, seeing it as a mystifying system of signs cloaking the essential, unmediated anthropology within which things and needs meet. This unmediated model is evident in the discourses of everyday life, and it seems to have remained as the dominant anthropology of everyday life. For example, the marketing departments of drugstore chains reproduce and simplify this anthropology by posting signs that represent the need as if it were intrinsic to the object itself, advertising such things as "beauty needs," "shaving needs," and so forth. As a committed modernist, Marx displayed an unremitting hostility to representation. This manifested itself especially in his view of the relationship between money and things.

> The name of a thing is entirely external to its nature. I know nothing of a man if I merely know his name is Jacob. In the same way, every trace of the money-relation disappears in the money-names pound, thaler, franc, ducat,etc.[3]

In effect, Marx opposed representation to the natural. Again, focusing on money, the exemplar of unnatural representation, he noted that the commodity passes through a second phase in its circulation in which it is "no longer in its natural shape but in its monetary shape."[4]

The Postmodernist Alternative

Marx's modernist impulse — the deep suspicion of representation — founders on what some contemporary theorists have recognized as the inevitability of representation or mediation. If one assumes that objects are never wholly present to the subject because they take on their meanings and identities not within simple acts of individual perception but within systems of representation, the way of theorizing economy must be altered.[5] Rather than constructing the domain of the cultural and the social as organized around need fulfillment, the conception of political economy is predicated on a construction of the social order as a system of sign exchange within which things are represented.

Marx's treatment of needs therefore serves as a convenient point of departure for contrasting the modernist and postmodernist approaches to political economy. While Marx emphasized the need-fulfillment properties of things and disparaged the commodity form, which he thought of as existing in the false world of appearances (represented in an exchange-value discourse), the postmodernist Jean Baudrillard deconstructs the "assumptive notions" implicit in the belief that there is "a real subject motivated by needs and confronted by real objects as sources of satisfaction."[6]

Baudrillard faults Marxist political economy for failing to question its "postulate of man endowed with needs, and a natural inclination to satisfy them"[7] and offers a different way of constructing subject/object relations, one he borrows from the linguistic model. "A consumer is never isolated, anymore than a speaker. . . . Language cannot be explained by postulating an individual need to speak."[8] Similarly, he argues, one cannot attribute meaning and value to a thing outside of a signifying system that differentiates objects one from another within a system of codes that also locates speaking subjects.

Most significantly, the abandonment of the Marxian anthropology of needs allows one to question whether it is the materiality of objects that determines their value, and several domains of modern social theory have contributed to this questioning. Taking off from a variety of theoretical influences, most notably modern versions of anthropology, psychoanalysis, and contemporary literary theory, the emphasis has been on theorizing what Jean-Joseph Goux has called the "dematerialization of economic value."[9] This turn in theorizing political economy is not merely a sign of disembodied intellectual ferment; it speaks to our present postmodern condition in which we have witnessed a shift in structures of power from control over land to control over signs (units of meaning).

The sociological and anthropological contributions to this dematerialization of economy hark back to Marcel Mauss's influential analysis of the gift, in which it becomes clear that the "economy" of gift-giving has less to do with the material value of the object given or exchanged than it does with the social positioning of the giver and receiver. What is exchanged in gift giving are signs, and the cultural norms surrounding the gift, both in archaic societies as well as modern ones, tend to repress the economy of gift giving. As Mauss pointed out, in gift exchange "the form usually taken is that of the gift generously offered, but accompanying behavior is formal pretense and social deception, while the transaction itself is based on obligation and economic self interest."[10]

Influenced by Mauss's analysis, some have elaborated models of society and culture in which the process of sign exchange figures prominently, and the radical separation of culture and economy, characteristic of both liberal/capitalist and Marxist political economy, is overcome. For example, Bourdieu, both in his analysis of peasant societies and in his treatment of the processes of distinction in advanced Western societies, has shown how "symbolic capital" is deeply implicated in all forms of exchange.[11] "Symbolic interests," he argues, cannot be separated from what are traditionally though of as economic interests. This approach allows him to move readily from political economy to problematics of power and authority by focusing on structures of domination arising from differential holdings of "cultural capital." What he shows is now the ability to hoard and control signs is at least as connected with positions of control as it is with the monopolizing of material wealth.[12]

Similarly, Baudrillard has developed a political economy of the sign, and Georges Bataille has theorized political economy on the basis of a model of ritual expenditure, wherein persons achieve distinction and value by spending rather than acquiring. This aspect of economy, the squandering of valuable resources, is shown to have an ontological depth, a fundamental connection with enduring human motivations and interpretations, in that it is related to processes involving both eroticism and death. [13]

The psychoanalytic contribution to the dematerializing of objects is also extremely significant. Paradigmatic in this regard is Freud's discussion of sexual perversions, in which he distinguishes the "sexual object" from the "sexual aim," the former being "the person from which the attraction proceeds," and the latter, "the act toward which the instinct tends." [14] Having set up these concepts, Freud concluded that "the sexual instinct is in the first instance independent of its object." [15]

Although Freud failed to heed the significance of this separation—he held onto the concept of the perversion, which assumes that there is a natural object of the sexual instinct—his analysis opened up the possibility of a radically innovative treatment of desire in general. [16] If desiring is not controlled by attributes of objects, one's search for an object's value must turn to a socially mediated, interpretive process wherein various psychic investments are made in objects because of the relationship of those objects to various psychically and socially mediated symbolic structures.

This aspect of Freud's contribution to the dematerialization of the object has been elaborated and extended by Jacques Lacan, who located desire not in the presocial, instinctual level but in the mediated, symbolic level of the psyche. For Lacan, desire is always desire of the Other. Object investments are always epiphenomenal to the desiring confrontation of the self with other selves. [17] Within such a model, the object does not take on value because of its physical properties but because possession of it represents a relation to others who have desired it or others with whom it is psychically associated (although this association may remain opaque to the valuing subject).

As is the case in Baudrillard's perspective, Lacan's model separates desire from needs and locates it in a process of sign exchange, which also assumes that the satisfaction promised by an object is a function of a symbolic relationship between selves and others, a system of mutual desire for recognition within which the desire remains unrecognized for what it is as it gets deployed on various objects. It is thus also a non-need-based form of desire, which, as he puts it, "takes shape in the margin in which demand becomes separated from need." [18]

Similar approaches to desiring have proliferated in a variety of disciplines, and one of those most apposite to constructing a contemporary view of political economy is René Girard's view that desire is essentially mimetic. Girard's mimesis model of desire, like others influenced by psychoanalysis, denaturalizes and dematerializes objects. About this he is explicit: "To affirm the mimetic nature of desire is to deny it any privileged object," [19] and "desiring mimesis precedes the appearance of its objects and survives . . . the disappearance of every object." [20]

Girardian desire is not evoked directly by objects but by the desire of another for an object. "What desire 'imitates,' what it borrows from a 'model,' is desire itself."[21] This approach to the object also implies a different way of locating subjects. For purposes of theorizing political economy, a Girardian model would have it that "rather than supposing the subject to be constituted prior to the exchange, exchange should be seen as the source of individual desires."[22]

From this notion of the mimetic dimension of desire, Girard envisions a social process in which each mimesis engenders a reciprocal desiring, with the result that the social bond becomes a function of a process of desiring signification and exchange of signs to which goods or objects are attached. Recent economic thinking has supported this implication of the Girardian view, for there has been a discernible shift in its focus from production to consumption, recognizing that the desiring process is primary, particularly in the age of mass communication and consumption. As it is aptly put in a recent formulation of the shift, "Economists increasingly understood that in their new science it was not that useful things were desired but that desired things were useful."[23]

A moment's reflection makes evident that modern marketing techniques operate on the basis of a more or less Girardian view of desire, one expression of which is that "the subject in the market place never views his desire head-on; he always reads it obliquely in the gaze of others."[24] In short, one is never alone in valuing an object. The gaze of the other perpetually intervenes in the process of producing desirability, and this is often an explicit thematic in the advertising of products (which are not "products" until desiring has entered the process to finish making them).

We finally come to a contribution to postmodern political economy that is not a theoretical tradition or practice but the very character of the age of postmodernity. The shift from the production and exchange of goods to the production and exchange of signs in theorizing political economy is intimately connected to some significant shifts in the structure of social space. An emphasis on consumption (and especially on consumer desire) rather than production is certainly in accord with the condition in which we find ourselves. Two dimensions of our age are important here. The first is spatial. What has increasingly replaced the former spaces of assembly in communities, where face-to-face relations of social, political, and economic processes take place, is electronic or broadcast space in which persons are interconnected with objects and other persons (political leadership, fashions, products, "public" issues, etc.) through mediated forms, through electronically transmitted representations.[25]

It was not the case that representational practices were absent from the social nexus in earlier periods; it is the case, rather, that our age has experienced a qualitative shift in which reproduction, the rapid repeatable production of meaning units, plays an amplified role and has produced an increased level of commodification of sounds, images, and a variety of other objects and experiences that reverberate through the social systems of signification. Exemplary is the change in the nature of playing space. The recreational space, which was once participatory, and the assembly spaces for spectators are now largely displaced by broadcast and other commercial display spaces (e.g., the shopping malls where "sport" has become more significant for recreational shopping, related to sporting fashions it encourages, than it is to the deep social agonistics it represented in earlier periods).

Such changes in modernity's social spaces are well described elsewhere. What is most significant for purposes of the analysis here is the second dimension of postmodernity. Closely related to the expansion and significance of the media, and thereby the space and speed of transmission, is the change in ideational structures. Gianni Vattimo has theorized this aspect of postmodernity well; it is the multiplication of the "centers of history," making it more difficult to maintain the dominance of single historical narratives. It is no longer possible to maintain, he states, a "universal history," such as the old Judeo-Christian history of salvation. "This is a result of the fact that the world of mass media—which is spread out far and wide across the face of the earth—is also the world in which the 'centers' of history have multiplied."[26]

This is, of course, merely a recent acceleration of a process begun much earlier when, for example, travels such as Marco Polo's to China in the thirteenth century had a marked effect on the European imagination of how different forms of life were possible. Polo's trip helped to territorialize religion and thus to disrupt the ecclesiastical authority system in medieval Europe by showing how extravagant and powerful yet very different cosmologies, based on different historical narratives, could exist side-by-side.[27]

Essentially, the Marco Polo travel story is the story of a profound media event that disrupted the spiritual economy of Europe by, among other things, territorializing, and thus desacralizing, forms of worship. In a sense, Isak Dinesen's *Babette's Feast* is also a story of a media event. It chronicles a disruption of a spiritual economy, as well, while at the same time exemplifying the various mechanisms involved in desiring's relationship to economy in general.

Babette's Feast

At one level, the story of the feast is a simple one. The summary on the back of the paperback edition captures the main narrative of both Dinesen's story and Gabriel Axel's screenplay:

Martine and Philippa are the daughters of a forceful priest of a Lutheran
sect. Reared to deny all earthly pleasures, they live out their lives
performing good work on behalf of the inhabitants of the tiny
Scandinavian village in which they reside. When Babette, the French
refugee to whom they have given shelter, asks to repay them by preparing
a sumptuous feast, they are forced to reconcile their father's teachings with
the elaborate and bountiful meal prepared by Babette for themselves and
other aging villagers.[28]

What should be added by way of summary at this point are two visits to
the village prior to Babette's arrival on the scene. The first is by Lorens Loewenhielm, then a young officer who had been living to excess (by austere
Scandinavian Lutheran standards), drinking, gambling, womanizing, and
falling into debt in his garrison town. Sent by his father to live for a month
with his aunt in the less stimulating environment of a small Scandinavian
village, he visits the home of Martine, Philippa, and their father, and falls in
love with Martine. However, the carefully controlled affect of the dean's
household defeats Lorens's hopes, and he leaves, having learned, he says to
Martine, that "Fate is hard, and that in this world there are things which are
impossible."[29]

He works hard to forget the episode, and toward that end concentrates
on building an illustrious career, which he succeeds in doing: "The day was
to come when he would cut a brilliant figure in a brilliant world."[30] This
imagery helps to set up the contrast in elaborate versus subdued forms of
signification, which is the main polarity in the story. It contrasts dramatically, for example, with the description of Martine and Philippa, who "had
never possessed any article of fashion; they had dressed demurely in gray or
black all their lives."[31]

The other notable visit is by Achille Papin, a world-famous singer from
Paris. While in the village, he discovers that Philippa has a beautiful voice.
Although her father, the dean, is shocked by the fact that Papin is a Catholic, he consents to Papin giving Philippa singing lessons. But Papin's hopes,
like Lorens's, are dashed. His plan to prepare Philippa for a career on the
opera stage is frustrated when she breaks off her lessons. Dinesen's description of the colorful Papin — "a handsome man of forty, with curly black hair
and a red mouth"[32] — is brilliantly constructed in the film. There, Papin's
(actor Jean-Philippe Lafont's) mouth is very large and evocative as he sings
with Philippa, urging her to join him in breaking the silence that the anti-
eroticism of her ascetic existence has imposed. His bodily and musical
gestures are rich, in stark contrast with the visual and tonal poverty of
Philippa's family and village life.

Papin is never to return, but he sends Babette to the sisters fifteen years
later, urging them to take in this political refugee who, because of her in-

volvement in the revolt of the Paris Communards, is sought by the French authorities.

All three visitors disrupt the enclosed spiritual antieconomy of the sister's home and village. Each constitutes, in effect, a media event. And, while the initial visit of Lorens Loewenhielm and that of Achille Papin fail to overcome, with their rich forms of signification, the stultifying silence and austere spirituality of the place, Babette's feast succeeds. The rich culinary rhetoric she deploys is reproduced in the awakening of discourse among the villagers, discourse that reveals and ultimately alters what Dinesen describes as the "ancient accounts" of the old worshippers.

Indeed, Dinesen's choice of figuration throughout the story encourages a political economy reading, for she continually juxtaposes the domain of the spiritual with the world of money, exchange, credit, and so on. For example, when Lorens looks at Martine, he has what Dinesen describes as "a sudden, mighty vision of a higher and purer life, with no creditors, dunning letters. . . ."[33] And later, when the sisters learn that Babette has won a lottery, they and their co-worshipers view lotteries as "ungodly affairs," and the actual winnings, the paper currency, as "ominous bits of paper" that threaten the spiritual, antieconomy of their village.[34]

This antieconomy is not an aberration peculiar to this kind of village and its devout congregation. Lutheranism in general, from which this devout little sect is an offshoot, was among other things a pious reaction against various forms of squandering or expenditure associated with Catholicism's lavish proliferation and brisk trade in costly objects related to forms of spiritual signification. As Bataille puts it, "Luther's doctrine is the utter negation of a system of intense consumption of resources."[35]

This austere, anticonsumption aspect of Lutheranism contextualizes the story both in the novelette and in the screenplay. The Norwegian (story version) or Danish (film version) religious enclave tends to resist or absorb attempts to proliferate forms of signification. One such form is the visual. As Dinesen sets the stage at the outset, although the village "looks like a child's toy-town of little wooden pieces painted gray, yellow, pink and many other colors," the sisters resist this display, "dressed," as noted above, "demurely in gray or black all their lives."[36]

Throughout the film, the contrast in the reduction versus the proliferation of signs is represented cinemagraphically. For example, the contrast between the sisters' understated clothes and Lorens's uniform is dramatic when he reappears as an older man (and a general) festooned with decorations and insignia. This is in keeping with Dinesen's description of the second visit of Lorens, who appears in his older version as "broad and ruddy, in his bright uniform, his breast covered with decorations." And the semiotics of his movements as well as his appearance is eloquent in contrast with the appearances and subdued body language of the old congregation. He "strutted and shone like an ornamental bird, a golden pheasant or a peacock, in this sedate party of black crows and jackdaws."[37]

This contrast in signification can also be read in the contrast of venues. Scandinavian villages, such as the home of Martine and Philippa, are places traditionally associated with a contraction of signification, and Paris, the home of Papin and Babette, with the density and proliferation of signs. Related to this difference in place are the differences in the economies of such places. The Scandinavian fishing village is typical of static, medieval economies in which, for purposes of the system of exchange, time stands still. Transactions are simple, and the extension of temporal boundaries offered in economies in which credit is extended is absent (recall Lorens's expressed desire to escape his creditors by temporarily retreating to a small village). As Pierre Bourdieu has pointed out, the social order is a temporal order as well, and what renders the kind of dynamic typical of the modern social order is the system of credit.[38]

This is yet another way this closed moral community survives. All systems and dynamics involved in signification, monetary and otherwise, are severely restricted. In addition, the provocation of desire is arrested by the relative absence of Others who, by positioning themselves with respect to new potential objects of desire, would provide models to stimulate desiring. When exotic others do penetrate the restricted economies of the village, the closed moral community wards off desire by invoking its restricted linguistic economy. This is not only the most persistent theme of the story but also the major dimension of the culture-economy interface with which one can analyze such stories or situations. Given that desire is mediated within the social process of signification, the operation of desire as it drives economies cannot be adequately evoked when language (or signification) is stifled.

Evidence of this restriction of signification abounds in the story. For example, when Papin leaves the village, Dinesen renders the posture of the two sisters thusly: "Of this visitor from the great world the sisters spoke but little; they lacked the words with which to discuss him."[39] And, when Babette offers the sisters a feast, the same linguistic poverty emerges: "They had no arguments wherewith to meet the proposition of cooking a real French dinner."[40] It is also evident that food itself is a system of signification, a culinary language that is restricted and impoverished in small Scandinavian villages and exuberant and rich in France. Accordingly, in the screenplay, Babette is shown being taught to make a drab and insipid fish soup by the sisters shortly after she arrives, setting up the dramatic contrast with the elaborate preparation and materials involved in the feast.

When faced with the prospect of the rich culinary language and the operation of desire it might evoke, the strategy of the worshippers is their traditional one. To contain a proliferation of worldly signs, they resist signification and mitigate desire by vowing to remain silent about the meal as they consume it. It would appear that their suspicion of speech is primary, being more profound than their suspicion of other forms of signification. As one of the worshippers puts it, "The tongue can no man tame; it is an unruly evil, full of deadly poison."[41]

But during the feast, a speech by Lorens disrupts the silence strategy and destroys the attempt of the worshippers to contain the various forms of signification attached to the feast. Lorens's speaking is infectious. He, like Babette, gives the group a gift: "Taciturn old people received the gift of tongues; ears that for years had been almost deaf were opened to it."[42]

Most significantly, Lorens's position in relation to language is essential to the functioning of desire at the feast. He does more than merely break the silence; his elaborate enjoyment of the meal, coupled with his discursive identification of the various dishes and wine (all elaborately represented in the film version) breathes life into a feast that the worshippers had tried to "kill" (as Lacan has pointed out, the past participle of *se taire*, "to fall or remain silent," is *tue*, which is also the third person singular of *tuer*, "to kill"[43]). It is also worth noting here the deep connection between eating and death at a symbolic level. Insofar as it is a form of consumption or expenditure, "eating brings death," says Bataille. Like sexuality, which Bataille gives the same treatment, eating and death are both primary forms of expenditure.[44]

Thus Babette and Lorens, both as outsiders to the restricted linguistic and culinary economies of the village, create a feast that turns into a disruptive event. Babette introduces a language of food, and Lorens assists by helping to make the culinary language voluble. With his intervention, the language of food is translated into other forms of talk as the worshippers break other silences that had been long held. Again, operating with a self-consciously economic rhetoric, Dinesen describes the worshippers as having had rancorous feelings toward each other based on the above-noted "ancient accounts." The volubility set off by the food and Lorens's place as a model for mimetic desire produces a review and, to some extent, a settlement of these accounts.

However, there are additional, very deep dimensions of the economy of the feast. At a very direct level, Babette's feast is offered in exchange for the sister's kindness in taking her in and making her part of their household. And, at the point at which the sisters try to resist the feast because of the disruption it represents to their moral economy, Babette explicitly evokes a balance sheet, noting that she had never made a request before. Obvious economy-related conceptions are also invoked with the arrival of the sumptuous goods from France, which contrast with the meager foodstuffs available in the local village store (a contrast that is emphasized cinemagraphically in the film version).

But there is a less obvious aspect of the economy of the feast that becomes evident only when one heeds a model of economy that is alien to the mainstream economic thinking, which emphasizes investment and saving. Babette's feast is a sumptuous expenditure, a squandering of wealth that, according to Bataille's model of economy, represents human motivation and desire at a deep, ontological level; it represents the pervasive human need to expend excess wealth or energy. This produces an economy of squandering that operates as a repressed economy.[45] The sisters want no payment for their charity but cannot resist the feast, which (like the sister's "charity") is a kind of payment that cannot be discussed as payment within the ordinary language of economy. Although such acts of expenditure in gift giving often function in systems of rivalry, Babette's feast is better understood as part of the economies of souvenirs, which also tend to function as economies at a repressed level insofar as the desire for souvenir objects is rarely placed within the discursive space of "economy."

It must be recalled that several things are being commemorated at the feast. Babette is enacting nostalgia for her past life as a famous chef in France, the group of worshippers are commemorating the life of their deceased pastor, and Lorens is reliving the turning point in his life, the point at which he placed career motivation above love and play. Apropos of all these recollections is Susan Stewart's theorization of the relationship of desire to economy in connection with souvenir objects and occasions. Noting that desire has a narrative dimension related to the longing for temporally distant things, she locates the economies of the souvenir in the symbolic consumption of objects from the past. In contrast with the more familiar notions of economy, which emphasize the materiality of objects and their "use value," which is a kind of value that is future oriented, is the past orientation of nostalgia for souvenirs.

> The souvenir speaks to a context of origin through a language of longing, for it is not an object arising out of need or use value; it is an object arising out of the necessarily insatiable demands of nostalgia. The souvenir generates a narrative which reaches only "behind," spiraling in a continually inward movement rather than outward toward the future.[46]

Once this narrativity of the desire involved in souvenir economies becomes evident, we are reminded of Lacan's point that desire, in the sense of the pleasure of possessing an object, is dependent on others, and we have yet another dramatic example of objects being dematerialized. Their value is not intrinsic but associational, related to past episodes of human association, emotional investment, and identity formation. Dinesen explicitly notes that Babette's cooking has been recognized as a dematerializing skill. As one had said of her former cooking at the Café Anglais in Paris, "this woman is now turning dinner at the Café Anglais into a love affair of the noble and romantic category in which one no longer distinguishes between bodily and spiritual appetite or satiety."[47]

Apart from the souvenir consumption involved in Babette's culinary performance, there are several souvenirs being consumed at her feast. The pastor, who is the original excuse for an occasion, is the first; the worshippers are re-collecting their association with him on the hundredth anniversary of his birth, and the celebration was to have been a rededication to the moral austerity and forms of renunciation of materiality that he had preached. Lorens, as noted above, is recollecting his fateful career decision, as well as the unresolved and unconsummated love in his life. All this is in addition to Babette's feast serving as a souvenir for her.

Beyond this series of recollections is the collective effect. The symbolic interaction of the different personalities at the feast have the effect of taking dead souvenirs and converting them into life. Death imagery abounds at the feast. There are those who have died during the revolt of the Communards in Paris; there is the deceased pastor, the extinguished love between Martine and Lorens, and the extinguished career of Babette. Moreover, the objects at the feast are redolent with death symbolism. In the film version, one sees delivered a variety of animals for the feast—a huge turtle, small quails, and the like, all under a death sentence as they await consumption. Most dramatic is the main dish, "Cailles en Sarcophage."

As a process, therefore, the feast involves the production of both life and death. First and foremost, Babette is expending or killing her lottery winnings, for the cost of the dinner is exactly the amount she has won. At the same time, she is severing her connection with the past. The feast is a last souvenir as she symbolically produces and expends her last connection with France and prepares to embrace forever her new home, having finally paid for it. She thus kills her identity as an exile and becomes a resident in Scandinavia.

The worshippers manage to extinguish the grip of the dead pastor, a grip that had enforced abstemiousness and silence. Babette's food, once enjoyed (through the mimetic contribution of Lorens) becomes life giving, as it is transformed into the gift of speech, and the worshippers kill off old grievances (the "ancient accounts") and celebrate their solidarity in a positive, festive way. For Lorens, what are killed are his regrets. His love for Martine, long dead (or sublimated in his career) is revivified and enjoyed, finally, in a nonmaterial or symbolic way, as a mutually affirmed, joint recollection. It is shown that Babette's cooking has once again produced a "love affair of the noble and romantic kind in which one no longer distinguishes between bodily and spiritual appetite or satiety."

Finally, a translation, which had formerly failed, is achieved. Where Achille Papin had failed in his attempt to bridge the gap between France and Scandinavia (to "translate" in Scandinavian, *oversette,* is, among other things, "to bridge"), Babette, with the help of Lorens, succeeds (and thereby creates a kind of belated success for Papin). The proliferation of signs, the rich system of culinary signification, succeeds in penetrating the closed and reduced signifying system of the Scandinavian community, opening it to more meaning and thus to more life.

What remains is to heed the economy lesson that Babette gives to the sisters. Upon discovering that Babette's winnings have been consumed at the feast, Philippa says, "Dear Babette . . . you ought not to have given away all you had for our sake." Babette responds, "For your sake . . . No, for my own."[48] And Martine says, "So you will be poor now all your life, Babette." Babette responds, "Poor? . . . No, I shall never be poor. I told you that I am a great artist."[49] Babette has produced another object that will be a lasting souvenir, one associated with herself as an artist. She goes on to explain that it is for her as it was for Papin, to enrich herself by giving happiness with her artistry. At the feast, she is able to be rich again through the expenditure and the effects it bestows.

Thus the story ends with many accounts settled. As silences are broken and, more generally, various restrictions of expression are overcome, signs proliferate, and people are able to "come to terms" with themselves and one another.

American Fictions and Political Culture DeLillo's *Libra* and Bellah et al.'s *Habits of the Heart*

Narrative and Political Culture

What does one seek to determine when investigating the American political culture? At a minimum, there is an attempt to be able to account for both tendencies and events, to discern both a general orientation toward public affairs and to anticipate how people are likely to act at different times and in different places. This would imply that at the most general level, interpretive strategies must attempt to construct the diversity of character types and to situate them in the different kinds of social space in which they are spawned and contained. Within such general strategies, however, the substrategies are manifold. One approach is the in-depth interview investigation familiar as a genre of the social sciences. Such is the highly acclaimed *Habits of the Heart* (hereafter referred to as *Habits*) by Robert Bellah and his associates.[1] Another is what Norman Mailer has called the "true life novel," a fictional recreation of events and tendencies, which also involves in-depth investigation—interviews, public documents, informants, and the like—but which then translates the "findings" into a coherent novelistic plot.[2] Such a strategy characterizes Don DeLillo's *Libra,* a gloss on both the life of Lee Harvey Oswald and those of others who may or may not have been involved in a "plot" to assassinate President Kennedy.[3] This latter strategic form, the novelistic biography, involves especially interesting complexities when one considers the relationship between actual plots and novelistic ones (a theme that has fascinated DeLillo for some time). But plots at the level of writing are not peculiar to explicitly fictional genres. When we compare the narratives in *Habits* with those in *Libra, our* plot thickens, for the juxtaposition will permit us to see that there is a relationship between the plot immanent in the textual practices of a supposedly nonfictional genre and its extratextual domain, the political orientations the text attempts to elucidate. It becomes evident that there is a "mythic plot"[4] in *Habits,* an investigation that purports to be controlled by its "nonfictional" dimensions—systematic interviews, "definitions," "concepts," and "data."

However, turning first to the investigation that confesses to its plots, it should be noted that despite the extravagant reactions of many to *Libra's* construction of a plot to kill the president, a seemingly direct challenge to the official encoding of the event by the Warren Commission, *Libra* does not offer a conventional conspiracy theory. It is not constructed as a who-dunit seeking to disclose the specific agents involved in JFK's assassination. It is, rather, an analysis of both the conditions of possibility for such events and of how we, in the modern (or postmodern) period, deal with the enig-mas of such events.

The assassination was, as expressed in DeLillo's first full reflection on the event, one of those "powerful events" that "breed their own network of inconsistencies, loose ends, dead ends, small mysteries of time and space."[5] But apart from the welter of remaining mysteries—"documents lost, miss-ing, altered, destroyed, classified. Deaths by suicide, murder, accident, un-specified natural causes"—is the most enigmatic part of the drama, the "main character." Again one of DeLillo's pre-*Libra* statements:

> "Lee Harvey Oswald" often seems a secret design worked out by men
> who will never surface—a procedural diagram, a course in fabricated
> biography. Who put him together? He is not an actor so much as he is a
> character, a fictional character who first emerges as such in the year 1957.
> . . . Oswald seem scripted out of doctored photos, tourist cards, change-
> of-address cards, mail-order forms, visa applications, altered signatures,
> pseudonyms.[6]

Insofar as the "Lee Harvey Oswald" we have come to know is fictional or constructed, a "fabricated biography," two dimensions of analysis are suggested for such a character. The first is one that is avowedly fictional, and DeLillo's choice of a novelistic biography, in his words, "a work of imagination,"[7] seems an appropriate response to an event that continues to be such a challenge to the national imagination. For example, Arthur Miller characterized its initial impact with the remark: "With the Kennedy assassi-nation the cosmos had simply hung up the phone."[8] The event continues to confound, for even after one investigator pursued its mysteries for over fif-teen years, it remained an "aberration in the heartland of the real."[9]

The second dimension that suggests itself is inquiry along the vectors constituting the "main character." If Oswald is "put together by others, a secret pawn"[10] (in contrast, for example, to Reagan's would-be assassin, Hinckley, to whom DeLillo refers as a "self created media event"),[11] the process of that putting together, which runs along the lines connecting

Oswald to his constructors, is the appropriate locus of analysis. Following this process leads DeLillo into a dense mapping of the American political culture, to an identification not only of the various "types" in the grid but also of the network of interrelations among them.

The "Plots"

Although DeLillo's Lee Harvey Oswald is partly a fictional character in that he is a character in DeLillo's plot, his novelistic character has a bearing on theorizing his life in the context of American politics. The narrative of how he emerges as a made subject amounts to both a powerful analysis of character and political culture and a penetrating account of modern life in the era of highly technical modes of surveillance and espionage, a modernity in which "sophisticated devices cause people to lose conviction," in which "we are more easily shaped, swayed, influenced."[12] Put simply in the words of a character in Libra, "Devices will drain us, make us pliant."[13]

This latter aspect of DeLillo's analysis helps to set up an apt comparison. In Bellah et al.'s Habits, we have another contemporary gloss on the American character, and we are offered another narrative of the shaping of types. Although Habits purports to be a piece of social theory, a nonfictional genre, it is in many ways also a work of imagination. Like Libra, it maps lives, and in producing accounts of the private and public lives of a (narrow) range of middle-class Americans, it situates these life narratives in a grand, covering narrative offered as an account of the emergence of the American political culture.

What is perhaps the most striking difference in the accounts of lives in the two works is the differing structures of the narratives. Habits is dominated by a theological or moralistic code. "How ought we to live?" the authors ask at the outset.[14] This turns out to be a largely rhetorical question, for they possess the answer before the inquiry commences. We ought to live a life of civic virtue, one in which we are all virtually political theorists with a communitarian, other-regarding value frame rather than an individualist, self-regarding one. Instead of entering public space with a model of self-interest, within a "first language" that is individualistic, one should operate with a "second language" that transcends self-interest by combining a transcendent, biblical morality with a dose of civic republicanism.[15]

Given this already-formed-answer to their moralistic query, individual lives are not so much presented and analyzed as they are judged. The narratives of the lives are remarkably flattened. They lack temporal sensitivity and spatial sophistication. Instead of a mapping of the competing situations, local spaces, discourses, media, and genres, all of which affect the building of a person's consciousness of self and others, emerging forms of awareness are represented with simplistic statements. For example, we are told that a particular "respondent" does not choose his goals on the basis of an analysis of current priorities but rather that they "are given to him by the traditions of his family and community."[16] This is more like a brief homily than a narrative of how it is that a person imbibes a value framework and a set of personal or social political discourses.[17]

In contrast with such foreshortened and simplistic background narratives is DeLillo's treatment of Oswald, whose "character" one observes in stages as it is constructed out of his experiences as a child, a student, a soldier, a defector, a father/husband, and a social activist, all in widely different venues—educational space, military space, metropolitan space, foreign/ideational space, and so on. Oswald, in short, is produced while on a complex intellectual and geographic odyssey that finally yields a man susceptible to participating in a history-making event.

This more complex kind of narrative proceeds within a wholly different kind of interrogation than that in *Habits*. DeLillo does not bring to his reading of a life the question of whether it measures up to a particular ideal of civic virtue. Rather, he poses the question of how the kind of experience of the structures that represent contemporary America—the technologies, the intelligence subcultures, the opportunity structures, the nature of military training, the pressures to achieve certain models of "manhood"—produces various types of persons.

While the authors of *Habits* are trying to identify a unified, coherent American character that would fit within an ideal model of civic space, De-Lillo constructs a system of colliding and coalescing character types and wonders about the coincidences that bring different lives together to spawn "plots" that seem to have a deadly logic of their own. "All plots end in death," one of his characters says (a line also produced in DeLillo's earlier *White Noise*).[18]

DeLillo looks at the relationship between plots and death, both through the construction of his textual plot and through what he analyzes, not because he is supporting an intentional, conspiratorial model of the JFK assassination but because he thinks that streams of experience that converge as the lives of various characters are diffracted through complex structures constitute a "plot" in the sense of a narrative that ends in death. Here the novel and life converge, as the fictional plot becomes the appropriate form of textual practice to accomodate deadly events.

Although *Habits* has very grammatically compressed narratives of individual lives that do not approach the richness of the way DeLillo constructs Oswald, as well as some of the other cast of characters, there is an elaborate master narrative that gives *Habits* its coherence as it collects the statements and typified forms of action of various middle-class Americans and moves them through its mapping of contemporary private and public life. This is the traditional "history of ideas" narrative.[19] The authors of *Habits* presume that systems of ideas at a philosophical level have had historical lives of their own, sustaining themselves since their invention and now manifesting themselves in the currently operating American self-understanding. This presumption produces specific inferences about "our [American] notions." For example, we have, they assert, a notion of an "unencumbered self" derived from the philosophies of Descartes, Locke, and Hume, "who affect us more than we imagine."[20] There is little attempt to discern how such models of the self are displaced and diffracted through the various resistant or at least affecting discursive practices of the modern age. Somehow they seem to arrive through history intact. Not considered by the authors are the different contemporary views of the self supplied in various genres of critical theory, in which the self is seen as fragmented and in contention as it is dispersed over a variety of dominant and peripheral discursive practices rather than existing as a homogeneous, centered steering mechanism with a historically seasoned capacity for consensual community.[21]

This inattention is not surprising, for *Habits* offers no politicized ground plan, no insight into domains that create forms of contention realized at the level of political discourse. Operating within an imaginative cartography that simply registers a difference between private and public space, *Habits* fails to acknowledge a modern spatiality (sets of practices constituting differences of place) in which the self is reproduced and maintained, for example, in such domains as merchandising space as a consumer, legal space as a juridical subject with rights, geopolitical space as a potential subversive or a potential victim of foreign others, and so forth. In contrast, *Libra* is extremely sensitive to the effectivity of space on the production of character. What we have, therefore, is a comparison of two extremely disparate accounts of the relationship between America as space and as character.

The Construction of "Characters"

The analysis of character in *Habits* purports to be inspired by Tocqueville's account of American individualism. Although Tocqueville emphasized equality and expressed ambivalence about American individualism, the authors of *Habits* emphasize the latter and, in keeping with the idealistic history of ideas grand narrative that animates *Habits,* they posit individualism as an independent ideational force "that has marched inexorably through our history."[22] However Tocqueville might survive both the revaluation and the idealistic narrative structure that the authors impose, what organizes much of the analysis is actually the pre-Tocquevillian epistemic space of the "classical age." As Michel Foucault has shown, the natural historians of the classical age—roughly the mid-seventeenth through the eighteenth centuries—saw "character" not as a product of a functional system of causality (this view belongs to the postclassical discipline of biology) but as a series of types through which the range of existing species could be assembled into a taxonomy.[23]

While *Habits* does not exhibit the almost total dependence on representation—a matching of names with visible organic features—that organized natural history, it does exhibit a preoccupation with types of character. And, perhaps most tellingly for purposes of locating *Habits* in the premodern, classical episteme, the authors fit Foucault's model of the classical episteme by locating at least part of their utopia space at the origin. Foucault has noted that for classifying or precausal systems of thought in the classical age, utopias were fashioned as dreams of origins.[24] The authors of *Habits* celebrate the nature of individualism at the origin of the American republic, regarding it as a founding source of all that is proper.

However, in disparaging the modern form of individualism, which they fear "may have grown cancerous,"[25] it is revealed that *Habits* stands with one foot in modern space as well, for although there is little analysis offered for the fall from the high origin, other than lack of an adequate political frame to translate private interest into civic virtue, *Habits* ends with the dream of an end to history, which is the structure of imagination that Foucault has ascribed to "the utopia of causal systems of thought," such as Marx's and Ricardo's nineteenth-century versions of the destinies of political economy.[26]

Although the analysis in *Habits* is remarkably bereft of Marxist or, more generally, critical social thought insights, it ends with a historical imagination that bears a structural similarity to nineteenth-century historical narratives. Under the rubric of "Transforming American Culture," the authors concede that change cannot come about at the level of pure thought, and although they offer no history of deprivation that will serve as a spur to action for their imagined actors—middle-class citizens— they posit the "morally concerned social movement" as the necessary condition for the recovery of civic virtue.[27]

It is clear why *Habits* produces almost nothing in the way of the conditions that might provoke a morally concerned social movement: there are virtually *no* conditions or situations in general that seem to have played a role in the constitution of the American character as the authors understand it. There is the oft-repeated lament that America lacks the moral community it had in its early, founding period. What once existed in abundance, "a conception of the community's interest," which would control and shape one's self-interest, is now "fragile."[28] None of the existing types in their taxonomy—the civic-minded professional, the professional activist, the urban cosmopolitan, or concerned activist—achieves adequacy. The only situation implicated in their discussion of these inadequacies is the shift from town to metropolis, which they hold responsible for a loss of community.

Why does *Habits* offer no analysis of the production of character, only a moralistic view of the inadequacy of existing types? In the final analysis, *Habits* is less a piece of social theory than it is a fable; it perpetuates a fable of community, an imagination of a lack of contradictions, antagonisms, and contentions underlying social and political life. The distribution of self-interest is not, for the authors of *Habits,* a result of the prevailing situations of modernity. It is a set of perverse perspectives in need of revision. "Community" is there to be discovered if the deficits of character, which exist independently of systems of technology, productivity, control, and the like, can be overcome. We are all in this together, and we can recognize this if "we"—the present cast of characters—can ascend beyond the currently entrenched "cosmopolitan value of relativistic tolerance" to a transcendent, higher "we," to a "commitment to the common good."[29]

In contrast with this remarkably depoliticizing fable of community is De-Lillo's trenchant mapping of modernity's "characters." Moreover, it is more than the kind of static structure that a "mapping" imagery suggests, for DeLillo treats character as something always in movement as it is shaped by various forces. Here, for example, DeLillo shows, through his textual practice as much as with an explicit thematic, how Oswald is constructed by the intelligence operatives led by Win Everett, the major planner involved in shaping a character who would be "slightly more visible than the others":

> They talked about Oswald as the subject in the same way they referred to the President as Lancer, which was the secret service code name. Habit. One wants the least possible surface to which pain and regret might cling— anyone's, everyone's pain. A thought for late afternoon.
>
> "Let me understand the sequence," Win said. "The subject leaves Dallas. He is gone, out of our operation forever. Then he turns up in the one place we would never expect to find him. He turns up out of nowhere, in New Orleans, in Guy Bannister's office, looking for an undercover assignment, the same fellow who defected to the bloody Soviet Union, who used his mail-order rifle to take a shot at General Walker, strolls right into the middle of the enemy camp."[30]

A lot is going on in this passage. Everett and associates are involved in crafting a gunman who is supposed to shoot at Kennedy but not kill him. Oswald is but one among several "subjects" or characters who can be shaped for the role. But, in keeping with *Libra's* plot, chance brings Oswald into their orbit again after they lose contact with him, just as chance made them misread his marksmanship—his army file showed a relatively poor average but a different kind of reading would have revealed that he was an excellent shot on certain occasions.

At the same time we learn how the emotional proclivities, along with their connected discursive practices (using code names), is involved in the style with which they craft a subject. Moreover, for purposes of our contrast, we can take note of DeLillo's use of "habit," which is not an aspect of national character but rather the kinds of discursive practices belonging to various molded subcultures. The "habit" of using code names is produced as a characteristic of intelligence types by the structure and situation of intelligence work.

Oswald is thus a "subject" both in the sense that persons must be impersonal subjects for intelligence types like Everett and his associates and in the sense that he is a passive grammatical subject with all that this implies when one moves from grammar to the power relations involved in the constitution of the self. *Libra* organizes a confrontation of types who are brought together only in part by explicitly formulated plans. Oswald and Everett are shaped in different milieux, their lives have involved different odysseys, and their resulting values and dispositions produce the conditions of possibility for the events that bring them together.

Subjects are shaped by more than other characters. In addition to a grammar and a rhetoric, which show the work of persons on each other in the production of character, is DeLillo's narrative, which sends Oswald on an odyssey through America's different spaces. In contrast with the homogeneous view of middle-class space we get in *Habits* is the disparate set of bounded areas that shape Oswald—educational space as it operates on a youth with a strange accent, the poverty space within which he is confined by the structure of inequality and the vicissitudes of his mother's occupational fortunes, the spiritual and ideational spaces of different subcultures. Perhaps the most dramatic shaping takes place in military space, which seems to function for DeLillo as an allegory for the more significant shaping effects of America's spaces. His description of Oswald in the brig, where he is sent after giving himself a gunshot wound to try to effect his discharge, is central to the role of space in DeLillo's plot. The brig is organized by white lines painted on the floor, and each line contains behavioral imperatives:

> You do not step on white paint an any time. Segments of the floor are
> painted white. Do not touch white. There are white lines running down
> passage ways. Do not touch or cross these lines. Every urinal is situated
> behind a white line. You need permission to piss.[31]

Two aspects of the shaping of Lee Harvey Oswald are represented in DeLillo's brig allegory. The first is the shaping effects of spaces controlled by others. Eventually Oswald adjusts to the tightly administered space of the brig. He manages to adapt to both the chicken-wire enclosure as a whole and the tyranny of the white lines within it.

The trick inside the wire was to stay within your own zone, avoid eye contact, accidental touch, gestures of certain types, anything that might hint of a personality behind the drone unit. The only safety was facelessness.

He developed a voice that guided him through the days. Forever endless, identical.[32]

The second part of the shaping effect of spaces, revealed while Oswald is in the brig, is the ideological instability of the made character. Oswald is ultimately "turned" by Everett and his associates because he is a susceptible character. That his habits are acquired from many very different situations and places is made evident in the structure of his enmity in the brig as it shifts back and forth between the guards and his fellow prisoners.

He hated the guards, secretly sided with them against some of the prisoners, thought they deserved what they got, the prisoners who were stupid and cruel. He felt his rancor constantly shift, felt secret satisfactions, hated the brig routine, despised the men who could not master it, although he knew it was contrived to defeat them all.[33]

This is the susceptible subject that the spatial odyssey has made. It is the subject as a "docile body," one shaped by modern disciplinary practices that have created what Foucault calls a "new political anatomy," a person/subject that is so susceptible to control that the economies of coercion are altered. It can be more easily turned to tasks.[34] Thus, far into the "conspiracy," DeLillo's version of David Ferrie, in a conversation with coconspirators, can reassure them that the same Oswald who shot at General Walker, a political reactionary opposed to administration policy, can be influenced to shoot at Kennedy, who is, ideologically speaking, a very different kind of target. "Leon's a type. He is willing to relinquish control at some point down the line," Ferrie said. "It just hasn't happened yet."[35]

And, just as they exploit Oswald's susceptibility to make him an Oswald that will act in the right way, they are also constructing a trace that will produce the right interpretation of the event that they want to impose after the fact.

We want to leave an imprint of Oswald's activities starting today and ending when the operation is complete. . . . [W]e create our own Oswald.[36]

Oswald is thus more of a script than an actual assassin. "As a shooter, Oswald was strictly backup. His role was to provide artifacts of historical interest, a traceable weapon, all the cuttings and hoardings of his Cuban career."[37]

Beyond Types: The Struggle of Ontologies

What produces political orientations? The authors of *Habits* suggest that political orientations have a profound ontological depth; they derive in part from enlightenment philosophical traditions and thence from ideas and moral notions about the self and the order that circulated and were institutionalized during the founding of the American polity. Then comes the fall from grace, the narrative of a loss of other-regarding communitarian value frames able to push people from a preoccupation with private interest to a form of civic virtue.

What is perplexing about this way of constructing a political orientation is that it does not countenance the distribution of difference that modern social, political, and economic structures produce. Modernity, argue the authors, has produced a change in the comprehensibility of structures, because "we have moved from the local life of the nineteenth century—in which economic and social relationships were visible and, however imperfectly, morally interpreted as parts of larger common life—to a society vastly more interrelated and integrated economically, technically, and functionally."[38]

The authors admit that modernity involves more than the fragmentation and the loss of the comprehensive, communitarian overview that is implied in the current powers of the managerial and therapeutic ethos our technological prosperity has helped to produce (and which is too narrow for their taste). They recognize that there are "those left out of that prosperity."[39] But their construction of the domain of the political does not register the differences modernity has produced, for example, the captive third world labor supplies in sweat shops in America's first world cities, produced by the globalization of "local" economies. All of modernity's patterns for creating differences produce, among other things, a cacophony of voices and perspectives, few of which are articulated through formal political institutions.

The voices chosen in *Habits,* all middle-class Americans, are represented as stable political orientations, "deeply individualist in their language,"[40] with seemingly powerful strands of what the authors see as founding "biblical and republican traditions in American politics" ventriloquating themselves through them. Could this be a function of the textual practice in *Habits,* which, despite the profusion of quotations from the interviews, is a relatively single voiced genre? The authors represent their respondent's views in the relatively homogeneous political discourse with which they construct their idealistic narrative of the history of thought working its effects throughout American history. Indeed, no voices contend in *Habits.* Each individual voice is cast as if it were groping within its discursive inadequacies toward a communitarian destiny that it would realize if it were to recognize the more transcendent political discourse of the authors existing deep within itself.

At present, the authors feel that the communitarian dimension of political discourse is fragile because we lack well-integrated towns. But, in general, political orientations are stable and relatively homogeneous, and the political problematic for these homogeneous voices is moral consensus, a harmonizing of interests or the political aggregation of positions through political parties and a national-level discourse.

In stark contrast with this view of the stability of American political orientations are the mobilization and clashings of political orientations that emerge in Lee Harvey Oswald's odyssey from his anonymous youth to his infamy as presidential assassin in *Libra*. That political orientations are radically unstable, a function of venues and their structures, is represented in a remark by Ferrie to Oswald: "You have to understand that there are things that run deeper than politics. Our political skin is just the thinnest outer crust. I was brought up a Catholic in Cleveland."[41] And Ferrie sees this instability in Oswald, recognizing that he is a professed leftist but also a Libran, one capable of seeing the other side, one who "harbors contradictions," for example, "a Marine recruit [who] reads Karl Marx." And to complete the Libra metaphor, Ferrie notes, "this is a boy sitting on the scales, ready to be tilted either way."[42]

Balance/imbalance in political orientation and thus susceptibility to be turned is how the coconspirators read Oswald, but the text as a whole represents the broader instability that underlies human agency. Each person and each different voice is a stream of experience helping to construct kinds of selves with potentials for varying actions that could be diverted at any point. Modern life, as DeLillo sees it, is not therefore to be seen as the progressive result of the refining of pervasive institutions and the development of coherent ideological/political positions. It is a series of fragments. Character and value orientations are like particles in modernity's accelerator— occasionally two or more collide and alter their directions. Doubtless DeLillo agrees with John Gardner's Agathon: "Values leap up before our acts like partridges."[43]

The Oswald-Ferrie collision is exemplary in this respect. Their interaction produces, among other things, a collision of ontologies. David Ferrie is a devout Christian, and his orientation toward events is apocalyptic. Joining the Bay of Pigs attack on Cuba for him was less a derived political necessity than a form of communion wherein he was to engage in a final act of spiritual self-confirmation. Both his personal events (losing his hair) and the public events in which he participates emerge out of a theological ontology in which he imagines his life to be preordained, sponsored by a higher power.

God made me a clown, so I clown it up. When my hair started coming out
I thought it meant imminent apocalypse. The bomb falling on Louisiana.
. . . The missile crisis came. This was the purest existential moment in the
history of mankind. I was completely hairless by then. Let me tell you, I
was ready. Push the button, Jack. The only way I could forgive Kennedy
for being Kennedy was if he rained destruction down on Cuba. I bought
ten cartons of canned food and let my mouse go free.[44]

Oswald, on the contrary, does not possess a notion of the transcendent.
He lives his life in the earthly maze that has shaped him, producing his susceptibility. Ferrie asks him:

"Do you practice a religion? Do you go to church?" "I'm an atheist,"
Oswald replies. "That's dumb," Ferrie states.

Oswald supplies a brief justification out of his neo-Marxist discourse:

"Religion just holds us back. It's the arm of the state."[45]

Given this kind of ideational commitment, how can Oswald be influenced by anti-Castro, intelligence types? The answer comes again in the
form of episodes into which Oswald seems to be drawn. He is not directed
by his atheism or Marxism. He is a drifter; actions find him. His participation in the "fair play for Cuba" chapter in New Orleans is as accidental as
other episodes in his life, for example, this, which occurs right after his
theological conversation with Ferrie:

Lee got into a shoving match out on the street with some Latin type who
had pock marks and a dangling silver cross. He didn't know how it
started. Even gripping the man's biceps and talking into his face, he
couldn't remember how the thing got started. A few people stood around
mainly for lack of other amusements. Then he was home in bed.[46]

This drifting, combined with his desire for connection with something in a
life in which he has achieved so little by way of self-mastery, moves Oswald
into the orbit of those who, with differing needs, desires, and thought structures of their own, move with him toward the event.

Moreover, these different characters construct different politicized objects. What is Cuba as a politicized object? It is subject to change as it is
thought and cathected differently by the various "characters." As Oswald
and Ferrie speak, for example, Cuba keeps changing size. Ferrie complains
that Kennedy's strike force was inadequate:

"You can't invade an island that size with fifteen hundred men."
"Cuba is little," Oswald responds.
"Cuba is big," Ferrie retorts as he continues his scenario.
"Cuba is little," Oswald responds again.[47]

And Cuba is more than a strategic entity; it's an object created out of the many different kinds of lives that drift through *Libra* and are brought together by coincidences. Ferrie confirms this view of political events, telling Oswald that he himself is a coincidence, a coincidence not in the sense that events are arbitrary but in the sense in which Ferrie's universe is a sponsored one:

> You're a coincidence. They devise a plan, you fit perfectly. There's a
> pattern in things.[48]

Ferrie's model, however, is not DeLillo's. Chance brings the coconspirators together, all drawn by different kinds of selves. "Cuba" is an object they share, but a different kind for each, according to how their characters have been shaped in their different spatiotemporal odysseys. For example, the head of the operation, Win Everett, seems to locate Cuba the way intelligence types in general do. Cuba is a threat to American security. But, as it turns out, "security" has a deeper, more personal resonance. To destroy Cuba is to overcome a kind of fear that operates across personal and ideational levels for him. Even as he plans the operation, we see him feverishly checking the security of his household.

> He checked the front door. The days came and went. Bedtime again.
> Always bedtime now. He went around turning off lights, checked the back
> door, checked to see that the oven was off. This meant all was well. . . .
> He turned off the kitchen light. He began to climb the stairs, felt
> compelled to double-check the oven, although he was certain it was off.[49]

And Cuba enters the silent struggle with his fear and anger, less as a coherent part of an ideological structure than as a personal asset in his struggle.

> A voice on KDNT said that our eight-nation committee of the
> Organization of American States has charged Cuba with promoting
> Marxist subversion in our hemisphere. The island is a training center for
> agents. The Government has begun a new phase of encouraging violence
> and unrest in Latin America.
>   He didn't need announcers telling him what Cuba had become. This
> was a silent struggle. He carried a silent rage and determination. He didn't
> want company. The more people who believed as he did, the less pure his
> anger. The country was noisy with fools who demeaned his anger.[50]

There is, then, a polyvocal poetics of Cuba distributed throughout the America of John F. Kennedy's presidency. DeLillo shows how Cuba has penetrated into the complex economies of desire that structure the American political culture. When Cuba emerges at the level of discourse, it undergoes a number of tropic displacements, such as the security game played by Everett at the two levels.

This poetics of Cuba is in keeping with the poetics of DeLillo's text in general. For example, Oswald's pseudonym, Hidell, gets translated imaginatively as "hiding," which describes the furtive nature of much of Oswald's odyssey. As Oswald travels, so do his thoughts, as they are diffracted and twisted by desire, which, in turn, is shaped by the spaces within which he moves.

It is not surprising, therefore, to find such a dramatic contrast in texts when we turn to *Habits,* which is shaped not by a self-conscious textuality but by the alibi of realism. The imaginative enactments of the "characters" in *Habits* are assumed to be their discoveries, and everywhere, the authors of *Habits* "discover" an inadequacy in their subject's discoveries, which they attribute to an impoverished political discourse. But they fail to assess their own discourse, the univocal, moralistic view of communitarianism, which they impose and then treat as a discovery.

The contrast therefore operates largely at the level of form. As a univocal discourse, *Habits* is centripetal in its tendency. Everything is pulled toward a verbal/ideological center in celebration of a unified American character that the authors imagine America presented to Tocqueville as well. What is it? "It is . . . a public image that helps define, for a given group of people, just what kinds of personality traits it is good and legitimate to have."[51]

Habits then goes on to decry the lack of such a good model in the modern era, but it offers no analysis of the current production of images, largely media images designed more to sell products than models of civic virtue. Perhaps more important, there is little sense of the diversity of lives upon which images may impact.

Habits recognizes differences among social groupings, but the problematic is moralistic rather than analytic, as the authors ponder how to describe social complexity in such a way as to find a language of the "common good." Rather than explicating the clash of different language practices, representing different kinds of selves, they imagine a common political language as a telos, a common moral destiny.

As DeLillo represents it, *different* types make *different* plans. His imagery suggests forms of isolation that make desperate men do desperate things, while *Habits* constructs isolation as a kind of moralistic independence. For example, in contrast with the angry, isolated Win Everett, *Habits* offers moralistic celebrations of independence: "Ours is a society that requires people to be strong and independent. As believers we must often operate alone in uncongenial circumstances, and we must have the inner strength and discipline to do so."[52]

This sounds more like how a therapist would seek to reassure a Win Everett than a language of analysis yielding expectations about how an Everett might act, how he might become a party to events. What is to be known for DeLillo is not how an Everett might plot but rather how plots have a force of their own as they collect Everetts, Ferries, Oswalds, moving them toward a rendezvous with each other and with death. Despite the incredible system of coincidence that brings Oswald continuously into the orbit of the coconspirators and ends with Oswald as an assassin, the plot is strong rather than arbitrary; chance works in favor of a coherent, well-connected plot, not against it. DeLillo puts his interest in plots, which he had already elaborated in his *White Noise,* into the mind of Everett:

> Plots carry their own logic. There is a tendency of plots to move toward
> death. He believed that the idea of death is woven into the nature of every
> plot. A narrative plot no less than a conspiracy of armed men. The tighter
> the plot of a story, the more likely it will come to death . . . He had a
> foreboding that the plot would move to a limit, develop a logical end.[53]

The Captive Consciousness

There are other shaping forces that *Libra* and *Habits* treat very differently. For DeLillo, perhaps the greatest popular culture event in American history is Jack Ruby's shooting of Oswald on television. He expressed this view through one of his characters in his first novel, *Americana.* There, in a discussion among television producers, someone suggests a radical departure for a TV drama, having someone urinate on camera. In behalf of the plan, someone says, "I honestly think we could take credit for expanding the consciousness of our nation to some degree." And a response comes from another, "Yes . . . it would be almost as good as Ruby shooting Oswald."[54]

Television, the major medium of popular culture, is an important part of modernity for DeLillo. As he does in his *White Noise,* DeLillo connects modern reality and consciousness to the televisual productions of the "real." For him, television's images and voices are agents occupying a terrain of effectivity on the level of many characters. And some characters seem to think in its slogans and clichés as well as those of other popular media. Whereas popular culture (or modernity in general) has very little shaping force on the "characters" in *Habits,* it looms large in DeLillo's "plot." Media voices are pushed aside in *Habits* by the ideas from the past that dominate its idealist, history-of-ideas narrative. When the idea of popular culture comes up, it is dismissed as a mere domain of inarticulate sensations.

> One sensation being as good as another, there is the implication that
> nothing makes any difference. We switch from a quiz show to a situation
> comedy, to a bloody police drama, to a miniseries about celebrities, and
> with each click of the dial, nothing remains.[55]

This the writers think is in contrast with the *real* source of culture, "to which we owe the meanings of our lives," the "biblical and republican traditions of which we seldom consciously think."[56] While *Habits* is obtuse to popular culture, *Libra* glosses its pervasive effects in two ways. First, as in his *White Noise,* DeLillo gives popular culture a speaking voice as it enters the narrative at various points (e.g., " 'Natures spelled backwards,' the TV said.").[57] The second appearance is through the image productions of the characters. Popular culture colonizes minds but it does not produce a uniformity. Like the many different streams of experience within which different types of persons combine or collide to produce events, popular culture is a multiplicity, registering itself in different ways on different types.

For example, early in the novel, after Win Everett and his wife make love, they wonder how representative and appropriate their after-sex conversations are as they lie side by side, listening to the radio. The radio presence is integral to their thoughts, for they wonder if others engage in the "moany-groany love talk" with which this medium has familiarized them.[58]

And as another coconspirator, Wayne Elko, tries to make sense of the Bay of Pigs experience, he turns to popular culture for a frame. In his case, it's a film:

It hit Wayne Elko with a flash and roar that this was like *Seven Samurai.* In which free-lance warriors are selected one at a time to carry out a dangerous mission. In which men outside society are called on to save a helpless people from destruction. Swinging those two-handed swords.[59]

The implication is that such imagery, which occurs after the event, could well have played a role in creating the susceptibilities and orientations productive of the event.

Of all the characters in the "plot," Jack Ruby appears as the most media/popular-culture-susceptible of all. Although DeLillo never states explicitly that Ruby's mentality is a popular culture construction, it is clear that Ruby has adopted the macho-male orientation that DeLillo represents as the Texas male mentality. When one of Ruby's waitresses is "grabassed" by a customer in his bar, he chases the man into the street and assaults him savagely.[60] And he is constantly asking his female employees if he looks "queer" to them.[61] Ruby's close attunement to media images is also represented in his self-presentation. For example, here he is as the TV detective:

Jack was wearing a dark suit and white silk tie, and he carried the snap-brim fedora that put him into focus, gave him sharpness and direction, like a detective on assignment.[62]

And he is described as one paying close attention to the popular culture media:

They listened to *Life Line* on the radio. It was a commentary on heroism and how it has fallen into disuse. Jack sat at the second mirror, his head lowered for maximum listening.[63]

This is not a man with a coherent political orientation, whether it be self-interested or communitarian. Jack Ruby is a cultural product, a man with a character reflecting a particular package of feelings and thoughts that popular culture supplies. In addition, and in keeping with DeLillo's plot, Ruby is a desperate man, deeply in debt to gamblers who aim to collect soon. He has an overdetermined susceptibility, like many of the other actors in the drama, whose lives the plot draws together.

Conclusion: The Politics of Genre

How is it that an explicit attempt to map the American political culture succeeds instead in disclosing the authors' mentality, while a novelistic biography, organized around one life, achieves important insights into that political culture? If we bracket the political imaginations of the writers — which are assuredly implicated in the difference — we confront the relationship between consciousness and genre.

The novel fits DeLillo's strategy inasmuch as his "plot" involves the interaction of different ideational types, all pulling away from what M. M. Bakhtin has called "the centralizing, centripetal forces of verbal-ideological life."[64] For Bakhtin, the novel is the exemplary centrifugal genre because it is "heteroglossic," constituted by many contending voices.

Within such an understanding of how the novel works, different social types would have to be represented as different linguistic orientations, and insofar as one pays attention to one dominant mode for constructing types — for example, the unifying, history-of-ideas discourse in *Habits* — the result is a form of writing that elides difference by representing social existence through a unified linguistic frame. But language, as Bakhtin points out, is diversified.

> At any given moment of its historical existence, language is heteroglot
> from top to bottom: it represents the co-existence of socio-ideological
> contradictions between the present and the past, between differing epochs
> of the past, between different socio-ideological groups in the present,
> between tendencies, schools, circles and so forth, all given bodily form.
> These "languages" of heteroglossia intersect in areas in a variety of ways,
> forming new socially typifying "languages."[65]

In pointing to the novel as the most heteroglossic of writing genres, Bakhtin was constituting the space of the novel as equivalent to a politicized version of social space. In mapping the tensions that exist in the many places from which different voices contend, the novel as a whole stands against modes of inscription that are univocal and spatially insensitive.

There are, of course, perspectives through which the novel can be read as pacifying and depoliticizing, for at a concrete level, some novels help reproduce extant forms of authority. For example, much of the depiction of property in eighteenth-century novels provided support for property ownership. In such cases, what is at one level simple background description operates at another as political legitimation for a landed class.[66]

But at the level of the ideology of form, the polyvocity or heteroglossia of the novel tends to oppose the modes of self-interpretation that secure and validate holdings, identities, and collective arrangements. DeLillo's *Libra* makes optimal use of this aspect of novelistic form. The clash of cosmologies, personal orientations, ways of construing objects, and modes for translating personal discontent into public interpretations creates a pattern of agonistics in which the mapping of novelistic space produces a highly politicized interpretation of the American culture and, at the same time, allows us to understand the conditions of possibility for plots in which a Lee Harvey Oswald becomes an assassin and JFK a victim.

In *Habits*, the combination of flattened narratives of individual lives and the restrictions of language to one moralistic, communitarian political code through which each voice is screened create a pacified, homogeneous social space. *Habits* emerges as a sermon disguised as an investigation.

Contrary to the impression left in *Habits*, thoughts proliferate in complex odysseys, resembling Lee Harvey Oswald's personal odyssey. They are twisted and turned in different directions as they confront and contest with other voices operating in different spaces. DeLillo's textual practice, in which the novelistic discourse twists and turns — for example, moving Oswald's pseudonymous Hidell into "hiding," into "Hidell means don't tell," and into "Jerkel and Hidell" (Oswald in his cell with his masturbating cellmate) — reproduces the twists and turns, the tropic extensions and contractions of consciousness.

Because the complex structures of political imagination are the subject matter of both *Libra* and *Habits*, it is to be expected that an explicitly imaginative genre will succeed better in giving imagination the kind of free play that is required to situate political culture. What we have, finally, is not a comparison between a nonfictional and a fictional genre but, ironically, in *Libra* and *Habits*, respectively, realistic versus moralistic and thus politicizing versus depoliticizing forms of imagination.

CHAPTER 6

Spatiality and Policy Discourse
Reading the Global City

The Spatialization of the City

In every age, the city has been the domain reflecting spatial strategies. For example, the medieval city was among other things a fortress. It was less appropriate to ask about policymaking *in* the city than to think of the city itself as policy. Its walled perimeter constituted a defense against predation from groups as diverse as outlaw bands and the mercenary armies of the great dynasties. When people were in the city, they were safer than when outside its walls, and discourse about the "city"—understood as protected space—was to a large extent oriented by the shape of the walls. There was relatively little ambiguity when one spoke of the inside versus the outside of the city.

Although there are still connections between warfare and the modern city, today they are more difficult to discern, not only because the contemporary state has displaced the ancient and medieval city's dominant position in the warfare nexus but also because the connections are less available to the gaze. In the present condition, the economic, social, political, and administrative practices of space that constitute the modern city are not represented in the form of visible structures, and, more generally, the connections between policy discourse and spatial strategies are less clear. As Paul Virilio has noted, it is no longer appropriate to think of the metropolitan agglomeration as bounded by a facade or a definitive spatial demarcation vis-à-vis the periphery. In effect, the city as geographic space has had its facades replaced by a set of nodalities implicated in a network of electronic transmission. Person-machine interfaces of communication and surveillance have produced a city based more on temporality of transmission than on immovable facades.[1]

Thus "spatial strategies," the practices of separation among spheres of activity that give places their meaning and value, have undergone dramatic changes, which challenge even the simplest grammatical proprieties of discourses related to city dwelling. What are imperiled are such statements as "X is in New York," or "X is in Los Angeles," which have become effectively ambiguated. For example, in a recent article on the style pages of the *New York Times,* "The Los Angeles Life on New York Time," the writer describes "a small army of Los Angeles residents" who awake at 3:00 A.M. in order to be at work at 5:00 A.M.[2] The rest of their schedule is similarly out of synch with that of other LA residents—for example, lunch at 9:00, happy hour at 2:00, bed at 8:00. These people are "stockbrokers, bankers, lawyers and news and entertainment people whose professional lives are keyed to New York and other Eastern cities." That they can operate in a geographically remote area is of course a function of modern technology, the increasing extent to which social, occupational, and other aspects of human relations are based on rapidly deployed electronic connections. Insofar as work relations depend on speed and the timing of communications, geographic space dissolves in favor of what Paul Virilio has called chronospace.[3]

In this kind of space, in which geography and temporality are imbricated, temporality is more geographically significant than ever before, for in modernity, A's distance from B in work- or war-related functions has become a question of the speed of travel, of weapons of information, and so on. Among other things, this new form of spatialization invalidates both the traditional discourses related to work and commerce and those related to international politics, "security policy," and the like. There are a variety of implications of modern spatial practices, particularly as they help one construct the city of Los Angeles as policy space, for in many ways Los Angeles is an exemplar of modern spatiality, but for the moment the attention is on the New York end of this "style" story.

What should not be lost in this story is the meaning of the *textual* space where these "Los Angeles residents" working in New York are described. The style pages of the *New York Times* are part of the relatively modern space within which buyers and sellers encounter each other. They are a symbolic extension of the display spaces produced by the age of merchandising in that they reproduce the social codes found in store windows and other advertising spaces, the codes within which consumers learn to locate themselves. Indeed, much of New York City is constituted as merchandising space though often disguised as something else. For example, even the artistic space of the museum functions as an indirect form of merchandising, for as Jean Baudrillard has pointed out, it serves as the "public backing" of the process of art consumption. "Museums play the role of banks in the political economy of painting."[4]

The Discursive Deficits

The kind of discursive practice implicit in spatial arrangements is rarely available as part of political understandings because in most contemporary policy talk, the shape of the arena within which policy is conceived is taken for granted. These arenas, the resultants of spatial practices, are not an audible part of policy talk. They exist at a silent level, or, to turn to a lexic metaphor, they are a series of power inscriptions that do their effective work without being read. They belong, in effect to a political rhetoric that is implicit in a society's spatial practices, as part of its "ground plan," which situates the sets of eligible speaker/actors who can produce meaningful and effective policy utterances and actions.[5] And, in general, they contextualize and render coherent the discourses that bestow meaning and value on things, actions, and relationships.

The shape of a society's spaces—leisure space, work space, public space, military space, and so forth—tends to remain largely implicit for a variety of reasons. One is of course that the shaping of such spaces takes place so slowly that few can perceive a process of actual boundary establishment or movement. However, part of the inattention to spatial predicates of policy discourse is positively administered. Dominant forms of social theory, for example both liberal and Marxist, fail, with some exceptions, to encode the spatial dimensions of human association.[6] For the dominant tendencies in both these theoretical traditions, space is either natural or neutral; it is either the empty arena within which political association and contention develop or it is the sanctified, historically destined places whose boundaries should remain inviolable.

Yet there are good reasons to resist this naturalizing of space. At a minimum, careful attention to the irredeemably contextual contribution of a speaker's or writer's situation to the meaning of utterances should provide a clue. The meaning and value that statements confer are inseparable from the mapping of persons within which the statements are deposited. Intelligibility is intimately connected to standing, to the sites and locations from which meanings are shaped. And the spaces from which discourse is produced are just as much constituted as sets of practices as the discourses themselves. Social relations thus form a complex in which spatial and discursive practices are inseparable.[7]

Those who use a discourse—an institutionalized practice through which meaning and value is imposed, reaffirmed, and exchanged—generally fail to discern the historically developed, presupposed practices, spatial among others, that ventriloquate themselves through the discourse. This is the case, in part, because, as Jacques Derrida has pointed out, our utterances seem to be wholly present to us: "The subject can hear or speak to himself and be affected by the signifier he produces without passing through an external detour, the world, the sphere of what is not 'his own'."[8] Nevertheless, the rhetorical contributions of space can be registered. At least their indirect effects are available to the gaze. What is often required is that one manage to suspend the usual aggressive practices through which everyday life is constructed.

For purposes of analysis it is useful to distinguish two levels of spatiality shaping the modern city, one that is relatively sightly once it is conceptualized, and one that is too remote to present immediate, perceptual evidence. To focus first on the former, consider today's urban pedestrians, who, although they conform to spaces that shape their everyday lives, nevertheless also contribute, with some of their movements, to the shaping of those spaces. To compare this level with that of the second, more remote level, one can turn to Anthony Giddens's conception of "time-space distantiation," where distantiation refers to "processes whereby societies are 'stretched' over shorter or longer spans of time and space."[9]

Giddens goes on to elaborate on how aspects of power, which reproduce structures of domination, are closely tied to the spatiotemporal extension of activities, so that what happens within a society or locale is shaped in part by the forces operating at the extremes of its extensions. For example, part of temporality is "the grounding of legitimations in tradition,"[10] and part of spatiality is the current set of "regularized transactions with others who are physically absent."[11] The greater the spatiotemporal distantiation of a domain, the more its activities defy sightliness. Accordingly, pedestrians can be read in two ways: in terms of the present operating forces whose effects they either reinscribe or resist, and in terms of the more remote forces, produced in earlier periods and in distant locales but which continue to exert pressure and control as they shape their movements.

In developing a perspective that fits primarily into the first aspect of the reading, Michel de Certeau has emphasized the extent to which New York pedestrians translate the more visually available dimensions of spatiality, those belonging to effects functioning in everyday life. While one could say that New York pedestrians are engaged in spatial practices, to say this is not to say, necessarily, that they are the initiators of these practices. Or, in de Certeau's rhetoric, New York's pedestrians are "the city's common practitioners . . . whose bodies follow the cursives and strokes of the urban 'text' they write without reading."[12] Certainly there are subversive or insurrectional aspects of "pedestrian utterances" and "perambulatory rhetorics," in that some who are on foot in the city (e.g., children) move in ways that create a counterrhetoric to that produced by city planners and architects.[13] But most intelligible pedestrian utterances serve to rationalize and even mythify the city, to deepen the boundaries of its spatial arrangements.[14]

To understand how this is the case requires both a particular conception of space and some historical distance. As a conception of space, what one needs is a recognition that "the spatial organization of human society is an evolving product of human action, a form of social construction," not just a neutral context in which human action is deployed.[15] And to gain some historical distance, it is necessary to recognize that one group of New York pedestrians, the shoppers, as opposed to the "street people," move, conceptually speaking, in a part of commercial space that was developed in the late nineteenth century. The most notable venue for this development was nineteenth-century Paris, which witnessed the development of such large department stores as Bon Marché. Along with the development of these stores came the development of merchandising, which represented a radical shift in the terrain connecting entrepreneur and buyer.[16] Whereas before, transactions were a process of bargaining between salespersons and customers (goods were not displayed with price tags), with merchandising came the production of browsing space, the right of customers to return purchases, and an ever-increasing amount of display space. Through merchandising, entrepreneurs shifted from merely announcing the availability of their goods to an activity that sought to stimulate an interest in them.

The space of shopping thus underwent a revolutionary change. No longer seen as haggling or transaction, the face-to-face contention between buyer and seller, the new commercial space involved the construction of a code or discourse for representing consumable objects, a code connecting the objects to a desired social space. Shoppers in arcades and on shopping streets could peer into store windows with goods displayed in a way that connected those goods with representations of social relations, and similar displays were erected within the stores. Shopping thus became the consumption not of an object designed to meet a need but the consumption of a social code that the consumer was encouraged to associate with displayed objects.

In its initial form the department store democratized social space, and to that extent was a social invention consistent with late nineteenth-century liberal democracy. The standardizations of presentation served to drastically lessen the social control role of the clerk in the presentation of goods. The movement of customers from one department to another made possible the commingling of social classes. With considerable rapidity the form of the department store itself became standardized (and later reproduced in the supermarket and other mass marketing enterprises). Class distinctions remained, but they were not encoded in the classification of goods. Coding goods by social class and in broader cultural frames became the duty of mass advertising. Training in the creation and utilization of these codes has become, finally, part of the educational process in the schools.[17]

This different concept of selling goods and the social space that its conception created is readily apparent in the movement of contemporary New York pedestrians. They move in such a space and consume a value-laden code with which the objects they see are associated. What directs their steps is not the need for a particular object but the historical production of a commercial space in which merchandising links desiring with social relations and thus with all the complexities involved in such relations—the libidinal and other economies of the family, the work place, public space, and so on. The disposition of shoppers, which helps to constitute the value of consumable objects, thus requires a decoding that turns our attention to a social space created within a still dominant discourse in which valuing and the social are complexly interwoven.

This complex commercial/social/desiring space extends from the street to museum displays, "style pages," and other spaces of commercial/aesthetic representation. Consumption fantasies of New York shoppers are provoked by exhibitions of "high culture" displays as well as what is represented in the "popular culture" domain (television, newspapers, magazines, etc.). The spatial practices of the sidewalks are therefore part of a social space that constitutes much of New York City as display space. Moreover, this commercial/social space, in which shoppers move, has historical roots antedating the emergence of the large department stores.

The Remote Forces Shaping Pedestrian Utterances

For conceptual purposes, it is useful to take this story of the modern/social/commercial space back further to the footfalls of a seventeenth-century pedestrian, for the world made in part by modern commerce is powerfully foreshadowed in a brief vignette in the life of Father Joseph. Aldous Huxley's *Grey Eminence,* an account of the production of the Thirty Years' War through the machinations of Cardinal Richelieu and his foreign emissary, Father Joseph, begins with a trek to Rome. As the Capuchin Father Joseph is walking (barefoot) toward Rome he is involved at once in a worldly and other-worldly activity. Although his mission is primarily political—he is carrying a message to the pope from the king of France—his inward disposition is spiritual. From the historical archive, Huxley constructs the inner life of Father Joseph as a spiritual practice of the self that was a form of "personalistic pseudo mysticism," an "active annihilating by means of which he hoped to be able to disinfect his politics."[18]

> "Love, love, love, Christ's love . . ." The little flame was alight again. He kept it burning unwaveringly, while he walked a quarter of a mile. Then it was time to pass on to operation—the repudiation of distracting thoughts and the resolve to banish them from the mind.[19]

Father Joseph's practice of the self is reflective of the shape of the medieval world from whence his mentality derives. This mentality, along with the fact that he is a part of a religious order involved in mundane political affairs, reflects the persistence into the seventeenth century of the religious, vertical spatialization of the world. As Foucault states in his rough retracing of the history of space, "The Middle Ages . . . was a hierarchic assemblage of places."[20] There was the sacred and the profane, the celestial and the supercelestial, and, what was most important for church authority, the earthly world was to be read as a symbolic reality with referents in the transcendent, heavenly world.

In Huxley's telling, Father Joseph, a representative of this medieval, vertical spatial mentality, is finally recruited by Cardinal Richelieu in a more horizontal reality, a struggle that both produces the Thirty Years' War and represents the triumph of a modern, geopolitical spatialization of the world. Despite Father Joseph's predilection for a holy war against the Protestants as well as non-Christian "heretics," he helps Richelieu put France on the Protestant side of the war in order to ensure French control of the European continent against the challenges of Catholic Spain and Austria.

Although geopolitics today is organized, as noted above, by some major changes in the practices of space, some aspects of traditional geopolitical spatiality persist. For example, the nation-state system, which Richelieu's policy helped to produce, has endured. It should be noted, however, that those involved in commerce have had an effect and a stake in the nation-oriented centralization involved in the turn toward state control. Historically it was the development of the nation-state that helped to protect and sustain commerce, and, in turn, it was commercial interests that helped to support state authority against the divisive pressures from the great landed estates. Huxley seems to be offering a subtle premonition of this future mutual facilitation, for he has Father Joseph pass another kind of pedestrian on his trek to Rome. This passage immediately follows the one cited earlier reflecting his practice of the self: "Headed in the opposite direction, a train of pack animals from the city jingled slowly past him."[21]

Father Joseph was on his way to participate in an exchange of commitments, which were connected to the old hierarchical arrangement of spaces. The pack animals and merchants were involved in an unmistakable journey. As the jingle attests, it was trade, and such travels helped to etch a world with a different shape. They operated in behalf of a horizontal, desacralized world, and this world, which was to triumph over the sacred, vertically oriented social space, would produce an ever-increasing traffic of commercial travel and a corresponding rearrangement of international, national, and various forms of domestic spatialization.

It is not sufficient, however, to simply note that the dominant spatial practice in modernity is horizontal, for within the horizontal orientation there is considerable contention over space. For example, there are struggles between proximate and distant centers of power as various municipal authorities and distant economic forms of power struggle to control urban space. Even within locales, spatial practices are complexly articulated with other forces. For example, with the more horizontal articulation of space in the present, there exists a critical intersection of space with systems of calculation. This intersection forms what Foucault has called "the forms of relations among sites."[22] One can easily exemplify such a critical geography with reference to that class of military objects called "conventional weapons," whose impact on understandings of geopolitical space involves the numbers held in relation to their proximity to strategically understood locations. And, of course, temporality is part of this calculation-oriented geography, for it brings into view the issues of mobility of weapons and their speed of delivery.

A Modern Version of Sacred Spatialization:
The Liberal Discourse

We have lost the vertical, medieval world, but we must not imagine that modern social space is wholly desacralized. Although the grand narratives belonging to ecclesiastical authority have been largely discredited and have thus lost their ability to produce the world's spaces, their replacements have had their sacralizing impetus. One of the major ones has been what can best be termed the liberal discourse on space, which has recently been reasserted by Michael Walzer. Characterizing liberalism as "the art of separation," Walzer describes the shift from the medieval, "pre-liberal maps" as a shift from a conception of society as an organic whole, wherein political civil society, church, and commerce are all interdependent, to a conception of society as a house with a modern floor plan. There are walls separating church, state, university, and other domains of practice, and this creates a politics in which people are free from unwarranted intrusions.[23]

In what is perhaps the most revealing statement in his narrative of the reconceptualization of society's spaces, Walzer states, "Liberalism is a world of walls, and each creates a new liberty."[24] This quite common liberal view is a remarkably depoliticized narrative of the production of modernity's spaces. A revealing alternative is provided in Gilles Deleuze and Félix Guattari's counterliberal narrative, influenced by Marx's notion of the counteracted tendency. Deleuze and Guattari figure the counteracted tendency in spatial terms, arguing that with every deterritorialization, such as the sundering of the space of dominance/subjection involved in the medieval church's control over both territory and the codes giving territory its significance, there are liberated new possibilities for economies of desire and energy to flow across old boundaries and reshape the world. But each deterritorialization is accompanied soon after by a "reterritorialization" in

which there is a "mobilization of dominant forces to prevent the new productive possibilities from becoming new human freedoms."[25] This reterritorialization is conducted, they assert, by the "apparatuses" of the capitalist
machine, such as government bureaucracies, legal structures, and city
planners.[26]

Walzer is not insensitive to the counternarrative, and his celebration of
the liberal "art of separation" contains a dialogue with his construction of
the Marxist gloss, which he renders as the argument that the liberal separations are a pretense. Walzer assumes that Marxism is constituted simply as a
desire to efface the separations, to tear down the walls and reinstitute the
organic connections of the "pre-liberal maps."[27] Apart from the impoverishment of the political conversation that results from the anemic representation of Marxist theory, what are evident from Walzer's discussion are the
discursive economies of his liberal talk. His liberalism consists in legitimating the arrangements produced by no longer evident forms of political contention. He treats the status quo as wisdom rather than attempting to disclose the struggles from which it emerged as a reified political victory.
Politics can go on once people have secured their holdings, and one can forget about the political process involved in establishing such holdings. One
can forget (in Foucault's dramatic imagery) "the blood that has dried on the
codes of the law."[28] One can, in short, render boundaries innocuous by
speaking unproblematically about "public" and "private" spheres, the
"work place," "recreational space," and so on. What is left of the political
process in this model is primarily a policing function that consists in the prevention of intrusions from one institutional setting to another. Clearly, there
is a significant operation of power and authority in the *production* of those
domains whose inviolability Walzer seeks to preserve. His version of the
liberal discourse depoliticizes modernity's contemporary ground plan and
serves as a legitimation rhetoric. It distributes discursive assets to those who
control the flow of goods, commitments, and, in general, all valued outcomes.[29]

Walzer's liberal discourse is thus insensitive to the politics of the production of modern spaces. It amounts to a resanctification of the ground that
the church lost to capitalist activity. "How do we draw the map," asks
Walzer, "of the social world so that churches and schools, states and markets, bureaucracies and families each find their proper place?"[30] In this kind
of account, in which a narrative of institutions locates existing arrangements
within a sanctified space of historically destined proprieties, there is no place
to register a politics concerned with how institutionalized spatial arrangements deploy power and control.

It was undoubtedly the Walzer-type discourse that Foucault had in mind
when he remarked that "contemporary space is perhaps still not entirely de-
sanctified." He was referring to the oppositions representing contemporary

practices of space taken as simple givens, for example, "between private space and public space, between family space and social space, between cultural space and useful space, between the space of leisure and that of work."[31] Rather than sanctifying what are politically relevant practices, one could turn to a variety of politicizing modes for extracting the political tendencies that inhere in the spatializing of modernity.

Most politically perspicacious are those modes that register spatializing practices. Walzer assumes that critical discourses, for example, Marxism, simply represent a desire for reproducing an "undifferentiated organic whole," but what critical analyses provide, rather, is a way to encode, among other things, the way that modernity produces space or the boundary-maintaining practices and the discursive legitimations aiding and abetting the control practices constituted by these spaces. For example, Foucault has shown how the development of a delinquent milieu, part of a new domain of the social, cannot be separated from the system of rules, penalties, and law enforcement practices that had a role in constituting such a domain.[32] While Walzer celebrates a system of laws, a distribution of legalities and illegalities, as a liberating phenomenon because it protects individuals from intrusions into their private lives, Foucault understands that such "private lives" are created by, among other things, the structure of penalties and their enforcements. For example, penalties are nested in a web of spatial practices organized around the primary opposition of public space versus private space, which is immanent in any understandings of "property crimes." In addition, Foucault recognizes that the system of legalities not only reinforces certain dominant and morally approved social practices but also creates some stigmatized and disapproved but nevertheless useful social spaces.

For example, from whence do these marginal social types who provide a ready source of information and instigative activity for law enforcement officials come? The prison, a relatively recent aspect of society's production of penal spaces, "has succeeded extremely well in producing delinquency, a specific type, a politically less dangerous and on occasion, usable, form of illegality."[33]

A Political Mapping of Urban Policy

Once we have such a politicized view of spatial practices, once we recognize that spaces are produced by various forms of power and authority and that, finally, the liberal "art of separation" is a mythifying, depoliticizing discourse serving to legitimate existing power arrangements, we are prepared to produce a political form of policy analysis. What is liberated is inquiry aimed at a politicizing view of the production of the boundaries that create spaces. Such boundary creation should not be viewed as an art, because space is not politically neutral. Henri Lefebvre, perhaps the theorist most responsible for politicizing modernity's spaces, has put the matter simply: "There is a politics of space because space is political."[34] It only appears to be politically neutral, he notes, because the production processes going into shaping it are no longer in evidence; what is left is space that seems natural because it has been used in familiar ways for some time.

> If space has an air of neutrality and indifference with regard to its contents and thus seems to be purely formal, the epitome of rational abstraction, it is precisely because it has already been occupied and used, and has already been the focus of past processes whose traces are not always evident in the landscape.[35]

Turning now to the Los Angeles side of the New York–Los Angeles nexus, it is time to explore the practices shaping Los Angeles. In so doing, the aim is to repoliticize what appears bland and normal by recovering some of the historic shaping of those spaces. For purposes of analysis, an advertisement for the sports channel ESPN provides an insight, not only into contemporary Los Angeles but also much of modern America, for its rhetoric has remote but significant origins that register themselves in the piece. The advertisement shows defensive back, Lester Hayes, of the Los Angeles Raiders football team. He is kneeling in the middle of the Los Angeles Coliseum while facing the scoreboard which shows that it is at the end of the third quarter of a close contest. The main caption reads, "Join our congregation this Sunday for an Inspirational Experience."

The advertisement is a virtual jumble of codes that bespeak modern spatial practices. To address these it is necessary to address what has been involved in the historical commodification of sport. The development of the modern stadium has played a role in this process similar to that evidenced in the development of the concert hall. In the case of the concert hall, the enclosure for performing music represented a significant change, which is described by Jacques Attali as one from music as dialogue to music as monologue, for the concert hall performance increasingly replaced the music associated with popular festivals, in which there was no separation between performer and audience.[36] Apart from the social and economic implications of confining musical space and controlling entry, the concert hall had a powerful political semiotic. According to Attali, it created an audience that affirmed by their silence "their submission to the artificialized spectacle of harmony—master and slave, the rule governing the symbolic game of their domination."[37] Of course, in the case of music, the development of the phonograph record had an even more dramatic impact on the space of music.

Among the effects of such commodified forms of musical repetition has been the delocalizing of the power configuration that had developed around the concert hall.[38] Music is now an intimate part of other spaces, not the least of which is the merchandising space discussed above. Similarly, the sporting stadium as an enclosed arena for sport is part of a historical rearrangement of playing space, produced as part of what Norbert Elias has called the "sportization of pastimes."[39] Just as the concert hall represents the diminution of the more participatory festival, the stadium represents the diminution of village play, a process that accelerated in the eighteenth century in England when bourgeois and aristocratic classes feared the insurrectional incitements of folkish pastimes. Games like Shrove Tuesday football, in which one village would try to kick a soccer ball through another, frequently ended in mass political protests against local extensions of centralized authority.

At one level, "sportization" meant creating and enforcing strict rules of the game in order to bring bourgeois notions of justice and fairness to the rough and often injurious village games. However, at another level it meant delocalizing the control of games in order to moderate the political effects of mass gatherings. The development from game to sport was thus intimately connected to policing peasant classes.[40] Of course, not incidental to the development of this new overlap between legal and playing space were gambling interests, which needed "fair" contests in order to encourage and control betting.[41] The stadium is thus an enclosure that represents a concrete version of the enclosing of playing space for political and commercial reasons. The replacement of broad-based forms of play and the concomitant radical separation of player and spectator is of course part of a long story that is incidental to the present point.

More to the point is the next step in delocalization that ESPN's invitation into the Los Angeles Coliseum reflects. Most of the viewing audience will visit the coliseum from their living rooms. Control over playing space in modern professional sports is now primarily a function of the modern aspect of the commodification of play, its electronic transmission to remote audiences.

Thus the invitation to join ESPN's congregation, an obvious reference to the competition that a Sunday telecast has with Sunday church services, is an invitation to a remote kind of solidarity, a feeling of oneness with people at a distance, all involved in a modern Sunday ritual. What is perhaps most ironic about the transmission of sporting activities to passive and isolated spectators referred to as a "congregation" is that the age of remote transmission is in effect an age that is effacing the ritual spaces in which people used to congregate. The kneeling, prayerful football player is an attempt to evoke this lost ritual space.

To be invited into ESPN's congregation is only symbolically to be invited into an arena (whose seemingly long expanse is attractive compared with the confined home and work spaces of most viewers). Professional sports activities developed most in urban areas because these were the places best able to draw large audiences. But now this aspect of urban space is being effaced in favor of broadcasting space, and the delegating power of this new space, remote from local political and legal authority, is clear.[42] For example, even the timing of sporting events now relates not to local work and traffic patterns but to the viewing patterns of a variegated, nationwide audience. All of this represents a new form of power that operates at the increased level of spatiotemporal distantiation that Giddens has described, power based on control over the spaces of communication and transmission, which have played a role in the globalization of the modern city.

The change in the spatiality of sporting contests therefore represents one of the major aspects of modernity. Just as there is no longer an organic connection between the game and most of its audience of remote viewers, who do not share the living space and other dimensions of shared identity with the players, the classes in the modern city have relatively little organic connection with one another. The contemporary structure of economic domination in the global city is based on increasingly remote nodalities of power and authority. Certainly entrepreneurs and laborers tended to live and play in different parts of the city in the past, but despite some spatial separation, their senses of self operated within a largely domestic or city-centered system of prestige. And whatever one can say about the injustices of past structures of economic inequality, which were certainly considerable, people in different parts of the status hierarchy were involved in a process of shaping one another and their local environment fairly directly.

As international capital has increasingly come to control the city's economy, local impacts on class formation and the place-shaping policy process have become attenuated. For example, the lives of economically dominant groups are shaped by the above-noted temporal exigencies of a work day dictated from remote domains. Middle-class and upper-class (predominantly white) groups segregate themselves into armed and closed communities—in fortified high rises or in walled, guarded enclaves situated astride ocean-view bluffs or on canyon rims, while increasing migration from the third world flows into older areas of the city. This group and the more tenured black residents share the urban core of Los Angeles and constitute much of the "dangerous other" against which the economically privileged groups have isolated and fortified their residences.

To the extent that any organically associated groups remain, one must look to the gang cultures arising from these economically marginal groups in the urban core, and, ironically, even many of these operate with connections to remote producer/entrepreneurs who manage the international drug trade. Given the fragmented, segmentalized, and globally dependent situation of life in Los Angeles, it is a challenge to summon up an appropriate grammar to situate the problem of "public policy."

"Public Policy" in Los Angeles

The Los Angeles Coliseum is only one of the spaces in Los Angeles that are remotely controlled. To understand most of what happens in Los Angeles it is misleading to use the ordinary descriptive language of public or urban policymaking, which speaks of "policy options" and various forms of "decision making" and ignores the nuances of the locations that determine possible participants in decisions. When thinking of policy in Los Angeles it is more appropriate to think in terms of "tendencies" rather than events or options, because policy in Los Angeles is more a function of the historical process through which Los Angeles and its residents have been shaped rather than a matter of local decisions.[43]

Nevertheless, the predominant orientation of most policy discourse operates within the misleading grammar that locates actors within Los Angeles's boundaries who produce policy outcomes. A recent *Atlantic Monthly* essay on Los Angeles is exemplary in this respect. The title of the article, "Los Angeles Comes of Age," inaugurates the "investigation" with a depoliticizing destiny narrative in which Los Angeles is seen not as something produced by spatial practices but as something drawn by a future place at the top of the urban heap. Los Angeles is figured as a city competing with New York to be the "greatest" city in the world, measured in terms of economic power, the prestige of its artistic community, and the notoriety of its political leaders.[44]

The writers recognize that Los Angeles has "problems," but the grammar of their policy discourse is the familiar one, a political science discourse that offers a mythic unified actor, a set of decision makers who strive to cope with traffic, pollution, and political integration. There is no narrative on the production of the problems (or the production of nonproblems) other than what is implied in the concept of "growth." It is thus the typical passive grammar of decision makers "faced with problems," rather than, for example, a more politically acute version that would inquire into the way public policy thinking tends to remain within certain narrow modes of problematization.[45] For example, "traffic congestion," which receives more space than any other "urban problem," is a middle-class problem, in that it accepts the already-produced segregation, housing, and shaping of the labor force that has arisen from the structures of real estate speculation, work force creation, city planning, and so on. Traffic congestion is a "complaint" from those who are in a position to vocalize; it does not access the production and distribution of such positions.

A much more politically sensitive perspective recognizes that the existence of a Third World labor pool is not simply something to mention but must be incorporated in a view of policy. But such stark dimensions of difference—third world labor in a first world city—pale in an orientation obsessed with identity. The article's policy codes remain ecumenical. There is a lot of talk about pulling together to solve problems, and the reasons for getting together register very little about the map of highly disparate levels of well-being and, most significantly, the produced levels of social disintegration that have been a result of a "policymaking" that has been complicit with the tendencies produced by forces extending from within Los Angeles to remote domains shaping it. What is offered as the big problem is to avoid missing opportunities assumed to be of general benefit, for example, the opportunity to control even more of the trade in the Pacific rim than Los Angeles has already captured: "There is no better time to build Los Angeles' role as a gateway."[46]

To the extent that there is talk of the political space of Los Angeles, it is represented as the political coalition of city council members. Ultimately, the *Atlantic Monthly*'s treatment of Los Angeles reads like a car rental advertisement. Los Angeles, the writers note, is the "second city," the Avis of the world of cities, and it's trying to be number one. Only cooperation by local decision makers can allow LA to fulfill this destiny.

There are other recent policy discourses on Los Angeles, which serve to illustrate the disenabling aspects of the *Atlantic*'s obtuse form of policy talk. First, and perhaps most important, what shapes Los Angeles life cannot be formulated without paying attention to dominant aspects of "late capitalism," which has, in Los Angeles, produced the "progressive globalization of its urban economy."[47] This is not the place for an exhaustive inventory, but, put simply, how people in Los Angeles live, and indeed what "decision makers" can control, is produced to a large extent outside of Los Angeles. One is foreign finance capital. There is, for example, the "Zaitech" phenomenon from Japan, which is the strategy of using financial technology to shift cash overflow from production to speculation. It is Zaitech that has been largely responsible for the financial and architectural structure of contemporary downtown Los Angeles.[48] Another is the modern version of warfare in the nuclear age. Much of Los Angeles's industry occupies military space in that there has been an increasing flow of money from the federal government into military-related manufacturing in the area.[49]

Related to the "outside" control of its economy is the fact that Los Angeles is one of the fastest-growing manufacturing centers in the world. This rapid growth is made possible by the dominant aspect of Los Angeles's spatial ordering, the situation—even acknowledged by the *Atlantic Monthly*—in which the inner shape of Los Angeles is constituted as a Third World labor force in a first world city.[50] In effect, Los Angeles has a domestic labor pool of Mexican and Asian workers who occupy very poor residential space and poorly remunerated labor space and who are largely excluded from effective legal and political space (among other things, most are not represented by unions and as aliens are excluded from legal privileges). In addition, the tremendous economic growth, along with the highly touted emergence of this second city, has not benefited another highly segregated group of the poor in Los Angeles, the black population. As Davis has shown, Los Angeles's blacks have in fact been increasingly marginalized by the "internationalization of the metropolitan economy."[51]

This is not the place to treat the racial segregation structure, which is intimately related to the Third World within a first world labor condition. Most disenabling from the point of view of political analysis are the predominant policy discourses, which focus on Los Angeles as a unified actor faced with problems and which see politics as the proper representation of the city's different ethnic groups. The spatial map of Los Angeles is a social map produced by the operation of various forms of power. To read the production of this map requires both a historical depth and a more politicized model of modernity. Some of the elements required have already been suggested above, particularly in reference to the brief discussion of the productive relation that obtains between law enforcement and the creation of a delinquent milieu. The recent heavy emphasis on problems of "law enforcement" makes it especially appropriate to conclude with a brief analysis of why the production of what constitutes policy in Los Angeles cannot be understood within the traditional law enforcement discourse.

Conclusion

Among other things, Los Angeles's policy discourse is increasingly occupied with its "crime problem." Although much of what produces modern "crime" and "delinquency" is what produces the modern city—the globalization of the city's economy; the marginalization of its poor, mostly "ethnic," classes; the recruitment (in LA's case) of a Third World labor force—the policy strategy has been reactive or, in Foucault's term, "carceral."[52] At its most concrete level, the paradigmatic carceral strategy is the prison, and Los Angeles's prison population is considerable. But, as Foucault has shown, the carceral does not end at the prison walls, for, in many respects, modern social science (as well as many of modernity's disciplinary agencies) is complicit with the prison; its form of knowledge practice has contributed to an observational gridding in which all members of society occupy segments that contribute to our knowledge of their contribution to work, to delinquency, to public acquiescence to public policy, and so on. Thus while Los Angeles's actual prison population is enormous, the carceral network is even more vast when more broadly conceived. Of late, the vast surveillance network involves policymakers and social scientists in an attempt to react to the most recent form of delinquency, the formation of Los Angeles's gang system, which controls much of the city's drug trafficking in the poor, ethnic neighborhoods.

How are these gangs to be understood? The traditional social science approach to delinquency has fashioned a space in the grid for "predatory criminal offenders," who, as one recent study notes, are "more likely to exhibit impulsiveness and disregard for others' feelings."[53] For this approach, delinquency is a "behavior," and although this disregard for other's feelings may well be essential to the success of corporate executives (e.g., Lee Iaccocca, by many accounts), it does not provoke investigations of its genesis in *this* social space. Rather, it is applied only to the behavior of "criminal offenders." For this social type, social scientists are busy theorizing about what else we "know" about such delinquents: the coherence of their families, school performance, and so forth. It is noted, for example, that the family is a "promising locus of explanation for and treatment of delinquent behavior."[54] Within such a policy discourse, which refines Foucault's grid, making more dense the surveillance crosshatch, the only policy options available relate to intervention by police, welfare, or other corrections agencies belonging to the carceral network.

Now, let us imagine another frame. First, one can view delinquency not simply as a behavior of marginal types but rather as precisely a function of marginalization, of the positive, administratively driven aspect of what constitutes the spatial practices of the city. Anthony Giddens has described a process that can be applied to what has produced Los Angeles's tribalized set of locales from which "delinquency" springs. Los Angeles's delinquent culture is not wholly self-made.

> Surveillance—the coding of information relevant to the administration of subject populations, plus the direct supervision by officials and administrators of all sorts—becomes a key mechanism furthering a breaking away of system from social integration. Traditional practices are dispersed (without, of course, disappearing altogether) under the impact of penetration of day-to-day life by codified administrative procedures. The locales which provide the settings for interaction in situations of co-presence (the basis of social integration) undergo a major set of transmutations. The old city-country relation is replaced by a sprawling expansion of a manufactured or "created" environment.[55]

Now, as noted above, Foucault has already explicated the intimate connection between policy and the delinquent milieu, but in contemporary Los Angeles, what has been made is no longer under control. There seems to be a new level of warfare between "youth gangs" and the police, whose traditional methods for controlling delinquency and rendering it usable are no longer effective (as has been recently represented in the film *Colors*). To understand the current police-gang warfare, consider the conceptualization of urban spatial practices offered by Michel de Certeau. Distinguishing strategies from tactics, de Certeau argues that strategies belong to those (e.g., the police) who occupy legitimate or what is recognized as proper space within the social order. In this case, they are part of a centralized surveillance network for controlling the population. Tactics, by contrast, belong to those who do not occupy a legitimate space and depend instead on time, on whatever opportunities present themselves.[56]

The drug business of Los Angeles's gangs amounts to the seizing of part of what is left of a possible economy in a greater economy controlled and policed by those who can function well in legitimated spaces. And, ironically, the very structure of modern Los Angeles, especially its high degree of racial/ethnic segregation, which has created a virtual tribalized order, has pushed "delinquency" further away from the traditional form of law enforcement control of it.

This situation of Los Angeles's gangs brings the narrative back to the place it began, the suggestion that, in the case of the medieval city, it is better to speak of the city *as* policy rather than speaking of policy in the city. In important respects, this remains the case despite the above noted changes in the spatial practices of modernity. Los Angeles is, in part, a city constituted as a system of internal war, a series of spaces informed by strategies and, in reaction, tactics. These actions and reactions cannot be drawn into traditional conversations about treating delinquency, cleaning up the environment, recruiting more ethnics into the city council, or strengthening the family.

CHAPTER 7

Strategic Discourse/Discursive Strategy
The Representation of "Security Policy" in the Video Age

The Disrupted Discursive Economies of Security Policy

The public disclosure of the Iran-Gate, arms-for-hostages trade in the fall of 1986 led to the raising of issues in the mass media that had earlier been treated only in more esoteric professional and academic publications. Agency was perhaps the most persistent theme. A central concern, it would appear, was how to identify the responsibility for operating the U.S. defense or, as it has been expressed in recent decades, "security" policy. It had become more evident than ever before to the public at large that there is a coordinated subculture of official, quasi-official, and unofficial military and ex-military, intelligence and ex-intelligence operatives who, in collaboration with foreign, free-lance profiteers, both conduct some aspects of strategic policy and contribute to the commodification of "strategic weapons."[1]

Although public questioning has focused less on the commodity than on the responsibility issue, any level of recognition that weapons are a commodity opens up access to an analysis that not only treats the issues of agency or control over strategic policy but also the complex interrelationships between strategy and political economy. The first important analytic step is to recognize that as commodities, weapons can be rendered as "texts" and thus be read, as Marx did with commodities in general.[2] In this case, however, the focus is on language rather than goods, on a discursive rather than a product economy. Therefore the question of value leads to a pursuit not to recover an originary "value" based on the labor power expended in producing weapons but rather to locate the conflicting discursive spaces within which different forms of value attach to them.

Accordingly a recognition that weapons are commodities helps to disclose a process of valuing that is congealed when "weapons" are understood wholly on the basis of the strategic discourse within which the value of a weapon is a function of its destructive power, its ability to survive someone else's destructive power, and its capacity to threaten. The strategic meaning and value frame clearly does not address the significance of weapons as something to be sold and therefore fails to make available an analysis of all of the "economies"—such as relationships with other products, structure of markets, and eligibility and capacity to enter them—that pertain to this aspect of their value.

One thing that recent events have made more evident than ever before is that the commercial and strategic spaces within which "weapons" are valued are not well coordinated and managed by a centralized state decision-making apparatus. From the point of view of legitimating "security policy," there are serious contradictions in the way official strategic discourse has represented it. That is to say, there are discursive disharmonies surrounding the circulation of statements about policy, and central to the structure of this disharmony are competing accounts of the forms of agency behind what gets constituted as "policy." Certainly, the U.S. transfer of arms to a supposed adversary is nothing new. For many years, although perhaps more frequently of late, weapons have achieved their "value" within both the international geopolitical/strategic discourse and the international political economy discourse. Indeed, "international relations" are governed at least as much by processes of capital formation and exchange, the creation and subjugation of foreign markets, as they are by state-controlled strategic defense expenditures, alliance formations, and levels of violence aimed at maintaining various patterns in modern geopolitical space. This is not surprising for structural reasons, among others. As Ernest Mandel has pointed out, arms transfers help to overcome one of the major contradictions in capital formation, that the rational firm that minimizes wages in order to maximize profits is also minimizing the capital with which laborers can become consumers for the firm's products. In the case of arms transfers, consumers come from a market outside of the sphere of the producer's wage-laborers, and, in addition, the state not only operates as a sales agent but also brings to bear its considerable powers of coercion to open up markets.[3]

However, not only is this state role becoming more of a media fact, whereas before it was consigned to radical or critical academic texts, but also it is becoming increasingly clear that the sales agency of arms transfers is not monopolized by official state leadership. The transfers operate through chains of relationships that extend in and out of governments, secret agencies, military establishments, and private enterprises. For example, the key operatives in the Iran-Gate, arms-for-hostages deal were simply employed in this specific venture, not newly created and assembled.

At a minimum, then, the role of governments in "international relations" cannot be understood within the dominant geopolitical, strategic understanding that continues to control the official discourse within which U.S. security policy is expressed both by government officials and by the various, largely complicit, discourses (those of academicians, journalists, "defense intellectuals," etc.) that purport to produce analyses of U.S. strategic policy. A recent episode in what we can call, for the sake of brevity, "U.S.-Thai relations," which involves another kind of commodity, is exemplary. Among other things, the state-centric grammar in the expression "U.S.-Thai relations" is misleading, for the forms of agency involved are more complex, matching the complexity of the delicate balances governing the interaction of geopolitical and political economy motives and legitimations producing the event.

The essentials were reported in an English-language Bangkok business newspaper in an article entitled, "State Department offers to aid Thailand fight cigarette lobby." With declining U.S. cigarette sales, U.S. cigarette manufacturers had apparently targeted Thailand as a market to help expand their exports. And, more specifically, R. J. Reynolds Tobacco International had begun, using high-level government pressure, to gain access to the Thai market. Among the threats signaled to the Thais was that R. J. Reynolds would have their "Generalized System of Preferences" revoked by bringing the case before the U.S. trade representative under the "Omnibus Trade Bill." The State Department intervened to restrain the firm, claiming that it preferred to see the issue placed in a more general, bilateral set of government-level negotiations in which the state could control the process and, undoubtedly, reassert the relationship between strategic and commercial interests.[4]

Barring a simple good cop–bad cop scenario, the episode does not fit neatly in the most extreme, neoimperialist exploitation frame. The tobacco company appears to have been inhibited by the State Department's intervention. Certainly there are often episodes of almost total compatibility between commercial and perceived "security" interests, which are pursued through state-level forms of coercion, but why, in this instance, is the State Department providing an "amicus brief" in behalf of the Thais?

There is a simple answer. Within the major strategic discourse, which locates the Thais in geopolitical space, Thailand is accorded the role of a local policing state. Using the locutions of Zbigniew Brzezinski, an avatar of geopolitical thinking, Thailand would be regarded as a "linchpin state," a key actor in a region that spatially fits ambiguously within attempts to draw lines in what Brzezinski and like-minded call the "East-West Struggle."[5]

Whatever may be the effects on shaping global events of the so-called East-West struggle, it has been until very recently the major reality in the American strategic discourse. But it is increasingly apparent also that "strategic" concerns are transected by commercial struggles, a reality that complicates answers to such puzzles in U.S. "security policy." What therefore become worthy of investigation are the various intersections between "strategic discourse" and the other discursive practices with which U.S. policy is thought, expressed, represented, and understood. Increasingly, the national security and military-strategy-oriented modes for representing policy are involved in a system of interpretive agonistics. One can identify a discursive economy—a terrain of competition among kinds of statements, in which the major discursive actor, the official strategic discourse, struggles not only to vindicate U.S. policy but also to contain representations of that policy. Contending with this official discourse have been a number of competitors. There are, for example, both the neo-Marxist and traditional liberal modes for representing policy that proliferates additional effective actors. The major additional actors in the neo-Marxist discourse are those with commercial interests, while in various versions of the traditional liberal discourse, the effective actors include the "shadow government" of military and intelligence types in and out of command structures who promote a covert strategic policy that defies the legitimate, regulatory structure for foreign policy that belongs to the textbook version of policymaking in a democratic state.

This stressful discursive economy is increasingly made available for public scrutiny because of the growing and increasingly technically sophisticated participation of the mass media, which has created the need for another level of strategy, a media or representational strategy for both the official strategic discourse and its various contenders. Moreover, the field of competition has broadened as documentary and fictional films and videos, as well as print journalism, have played an expanding role in the struggle to interpret U.S. policy. As a result, the public is able to view documentary genres, such as congressional hearings on excesses of U.S. intelligence policies and news coverage of actual battle films and of remote victims in exotic locations, and fictional genres, which, like various documentaries for mass consumption, reinterpret past "strategic" episodes (the Vietnam War) and current international political dynamics (the U.S.-Contra relationship, which has been a subject of film and television drama).

This form of intervention into the discursive struggle has altered the economies of both official and counterofficial discourses, for it has moved the public more and more into a juridical space, into a place in which a judgment of U.S. policy, less controlled by the White House media team, can be made. These media-related alterations in the discursive economy have provoked changes in the discursive strategies surrounding attempts to vindicate policy, especially those connected with the delicate balance between what have been traditionally overt and covert dimensions. This aspect of strategy is a major focus of the analysis below. Before treating this, however, it is necessary to return to the initial concepts of the investigation in order to explicate the significance of the very expression, "strategic discourse."

"Strategic Discourse"

In the modern period, talk about "security" is wholly intelligible, but what are the conditions of this intelligibility? To raise this question effectively, it is necessary to elaborate what is meant by the idea of a "discourse," which is a linguistic practice that puts into play sets of rules and procedures for the formation of objects, speakers, and thematics. This "putting into play" is an important part of the identification of "discourse," as contrasted with the more general interest of linguists in the rules that govern utterances, for the concept of discourse involves concrete, temporarily and spatially located instances of language practice, as well as signaling a concern more with the constitutive role of statements than with their referential function.

In order, therefore, to move toward more specificity, it is useful to examine a particular historical period. For example, in his attempt to provide the spatiotemporal predicates of modernity's discourses, Michel Foucault has briefly traced the history of Western space, noting that "in the Middle Ages there was a hierarchic ensemble of places: sacred places and profane places; protected places and open, exposed places, urban places and rural places."[6] In addition to these places, which "concern the real life of men," there were places that provided an ethos, a mythos, and a logos, that is, transcending systems of ideational support, which had effects on the understanding of these more concrete places:

> In cosmological theory, there were the supercelestial places as opposed to the celestial, and the celestial place was in its turn opposed to the terrestrial place. There were places where things had been put because they had been violently displaced, and then on the contrary places where things found their natural ground and stability. It was this complete hierarchy, this opposition, this intersection of places that constituted what could very roughly be called medieval space, the space of emplacement.[7]

This model of medieval space, along with a historically specific understanding of temporality, provided the ground plan or context for the various discourses with which individuals, social groupings, and events were given their significance in the Middle Ages. For example, because of the presumed connections between supercelestial and terrestrial places, actions and events were accorded symbolic significance; earthly happenings were interpreted as reflective of a domain of a superearthly action of divine will. And, accordingly, the eligible and legitimate interpreters of the significance of earthly events were those whose positions rendered them intimate with the divine plan.

Thus a medieval cartography provided the support for a set of discourses that regulated daily life, and it was not until the seventeenth century that the vertical space, managed by a global network of ecclesiastical authorities, received decisive competition from those with more geopolitical imaginations and intentions functioning within a more horizontal cartography representing an emerging system of state power. One very plausible view has it that it was the emerging powers and events connected with the Thirty Years' War that were most decisive in the displacement of the medieval imaginative geography.[8]

What is most significant about the medieval cartography and its related set of authoritative discourses, for the purpose at hand, are the resources it bequeathed. If we take a politicized view of discourse, our attention is not simply on its referents—the things to which it referred, such as divine will, supercelestial space, and the like—but on the assets it provided for specific kinds of speaker/actors. In general, discourse can be viewed, as Foucault has noted, as an "asset" to be assessed within an economy of linguistic practices, a circulation of silences versus volubilities and of dominant versus subjugated modes of statements and knowledge practices. This is a view that places discourse within an economy of power relations rather than within a simplistic epistemological frame that emphasizes fidelity of representation or expressions of a deeper reality.

In sum, this Foucauldian view of discourse opens up a space for the political analysis of statements, for it provides a strategic view of discourse within a metaphor of political economy rather than epistemology:

> To analyze a discursive formation is to weigh the "value" of statements, a
> value that is not determined by their truth, that is not gauged by a secret
> content but which characterizes their place, their capacity for circulation
> and exchange, their possibility of transformation, not only in the economy
> of discourse, but more generally in the administration of scarce resources.[9]

One immediate implication of this understanding of discourse is that it renders obvious the redundancy of the very expression "strategic discourse," for discourse, so conceived, *is* strategic. Of interest here is the strategy inherent in the spatializing effects of modernity's discourses, which become evident when compared with earlier "strategies." Thus it is useful to show that what has replaced the above-elaborated medieval discourse on space, which constructed a more or less vertical world and system of authority, is a horizontal, geostrategic mode of representation, a cartography and accompanying set of discourses that renders the world as a space of strategic struggle among nations.

There are therefore two senses in which the geopolitical discourse is strategic. First, it is strategic at an explicit or recognized level in that it maps the world into warring camps and strategic alliances. At a second level, it is strategic in the sense that it participates in a linguistic or discursive economy of power and authority by holding sway over other possible representations of the world. By aggregating the world into national units and blocks, for example, it licenses particular forms of political recognition at the expense of other possible forms. As I have noted elsewhere, to refer to any area in the geostrategic mode of representation, such as "Latin America . . . is not just to refer to a place on the globe, it is to help reproduce an institutionalized form of domination, one in which the minority, hispanic part of the populations of the region control the original indigenous groups."[10] The institutionalization of the state-centric discourse incorporates a form of silence. What is not registered in the modern geopolitical discourse is the historical process of struggle in which areas and peoples have been pacified, named, homogenized, and fixed in modern international space.

But as has been noted, the dominance of the purely strategic mode for representing U.S. policy is under increasing pressure. It faces strong counterdiscursive pressure from a political economy discourse within which global politics is determined more by the activities through which states reproduce their politico-economic practices rather than through their concern with defense from attack, although certainly the modern concept of "security" tends to elide the political economy and defense impulses. Because, for example, U.S. national policy operates in behalf of specific commercial interests, discursive strategies emerge that try to convert the effects of state agency into more ideologically acceptable channels — for example, converting commercial transactions, whether arms transfers or otherwise, into national-security-related actions or by representing the state's role in exchange within a grammar that registers no differentiated class interests. For example, should the complex connections between R. J. Reynolds Tobacco International, the State Department, and Thailand receive widespread domestic media coverage, the construction of a rationalizing discourse would be put into play to impose a unity of actors and purpose — primarily geostrategic — on the interpretation of events, much as the official discourse has done with respect to the seeming affronts to security strategy of our pattern of arms transfers. In addition, then, to discourse *as* strategy there is another level of strategy, one that attempts to contain challenges to the dominant discourse.

Strategic Containments

At the level of discursive production, a subtle economy is involved that comprehends attempts at controlling interpretive frames, an economy that pervades U.S. discursive production and is connected not only with specific policy domains but also with the rationalizing of the political system as a whole. The generalized liberal discourse within which the predominant U.S. political understanding resides constitutes a containment strategy in itself. It contains political controversy by representing its system of exclusions as opportunities or freedoms. It fails to recognize the privileged values and strategic advantages that emanate from the capitalist/liberal version of space, the various divisions of real estate, activities, and social spaces that define the society and its distribution of holdings.

The liberal self-understanding depoliticizes the existing mapping of privileged and deprivileged spaces by converting privileged turf into such things as "freedom from unwanted intrusions."[11] Of course, this covering understanding of political space, which sacralizes the society's boundaries (naturalizing private property, divisions of work space from leisure space, etc.) produces a need for other levels of discursive strategy, for systems of exclusion, especially those that govern such things as industrial production and thus the shape of work space, inevitably produce resentments. As resentments deepen and new ones are formed through the vicissitudes of the differential allocation of well-being, it becomes necessary to shore up official legitimations.

Therefore the contemporary state discourse on the economy deflects attention away from the recent decade of transference of wealth dramatically upward by emphasizing dangers to our system of productivity as a whole. A state that under a recent administration has encouraged predatory capital, attacked organized labor, and deepened the impact of inequality by disqualifying economic victims from welfare payments emphasizes domestic weaknesses in the system as a whole in such things as failures of the educational system to develop the intellectual requisites for reproducing an effective and loyal labor force and threats to the general economy from other nations whom it charges with unfair trade exclusions.

This latter discursive strategy requires an extraordinarily deft touch, for, on the one hand, the role of the state as an economic actor must be minimized to be legitimate within the capitalist construction of the state, but, on the other, its overt actions on behalf of the economy as a whole produces media coverage that threatens to expose its more covert actions in behalf of particular domestic economic interests. And what is further threatened is its attempts to radically separate its role in military and defense policy from its role in using state power both to maintain "the sphere of social reproduction required for maintaining the U.S. way of life"[12] and to further the interests of the defense industry, as well as other U.S. industries (such as the top soft drink companies, whose contracts in the Soviet Union and China were negotiated with White House assistance). In short, containment in the face of anomalies and contradictions is a major dimension of the discursive strategy through which the strategic discourse in particular and state policy in general is legitimated.

The Media and Strategies of Representation

We are now prepared to deal with the added complexities created by the forms of media expression through which both the official discourse and its various supporters, competitors, and detractors are produced and transmitted. The media alter the discursive economies of the strategic discourse and intervene within what is the most delicately balanced domain, the interplay of presences and absences realized in the form of the overt versus covert strategies of "security" and other aspects of state policy.

To understand the place of the media in this discursive economy it is useful to explore the structure of another overt/covert structure, treated in a masterful sociological analysis of a communication dilemma of governments involved in domestic terror.[13] The analysis is predicated on the recognition that government services for terror are bureaucracies not unlike postal and educational hierarchies that function within a complex system of dependency with the top layers of governance. This is a complexity that imposes what are often "paradoxical relations of publicity and secrecy" with respect to the mass public, because it is necessary for purposes of maintaining state-level legitimacy that top rulers not be implicated in lower levels of implementation.[14] Succinctly stated by the analyst, this is the contradiction between "publicity and secrecy in the practices of intimidation."

> In a police state the majority of citizens know that in their country a state service for mistreatment exists, and yet that has never been made public in so many words. It is public secret private knowledge. This twilight zone is the essential mark of terrorist regimes. This must be so, because if the existence and manner of operation of the terror apparatus were the subject of public debate, then the citizens would inevitably try the terrorist practices against the confessed ideals of the regime. But if the methods would remain completely unknown, then they would not achieve their intimidating effect.[15]

Here we have in basic structure an expressive economy that arises from a contradiction that operates in other domains of the implementation of state policy. In the case of the United States' large-scale covert machinations—intelligence gathering, arms trading for strategic and economic advantage, regime destabilization, political assassination, disinformation, and the creation of extralegal discretionary funds—it is regarded as positive by much of the U.S. public that we have an intelligence service that acts along with the executive level's more overt dimension of strategic policy. And further, many endorse the methods employed by intelligence services: political assassination, dubious commercial enterprises, torture and other brutal interrogation techniques, and the employment of "criminal types" as operatives.

But by and large, it is felt that these operations should not involve a chain of command that extends to the president and his immediate advisors; they should remain above such methods in order to maintain credibility. At most, the office of the presidency should retain enough control so that there is in general a close fit between public assertions from the state and the implementation of policy. The more brutal methods of intelligence services can be condoned as long as fundamental policymaking does not violate the grammar of a centralized state-as-actor model of policymaking. It must remain credible to say that "we" have such and such a strategic policy.

In order to have the overt/covert economy operate appropriately, certain discursive strategies for representing the relationship must be maintained. The president and his staff must be regarded as being in control of foreign policy, if not of all the details of its implementation. That policy must not be seen as duplicitous; for example, the use of force or intimidation externally must be seen as operating in behalf of "national security," not on the basis of private commercial interests or even partly on that basis. To maintain the credibility of its strategic discourse, the U.S. state must therefore manage the articulation and expression of policy, and because of recent contention in congressional hearings, as well as elsewhere, surrounding the proprieties of the covert dimension of policy, it must either contain expressions of the relationships between overt and covert policy, or it must actively produce representations aimed at preempting or responding to modes of representation that are hostile or at least incompatible with the constructions it desires.

Therefore, the textuality of official discourse is taken up with strategically affecting the interpretation of policy structures, ideals, and implementations. The textual strategies are produced in the form of narratives, rhetorics, and grammatical constructions and as forms of expression—verbal utterances, video images, or combinations of these. And because these same strategies belong to challenging interpretations of policy, the articulations of official discourse are often in the form of counternarratives, counterrhetorics, and alternative grammars aimed at discrediting various models of agency or responsibility that nonofficial sources ascribe to U.S. policy. Moreover, the shape of the discursive strategy of official discourse must involve the appropriate media, as well as textual mechanisms. At times it will respond with narratives about the course of events when what is at issue are historical sequences leading up to an action, and at times it must respond with graphics and videos when what is at issue is what was perceived before an action was taken. Given the increasing availability of at-the-scene video footage carried by television into millions of U.S. homes, those in charge of official discourse have become increasingly sophisticated in the use of images and the creation of favorable verbal scenarios to accompany them.

What remains, then, is to characterize the role of these representational strategies employed in behalf of the United States' strategic discourse in a modernity in which technically sophisticated media are so pervasively involved. It is appropriate to say, indeed, that the economy within which the strategic discourse operates is qualitatively different from that in earlier historical periods.

Strategic Discourse in the Media Age

If we go back to the earliest forms of mass media, we observe that newspapers did not achieve anything like wide popular circulation until the early twentieth century. For example, in England, a majority did not read Sunday papers until 1910, dailies until 1920.[16] Print journalism during this period, which covered World War I, functioned in a wholly pious way. For example, the battle of the Somme, commanded on the English side by Sir Douglas Haig, resulted, from poor strategic planning, in approximately 60,000 killed or wounded out of 110,000 attackers.[17] While "the Somme Affair" was referred to by the English troops as "the Great Fuck-up,"[18] the press reaction to this and subsequent disastrous battles was to attempt to build morale. Accordingly, an English paper responded to Haig's disasters with the following: "Be cheerful. . . . Write encouragingly to friends at the front. . . . Don't repeat foolish gossip. . . . Don't listen to idle rumors. . . . Don't think you know better than Haig."[19]

At a minimum, the press was not altering the discursive economies of the military/strategic discourse at this stage. It was not until late in the cold war period that Western print journalism and other media began playing a counterdiscursive role, putting into circulation representations of the international strategic and commercial map that did not coincide with those of official discourses. However, what is perhaps the most significant part of the story from the point of view of the added economies imposed by the media explosion is the role of popular visual media. At an early stage, one visual medium, the National Geographic Society's maps, were implicated in helping to *produce* the strategic discourse rather than merely influencing its representational practice post hoc. The invention of the geostrategic reality called Southeast Asia resulted from an interaction between the National Geographic Society, which made twenty million maps from 1941 to 1944 in order to allow the public to follow the movement of U.S. forces in the Pacific, and "the Pacific Command." Although the expression "Southeast Asia" preexists the maps, pressure to standardize it came about when allied war strategists were queried by the mapmakers who wanted to represent strategy geographically for mass consumption.[20]

At present, the mass media, visual and otherwise, are far less complicit with those who promote geopolitical, strategic representations of the globe, and the symptoms of this modern shift in discursive economies is evident even in the articulations of those who are the most slavish adherents of the dominant strategic discourse. Especially instructive in this regard is the reaction of a branch of the academy that operates within the discursive economies of strategic thinking very much the way the nineteenth-century "vulgar economists" identified by Marx produced a discourse that merely celebrated the capitalist legitimations for the system of exchange.

Writing in *The American Defense Annual,* which could well pass for a branch of the White House press corps, one "defense intellectual" reflects on the Iran-Contra, arms-for-hostages affair as if it were merely a threat to the legitimacy of President Reagan's administration. "The Iran-Contra scandal of late 1986 cast a pall over U.S. foreign policy for the remainder of the Reagan administration."[21] Unlike more perspicuous analyses that have shown how the Iran-Contra revelations are simply a window on some massive contradictions within what gets constituted as "foreign policy," the remainder of the analysis is pious and reassurance-seeking.[22] But what is especially significant is the degree to which it registers a concern with media imagery, noting that "despite the conspicuous involvement of many active-duty and retired military officers in the Iranian arms controversy, the U.S. military establishment continued to enjoy broad public support."[23] Further, reflecting on the air force raid on Libya, the analyst refers to it as "a clear military success," but worries about the public relations effect of civilian casualties shown on video broadcasts around the globe. "The picture from Tripoli of wanton death and destruction suggested to many outside observers that there might be some moral equivalence between terrorist and antiterrorist, an outrageous but nonetheless powerfully felt emotion."[24] Here is an analyst secure in his feeling that his form of global partisanship is morally superior but who nonetheless frets about the additional modes of resistance to its command of perceptions made possible by the visual media. This is symptomatic of the more general change in the representational environment, as visual media markedly influence the discursive economies of U.S. policy.

It should be noted, however, that the problem facing the moral and strategic purity of the official version of the strategic discourse goes well beyond the growing influence of the news and other documentary media. In many respects, various aspects of popular culture provide counterdiscourses to the official strategic discourse. Perhaps most notable is the TV detective drama "Miami Vice," whose narrative is primarily taken up with the actions of two Miami narcotics investigators. Apart from the program's commodified aspects, which promote styles of music, clothing, automobiles, and pleasure yachts, it nonetheless supplies a more sophisticated reading of global politics than the typical "international relations" textbooks and commentaries written by the "vulgar economists" of the strategic discourse. Well before the Iran-Contra scandal, "Miami Vice" ran a "fictional" version of the United States–Contra connection, showing it involving the slaughter of innocent peasants, drug dealing, and personal aggrandizement with the complicity of official and quasi-official U.S. military and ex-military types (one of whom was played by the legendary Gordon Liddy of Watergate fame). The interesting question that arises was well posed by one television critic: "What . . . were tens of millions of prime-time viewers to make of the 'Miami Vice' scenario that was portraying assorted fictional Contra-supporting corporate and government leaders as, at best, scheming liars?"[25] Part of what is threatened in this particular "Miami Vice" episode is the credibility of the role of "active-duty and retired military officers," whom the *American Defense Annual*'s "analyst" is so eager to vindicate, but, more significantly, the attempt to support discursively a strategy that suggests that the bulk of our "foreign policy" is overt and thus subject to public validation is called into question. As the "defense intellectual" puts it, expressing perhaps more of a pious hope than a conviction, "the United States has a predilection for the overt use of military force as opposed to covert action."[26]

"Miami Vice" has challenged another important aspect of the strategic discourse. There have been several episodes showing the complicity in drug trafficking among U.S. banks, U.S. political officials, foreign public officials, and domestic and foreign policing authorities. Indeed, a major theme of "Miami Vice" is the ineffectiveness of local drug investigators who operate within legally fixed boundaries against a form of commerce that exists along global commercial and political vectors, managed and supported by public officials as well as powerful, "legitimate" commercial interests in the United States and abroad. Certainly this is a version of world politics, available for mass consumption, that is at odds with the version being promoted by the official discourse.

The growing existence of a variety of visually oriented media — including several films with anti- and unofficial versions of the Vietnam War, as well as of the "civil war" in El Salvador — has produced a media awareness and sophistication that official discourse has been pressed to counter or anticipate. In order to consider the various strategies of containment, counterargument, and media productions that have become part of official strategic thinking, it is important to consider more closely the economies attached to genres that have a visual component.

Ideological Contentions around the Visual

Exemplary for purposes of analysis is one of the oldest quasi-visual genres, the play, for because of its visual as well as verbal text, it places its audience in the kind of juridical space that is unavailable to, for example, readers of a

story or novel. As Fredric Jameson has pointed out, in a play there is a separation between the domains of facticity, between "the brutal visual facts,
the moments of pure happening," and "its area of assumption: the speeches
in which these events are taken up into language."[27] Thus, for example, the
audience of a Molière comedy is able to judge the gaps between the pretensions and hopes of various characters, whose pride and ambition impose delusional interpretations on events, and a more coherent and effective version
of events.

A typical character is Arnolphe, in "The School for Wives," who thinks
he has avoided the risks of deceit and infidelity involved in marrying a
younger wife by contriving to control his fiancée's education, making sure
she is kept innocent of all intrigue.[28] Arnolphe's assumption, throughout
most of the play, that his plan has succeeded is belied by the events involving mostly a growing love affair between Arnolphe's fiancée and a young
suitor, to which the audience is privy. However, apart from the play's demonstration of the knowledge-effect of the interaction between verbal script
and visual event is the strategy of ideological containment that structures the
play as a whole. While the visually available sequence of events is percepti-
bly subversive to Arnolphe's strategy of producing a docile and obedient
young bride, the more general possibility of the play's subversion as a
whole is overcome by a twist in the plot.

It appears until the last scene that were Arnolphe's betrothed to marry her
young lover, the match would be in violation of the reigning notion that
marriages should be chosen by parental agreement rather than controlled by
the emotions of the marriage partners. However, through a series of coincidences, it turns out that the match between the young lovers is approved
by an agreement between their respective parents, although they had been
unaware of it. Therefore, through this surprise turn in the narrative, the apparent conflict between a love match and an arranged marriage disappears,
and the play's potential political subversion—its possible affront to the official politics of sexuality—is contained. Molière manages a potentially subversive genre and plot by making the written text finally overcome the apparent subversion to which the presence of the visual dimension has
contributed.

We can now turn to the containment strategies surrounding official strategic representations. Structurally, the dilemma faced by official discourse is
similar to that of Molière, inasmuch as it must produce an accompanying
text that will overcome the possible subversion of visual representations.
With audiences of "security policy" increasingly becoming also spectators
who are drawn into a more effective juridical space by video and film, those
who produce and manage the official strategic discourse are involved in a
video war and a series of argumentative commentaries to overcome what
appear to many as disjunctures between professed policy and that which is

implemented. What has resulted, in short, is a struggle over visual representations.

At times the official discourse's video strategy is wholly offensive or preemptive. For example, the Monday after the Reykjavik summit meeting between Reagan and Gorbachev, after the Strategic Defense Initiative (SDI, or "Star Wars") capability had proved to be an impediment to an arms limitation agreement, a media "security analyst," John McWethy, aired a three-minute special on the U.S. SDI capability. With the aid of various video techniques, he turned what was at that stage (and undoubtedly remains) a mere "technological dream" into a fully functional reality.[29] Various video sequences involving weapons being fired, trajectories being simulated, and scientists working in white laboratory smocks were contextualized by McWethy's statements about SDI's capability being of a greater order of firepower and precision that what is witnessed.[30] Through a variety of juxtapositions of verbalizations and jump cuts between weapons fired and scientists working, McWethy transformed the "contemplated into the real."[31]

However, other attempts at containment in various domains of the strategic, security–oriented discourse have operated in a different economy as a result of the presence of video. For example, in Israel, official struggles to contain images have reached a frantic level because of the leadership's felt need to counter the image that its military operations recently in Lebanon and now in the Gaza strip involve extraordinary levels of brutality. Recently, the representational issue arising from Israel's policing operations extended to the emotional demeanor of Israeli soldiers when, as a writer reported, controversy erupted over the question, Should soldiers be allowed to cry at funerals of their comrades?[32]

The clash of representational positions arose because, on the one hand, "wet eyes" have been seen as the "hallmark of the sentimental old-type exilic Jew," which many now contrast with the New Jew who is too tough to shed tears.[33] But, on the other hand, the "security policy" discussion in Israel is receiving such hostile world reaction, in part because of video coverage of the shooting of civilians and the destruction of residences, that the representation of inhibitions and remorse of any kind becomes an important accompaniment to the policy. What is especially noteworthy in the Israeli case is that a cultural conflict over the contradictory values of sentimentality and toughness has produced what the writer has termed a "shooting and crying literature," which constructs the character of the Israeli soldier for domestic consumption.[34]

In the case of the United States, with rare exceptions, violence in behalf of "security policy" is delivered with the kind of technology that distances "fighting men" from their victims. As a result, the representational strategies and strategic commentaries in response to free–lance and other uncontrolled representations differ. In the U.S. case, visuals of "fighting men" are displaced by graphics showing the trajectories of missiles and planes and occasionally actual film footage of air-to-air and air-to-ground strikes. From the point of view of the textuality that must accompany such visual displays, it is analytically useful to heed the narrative, rhetorical, and grammatical mechanisms discussed above. And, in order to treat the special significance of the added economies of video coverage of international events, it is important to do so with a contrast between structures of official discourse at a point earlier in the video age and a recent, relatively well filmed event, for which the shooting down of two Libyan planes by U.S. aircraft in January 1989 serves excellently.

The contrast with this event is provided by the now famous Gulf of Tonkin incident, which was used as the pretext for the U.S. declaration of war against North Vietnam during the Vietnam War. The public was first informed of the event with an announcement from the office of the Pacific Command in Hawaii, which began:

> While on routine patrol in international waters at 020808 GCT (1608 local time) the US destroyer *Maddox* underwent an unprovoked attack by three PT type boats on Latitude 19–40 North; longitude 106–34 East, in the Tonkin Gulf.[35]

At this initial stage, official discourse was totally in control of the narrative strategy, beginning the story with the attack on the destroyer. Immediate press coverage by the *Washington Post* did report, in a cursory way, earlier episodes suggesting hostile action against the North that might be related to their hostilities toward the destroyer, but by and large newspaper coverage at this stage supported the primary narrative and rhetorical dimensions of the above official release—that the attack was "unprovoked" and that the destroyer's prior conduct was "routine" (as compared, for example, with provocative).

Among what remained, for purposes of extending the plot into the U.S. entry into the war, was a grammatical strategy, which emerged in President Lyndon Johnson's address to the Congress, in which he converted an ineffective firing at the destroyer into an attack on "us," where "us" included our allies, the United States (especially its women), and the "free world" in general.[36] Given the absence of observational evidence, either actual videos or graphics simulating the encounter, and given relatively little by way of counterdiscourse (especially narrative sequences including U.S. provocations), the representation of the incident was almost wholly controlled by the administration's official chronologies, its rhetorical moves, and the grammar with which it linked the threat to the ship with an imminent threat to the lives and liberties of all Americans and their friends. Only well after the incident, and indeed after the hostilities and destruction wrought by full-scale American participation in the war, did investigative journalism impeach the official discursive strategies.

The interpretive dynamics surrounding the January 1989 downing of Libyan planes is more typical of the current discursive economies that media have added to the situation of the strategic discourse. As was the case in the summer of 1988, when a U.S. ship shot down an Iranian passenger plane, the widespread visual representations of the event offered to the public both shaped and in some ways discredited the attempts of the official discourse to contain interpretations of the event.

Perhaps most central to the U.S. vindication of its action is a construction of the episode literally from the point of view of the pilots who brought down the two planes. Official discourse, in effect, was obliged to produce a grammatical strategy in which it had to construct perceiving subjects (the pilots) on the basis of a narrative of their training, a story about how what they saw was to be interpreted by them on the basis of how they had been trained to interpret the actions of potentially hostile aircraft. But in so doing, official discourse had to contend with other viewing subjects, the public spectators of the videos of the episode, and with a variety of conflicting narratives based on other views of official videos and on films and photos supplied by others.

Among what became available in the conflict over establishing an interpretation of the event was a videotape from a Navy F-14 accompanied by a dialogue between the two U.S. pilots. Although this video tended to confirm the U.S. claim that the Libyan planes were armed, the subsequent media coverage of the event raised serious doubts as to whether the decision to fire at the planes was preemptorily made, given the rules for pilots in such situations. In any case, as in the situation of the audience/spectators of a play, who are able to compare statements with actions, the domestic and foreign publics in this case became involved in judging such things as the relationship between the trajectories of the Libyan aircraft and the pilots' interpretation that they were under threat. Like playgoers, therefore, spectators of this event were placed in a position to try what it heard from the pilots and the subsequent official discourse on the basis of what it saw.

Among other things, it became a more difficult rhetorical problem for the official discourse to demonstrate that planes that one could see had never fired a shot ought to be regarded as participants in the more general activity ascribed to Libyans: terrorism. Certainly aspects of the episode remain contentious, but for present purposes what emerges is a new way to consider the representational strategy surrounding strategic discourse. Having moved full-scale into the video age, official discourse must now operate within an altered representational economy that it cannot wholly control. It must be a participant in a contentious series of encounters over the interpretation of visual images as well as verbal scenarios. Accordingly, the modern textuality of official discourse, the modes through which it represents events, must occur in an environment in which the media moves the public increasingly into a critical juridical space. And, in case one might object, after all that is made here of the effect of witnessing, that no one is watching very closely, I offer a small exhibit in defense of the analysis. The following letter to *Newsweek* was submitted in response to the stills it ran from the videotapes of the Libyan plane event:

> I am nine years old, and I study jets day in and day out. I have a huge collection of books, models and posters. Your picture showed an F-14 Tomcat firing a missile. It isn't a Sparrow, as you stated, but a Phoenix missile. I thought you should know this.
>
> Erich Anderson
> Twinsburg, Ohio[37]

CHAPTER 8

The Politics of Fear
DeLillo's Postmodern Burrow

Video is a weapon that takes over consciousness itself.

Paul Virilio

Kafka's Burrow

By the time Franz Kafka wrote his story "The Burrow" (early in this century), the age of merchandising had arrived, and people in industrial societies were beginning to experience a saturation of private, commercially oriented appeals, along with all the publicly disseminated codes aimed at producing docile, officially approved forms of citizen consciousness. Our "postmodern condition" experiences a density of messages and images, a cacophony of codes, competing for pieces of contemporary consciousness on a scale that far exceeds the situation in which Kafka wrote. It represents a qualitative shift in the relationship between the cultural and the social that perhaps justifies the concept "postmodern." Nevertheless, Kafka had already realized as keenly as anyone ever has that a simple notion of enlightenment, the idea that our condition can be clarified by enlightened contemplation, is misguided. He recognized that, especially in our century, consciousness can be more of an enemy than an ally.

Of course, this recognition is predicated on a Nietzschean view of consciousness, the view that there is no intelligible world to be known, for "the world" is fundamentally disordered; it is a container of opposing forces. Insofar as there is intelligibility, it is a result of intelligibility systems that humans impose. Within such a view, the domain of the nonintelligible is an agonistic arena of alternative possible systems of intelligibility.

If intelligibility is a human practice rather than an independent feature of the world, consciousness must confront a dilemma. Thus, the creature in the burrow, who is digging a complicated maze as protection from the predators it imagines to be operating both outside the burrow and under it, is represented as one who cannot distinguish the extent to which the "dangers" impinging on the inner space it has created are from the "outside" or are produced by its own (interpretive) activity. At the outset, the creature tries to control its fear:

> But you do not know me if you think I am afraid, or that I built my burrow simply out of fear. At a distance of some thousand paces from this hole lies, covered by a movable layer of moss, the real entrance to the burrow; it is secured as safely as anything in this world can be secured; yet someone could step on the moss or break through it, and then my burrow would lie open, and anyone who liked—please note, however, that quite uncommon abilities would also be required—could make his way in and destroy everything for good. I know that very well, and even now, at the zenith of my life, I can scarcely pass an hour in complete tranquility; at least at one point in the dark moss I am vulnerable, and in my dreams I often see a greedy muzzle sniffing around it persistently. [1]

Eventually, the creature becomes aware that the sole evidence of the existence of its enemies is noise. Beginning in a romanticized state of silence and tranquility, as its efforts to create an impregnable burrow proceed, the creature draws disparate conclusions about the whistling it begins to hear in the walls. Its inability to determine whether the noises are produced by its own burrowing or by a predator can be read allegorically as pertaining to interpretation in general. Interpretation of the object world, which is required for the creature's rational planning for its defense, encounters the dilemma of intelligibility: how to discover how what is known can be reliably separated from the ideational enactments of the knower, how, in short, to distinguish the perception of objects from the object effects of perceptual acts.

It becomes evident, finally, that the shattering of the creature's tranquility bears on the issue of consciousness itself. The creature's consciousness turns out to be constitutive of the "danger." The mind, in its contemplative mode, cannot offer tools for coping with the world inasmuch as it is implicated in the enactment of that world.

While there is no definitive solution to the dilemma of intelligibility and its implications for creating a rational order to contain and channel one's fears in nonobsessive, effective ways, Kafka's solution was constitutive of his work; he wrote in a style designed to provide escape routes out of the mazes produced by the prevailing systems of intelligibility, the objectifying intellectual structures that immure us within prevailing danger codes. Kafka did not want to be the "old architect" that the creature in his burrow had become when, in its old age, it was resigned to the insecurities its own consciousness had created:

Between that day and this lie my years of maturity, but is it not as if there were no interval at all between them? I still take long rests from my labors and listen at the wall, and the burrower has changed his intention anew, he has turned back, he is returning from his journey, thinking he has given me ample time in the interval to prepare for his reception. But on my side everything is worse prepared for than it was then; the great burrow stands defenseless, and I am no longer a young apprentice but an old architect.[2]

In short, rather than an old architect, one who simply reproduces the danger codes contained in the prevailing systems of intelligibility, Kafka was a wily and cunning writer, who identified with his version of Ulysses (see chapter 3).

The Postmodern Burrow

The more radical postmodernist modes of theorizing and writing are also designed to provide escape routes, and, arguably, the textual strategies must now be more radical because the postmodern burrow is a more densely articulated maze. Kafka anticipated these forms of writing by exploring the inner space of consciousness and demonstrating its ambiguities and uncanny relationships with the spaces outside of consciousness. But where postmodernist fiction departs from Kafka's ambiguities and enigmas is in its representations of the tangle of codes that represents modernity's spaces. It draws its impetus from the postindustrial age of esoteric structures of communication and information, positing an extreme breakdown in the legibility of modern society and its spatial practices (the complex sets of boundary practices that carve up and administer activities) and representing the extreme difficulties one has in locating the self in history, in the modern city, and in the complex sets of codes that bear on issues of survival. Like Kafka, postmodernist writers recognize the dilemma of consciousness. What they add is the recognition that the modern consciousness is organized less on the basis of one or more dominant, universalistic codes, such as the spiritual or scientific, and more by a jumble of representational practices, a variety of film and television images along with vocalized and written scripts that have colonized modern thinking. Thus, for example, novelist Manuel Puig represents a young Argentinian boy's musings about sexuality and romance with an imagined interaction he has with the Hollywood film star Rita Hayworth.[3]

At a minimum, the postmodernist writer is not driven by the old notion of consciousness raising, working instead within the conceptual space opened by Kafka's suspicions about the complicity between consciousness and the objects it represents. But in order to appreciate the contribution of postmodernist fiction to locating the self in the postmodern order, it is necessary to map certain aspects of that order, to isolate the historical situation within which such writing can register important effects. For example, one cannot understand the contemporary, fear-driven issue of "national security" outside of the context of what is thought to be at stake, of "who" it is that must be made secure from various internationally inspired forms of danger. Therefore, before turning to an exemplary postmodernist writer, Don DeLillo, who has been termed, among other things, a "connoisseur of fear,"[4] it is necessary to elucidate both the present and the radical postmodernist mode of theorizing it. This has been provided in Foucault's genealogically oriented investigations, which are designed to denaturalize and politicize the present by showing how remarkable its structures and techniques of power and authority are when placed in historical perspective.

Genealogies of the Present

Historically, the democratization of safety or protection has been a mixed blessing. One dominant political narrative, in which the development of civil society has led to an increasing protection of persons from arbitrary state power, tends to read wholly favorably. The sovereign and other representatives of the state have been increasingly limited, and their power has been displaced by a broad process of deliberation, which extends to policies that can put populations at risk in peace or war. However, there are other scenarios that emerge from this displacement in the collective identity of a society. It can be shown, for example, that the historical displacement of sovereign power has not meant that representations of safety are now deposited in the hands of individuals who can locate themselves unambiguously within fields of local and remote forms of danger. Although it is no longer an individual sovereign who can exercise power over life and death, the modern defense of the society as a whole carries with it imperatives that distribute dangers and risks that must now be read within an ideational terrain that is more dense than ever. Death remains effectively if not officially on the policy agenda. What has changed, as Foucault has pointed out, is that what is at risk is no longer the safety of the sovereign but the existence of the social body as a whole. What is to be protected is the "population," which is a relatively recent form of collective identity, inherited from the eighteenth century and now an integral part of the grammar of modern "security" policy.

> One of the great innovations in the techniques of power in the eighteenth century was the emergence of "population" as an economic and political problem: population as wealth, population as manpower or labor capacity, population balanced between its own growth and the resources it

commanded. Governments perceived that they were not dealing simply with subjects, or even with a "people," but with a "population."[5]

This aspect of modernity, which Foucault has helped to isolate, is not clearly encoded in policy talk, in the discourses with which we construct problems related both to sudden annihilation or to a more gradual debilitation from the effects of the toxicities used, ironically, in the name of more vitality (energy, defense, etc.). This is because that talk is aimed outward at constructions of the world rather than inward at what we have become such that we can have such a world. Although within various forms of official discourse there is only a dim recognition of the relevance of our cultural condition, of both what and who we are and of the forces constructing our imagination of what is to be feared in the postnuclear age, in which a politics of exterminism is possible, our intellectual and artistic discourses are increasingly aimed at alerting us to the consequences of the unprecedented capacity for the destruction of human life.

An Exemplary Modern Conversation about Fear

More of the implications of how "we" in the contemporary age have fear emerge in a conversation, reported and analyzed by Barry Lopez, that occurred between a Danish anthropologist and an Eskimo shaman in 1924. What is most evident in Lopez's treatment of the conversation is that Eskimos use fear rather than belief as an epistemological category. This is the case, Lopez implies, because their experience of their surroundings is more intimate or less mediated than that of the citizen of modern, industrial societies.

> Eskimos do not maintain this intimacy with nature without paying a
> certain price. When I have thought about the ways in which they differ
> from people in my own culture, I have realized that they are more afraid
> than we are. On a day-to-day basis, they have more fear. Not of being
> dumped into cold water from an umiak, not a debilitating fear. They are
> afraid because they accept fully what is violent and tragic in nature. It is a
> fear tied to their knowledge that sudden cataclysmic events are as much a
> part of life, of really living, as are the moments when one pauses to look at
> something beautiful. A Central Eskimo shaman named Aua, queried by
> Knud Rasmussen about Eskimo beliefs, answered, We do not believe, we
> fear.[6]

Some might file this interaction under the simple notion of misunderstanding, but, if read appropriately, the shaman was supplying the beginnings of a very powerful interpretive reflection. In offering a less-than-obvious translation, he was also both contrasting two cultures and supplying a penetrating reading of modernity. The response turns the questioner back on himself, encouraging reflection on the ontological conditions and premises of the question. What, one must now ask, has made the concept of belief so central to social sciences such as anthropology, and what are the social, cultural, and historical contexts of such questioning disciplines? In short, Aua has provoked a phenomenological moment in the conduct of an inquiry. He has encouraged a questioning of the complex interrelations between a practice of inquiry and the historical practices out of which it emerges. With such a questioning, we are set on a track that helps to disclose the contemporary politics of fear.

The effective distance that the shaman's remark provides us is similar to that which Foucault's revision of the traditional Kantian questions has provided. Shifting the ground of knowing from the "what" — Kant's "What can I know?" — Foucault sought to situate knowing within the reigning practices of subjectivity within which "knowing" is practiced. This construal of knowing as a practice is linked, for Foucault, to particular times and places, to the subject's situation rather than merely its formal structures of apprehension (Kant's exclusive focus). Thus, the question emerges in Foucault's version as, "How have my questions been produced?"[7] Moreover, this "how" has considerable historical, ontological, and social depth, for it is meant to evoke, at once, both the peculiar set of practices that constitute the present human condition and the process by which that condition has evolved through a complex process of interactions between chance occurrences and political, social, and administrative tendencies.

What is therefore most revelatory about the question posed to the Eskimo shaman along with his response is the remarkable difference between an epistemology of fear and an epistemology of belief. At a simple level, Aua was saying that for Eskimos beliefs are an extravagance rather than a mode of knowing and appraising. The daily survival demands within which the Eskimo operates render fear as the appropriate knowledge vehicle, because it implies a high degree of alertness to immediate danger. By contrast, in the modern, postindustrial condition shared by Rasmussen and us, "danger" is bureaucratized. There is an extremely dense layer of mediation between what one might be advised to fear (i.e., fearing is as elliptical as my advisory metaphor) and what one's moment-to-moment experience appears to be. That is not to say that fear ought not to be an effective epistemological category for us. It is to say, simply, that for complex reasons, it isn't. Part of this complexity has to do with how we sequester death rather than confront it. But this is an issue to be treated later.

What remains to be discussed in connection with this exemplary conversation between Rasmussen and Aua is "belief." Without attempting an extensive genealogical treatment of this modern (cognitive) attribute, it should suffice to note that "belief" has become an increasingly important dimension of the modern, psychologized self because of the extent to which "we" in modernity have a complex, institutionalized relationship to both individual and collective aspects of survival and protection. The process of creating, administrating, and legitimating "security," "protection," "safety," and the like rarely involves face-to-face, reciprocal relationships. Because both individual and reciprocal approaches to treating danger have been displaced, and because there are competing meaning frames, as well as institutionalized "policies" involving media such as print, visual signs, and voice-at-a-distance, we have "beliefs." "Beliefs," in short, are phenomena that are intimately connected to a variety of institutionalized interests and procedures involved in indirect influence.

This scenario about the cultural and political foundations of interest in "beliefs" is predicated on the modern gap between experience and knowledge. For example, in the case of whatever health hazards may arise from various electronic emissions, one must rely on various knowledge agents, who are nominated within a complex web of medical, scientific, and public policy discourses, all having varying degrees of authority over the representation of the potential dangers. Living in a world in which danger is mediated, persons interested in focusing their fears effectively must become consumers of representations, hence the displacement of an epistemology of fear by an epistemology of belief. For a variety of reasons, agents on both sides of dangers—the potential victims as well as the represents and explicators—tend to occult as often as they disclose them. But doubtless what is chiefly implicated on both sides is mortal danger's status in modern representational practices. It would be less appropriate to say that such danger has a "bad press" than to say that it lacks an effective press. This allows whatever/whoever has authority over life and death and the processes by which mortal fear becomes focused on real or imagined objects to escape contentiousness, to operate in an atmosphere in which fear is depoliticized. As Jack Gladney, the narrator and "main character" in *White Noise* says, while scanning the television to get the news after having fled from an "airborne toxic event,"

> Everything we love and have worked for is under serious threat. But we
> have looked around and see no response from the official organs of the
> media. The airborne toxic event is a horrifying thing. Our fear is
> enormous. Even if there hasn't been a great loss of life, don't we deserve
> some attention for our suffering, our human worry, our terror? Isn't fear
> news?[8]

Don DeLillo and the Repoliticization of Fear

In *White Noise*, DeLillo produces a powerful thematization of fear and death. But this is not a traditional consciousness-raising novel aimed at alerting people either to imminent dangers or their dire consequences, as is the case, for example, with Nevil Shute's *On The Beach,* a best-selling depiction of the death of the human race as a result of nuclear war.[9] In Shute's book the reader learns, among other things, that even Australia is not safe from the radiation fallout of a nuclear war, and such themes were popular enough to produce both a follow-up film and comic strip. The media history of Shute's story is more of a DeLillo-type theme than the dangers toward which it gestures. DeLillo's novel does its work not by raising consciousness but by revealing the dilemmas and aporias of consciousness, by showing in general the extent to which consciousness is owned and operated by modern, media scripts—for example, Gladney hears one of his children mumbling "Toyota Celica" in her sleep—and in particular by showing the way modern fear remains ineffectively focused because, in a fundamental way, our epoch has rendered "real" danger illegible. Its signs are softened and commodified. Advertising, modern consumer society's most pervasive and energetic emitter of signs, forms danger into merchandising. In an analysis of the events surrounding the assassination of President Kennedy (and other similar events) DeLillo discusses this softening and commodifying of danger in a passage that anticipates much of the thematic in his *White Noise:*

> One of advertising's unspoken rules is to absorb social disruptions and dangers into the molded jell of mass-brand production. This is the philosophy of total consumerism. Black rage becomes the tacit subject of commercials for Lite beer. The ex-athletes who appear in such commercials, large black men tutored in snarls, intense stares, various intimidating gestures and expressions, serve the consumer culture by debasing righteous anger. They allow it to be incorporated into the living-room world of sitcoms and game shows. The mean looks and gestures they are asked to supply in a given commercial's scenario are ways by which the culture softens the texture of real danger, changes real things to fantasies, undercuts meaning and purpose. We consume social threats and problems as if they were breakfast food.[10]

DeLillo is aware that the America he is thematizing is a postmodern culture inasmuch as he recognizes the "radical structural difference" (as Jameson has put it) involved in the change from earlier stages of capitalism to the modern, information/consumer stage.[11] What DeLillo adds to this recognition is a postmodernist style. America, for DeLillo, is not a *thing* to be depicted; it is a system of "codes" in the two important senses of that term. In the first instance, the codes are the set of messages emerging from the electronically communicated images on which he dwells in *Americana* (his first novel) or the noises and advertising slogans that populate people's consciousness throughout *White Noise.* And, according to DeLillo, the more sophisticated the technology becomes, the more controlling and determining the codes become. "Sophisticated devices," he states, "cause people to lose convictions. We are more easily shaped, swayed, influenced."[12] He elaborates this perspective by updating, into our present technologically sophisticated surveillance situation, the Kafkaesque condition of one who is subject to criminal investigation. Mudger, the investigator/security agent in *Running Dog,* puts the case clearly:

> When technology reaches a certain level, people begin to feel like criminals
> . . . someone is after you, the computers maybe, the machine-police. You
> can't escape investigation. The facts about you and your whole existence
> have been collected or are being collected. Banks, insurance companies,
> credit organizations, tax examiners, passport offices, reporting services,
> police agencies, intelligence gatherers, devices make us pliant.[13]

There is, of course, a normative force to "codes," which is the second sense of the term, that emphasizes a code as an authoritative rule (as in "the penal code"). Technologically assisted information systems of codes seem to have a more powerful regulatory force, and modern reality, for DeLillo, is an overlapping set of information systems. We live in a postmodernist burrow, a maze constructed by the codes—at once informational and regulatory—that emerge from intelligence organizations, media messages and consumer products, banking and commercial systems, and so forth. For example, as Jack Gladney is in midnarration in *White Noise,* we get this message:

> PLEASE NOTE. In several days, your new automated banking card will
> arrive in the mail. If it is a red card with a silver stripe, your secret code
> will be the same as it is now. If it is a green card with a gray stripe, you
> must appear at your branch, with your card, to devise a new secret code.
> Codes based on birthdays are popular. WARNING. Do not write down
> your code. Do not carry your code on your person. REMEMBER. You
> cannot access your account unless your code is entered properly. Know
> your code. Reveal your code to no one. Only your code allows you to
> enter the system.[14]

This is more than a message for the characters in *White Noise;* it is the condition against which DeLillo writes. Like Kafka, his writing is aimed at escaping from closed systems, from the web of codes that remain unread because they are confused with the "real."[15] What DeLillo's recent fiction, particularly his *White Noise,* seems designed to do is to deconstruct the maze, a deconstruction effected not with simple, unreflective statements about the maze but with a variety of narrative, grammatical, and rhetorical strategies that first construct it and then deconstruct it.

One of the first and most essential textual strategies is DeLillo's construction of characters. For example, in a discussion of his *Players,* he refers to his work as "pure fiction" in that his characters "have been momentarily separated from the story telling apparatus; they're still ideas, vague shapes."[16]

And the characters lack a consistent, coherent personality, operating more as linguistic vehicles than self-contained and controlled identities. What De-Lillo says of his characters in *End Zone* is a persistent pattern in his *White Noise,* as well. "Some of the characters have a made up nature. They are pieces of jargon. They engage in wars of jargon with each other. There is a mechanical element, a kind of fragmented self-consciousness."[17]

In *White Noise,* this strategy is enhanced by creating separate voices for various media, as well as for persons. One reviewer mistakes this textual strategy, which represents postindustrial society's fragmentation and diffi-cult-to-discern codes, for poor character development, complaining that DeLillo does not "render as faithfully as possible, the feelings his characters would be likely to have in the situation he has them in."[18]

DeLillo is not after pure feelings (whatever those might be) but is pursu-ing the delirium one experiences in trying to focus feelings in a world of names and codes that prevent feelings, especially fear and dread, from ef-fectively situating themselves in systems of self-interpretation that connect with practical experience and likely consequences. In *White Noise,* as in other novels, even though characters narrate, they do not control the flow of discourse. Committed to a view that "style and language reflect the land-scape," DeLillo interweaves his character's musings with the media voices that construct modern meaning systems. To deconstruct such systems, one must first represent them. The seemingly bland and impenetrable facticity of the world must be placed in a centrifuge to separate out the many layers of codes, the maze constructing that facticity. Kinnear, an anarchist in *Play-ers,* recognizes the layers of complex codes constituting intelligence/surveillance relations, financial relations, and so on. "It's everywhere . . . mazes . . ." And, a moment later, "Behind every stark fact we encounter layers of ambiguity."[19]

In *Players,* DeLillo gives us a glimpse of some of the layers underlying what appears as the simple fact of money by representing the gap between the direct, tactile experience of holding it and the complex modes for as-sembling and transmitting financial holdings. DeLillo has Lyle's gaze, in *Players,* pierce the "paper existence" of money:

> He'd seen the encoding rooms, the microfilming of checks, money moving, shrinking as it moved, beginning to elude visualization, to pass from paper existence to electronic sequences, its meaning increasingly complex, harder to name. It was condensation, the whole process, a paring away of money's accidental properties, of money's touch.[20]

Here is how DeLillo works, dissolving objectivities into the processes — particularly the contemporary electronic processes — that constitute them. And, recognizing that the modern world is populated less by things than by simulacra, DeLillo has the action in *White Noise* hover ambiguously across television and face-to-face relations as the distinction between the real and representation breaks down. DeLillo decodes modernity in both important senses. He displays the informational and communications systems, the mediating structures that produce meanings, and he challenges their authority. It is his style, his way of playing with the codes constructing modernity that is his functional vehicle.

Confronting the dilemma of codes—mastering them without being mastered by them—DeLillo's rhetorical moves, some of which are very spare gestures, provoke powerful reflection on modernity's closed system of codes, which, among other things, are complicit in obscuring danger and death. His analyses are delivered less in the form of conventional plots and more in revealing linguistic fragments, which reflect the fragmented nature of modern subjectivity. For example, in *White Noise,* there is a reference to two women who are reunited on television—they had been "twin sisters in the lost city of Atlantis 50,000 years ago"—and are now "food stylists for NASA."[21]

This fictional but highly plausible vocation conveys the general level of merchandising mediation for even such basic human functions as eating. That NASA is the venue for this new profession conveys the banality and bureaucratized collective inattention of systems for hastening danger and death. It implies, moreover, that this banal commodification of food services, mixed with a death machine, constructs our postmodern defense system (our burrow) as an intricate web of complicit practices that diffuse rather than focus danger and death.

DeLillo is showing, with a seemingly trivial aside here, that even our agencies directly implicated in creating potential for mass destruction are "agencies" in a highly dispersed, cultural sense. People whose vocations seem very distant from death are part of a penumbra of banal practices that, though not as effective as the main agents of death and destruction, all contribute to the phenomenon. The ritual space within which societies used to cope with death, making it intimate by confronting it and delimiting its meaning from all that is nondeath, is displaced by processes producing radical nonintimacy. Discursive and nondiscursive practices serve to defer attention to death-related services by making them quotidian rather than decisive and extraordinary.

DeLillo also conveys an image of postmodern society with a postmodernist grammar. Individual subjects are not responsible for apprehending objects or creating actions. What are objectified or enacted throughout *White Noise* are vague tendencies produced out of the same milieu that produces the fragmented and ambiguous system of subjectivities, of which each character is a representative.

There is, nevertheless, a rough plot to *White Noise,* which is meant to reflect modernity's most powerful plot, the production of death. As Gladney puts it early in the novel, "All plots tend to move deathward," but even this seemingly ideationally committed pronouncement turns out to have been ventriloquized through an unwary speaker who, reflecting on it six lines later, says, "Is this true? Why did I say it? What does it mean?"[22] This desultory and unfocused relation to death pervades the story, as almost every banal activity seems to have a contrived, oblique relation to death—for example, there are elderly students in a posture class, about whom the narrator remarks, "We seem to believe it is possible to ward off death by following rules of good grooming."[23]

At its most general level, the novel centers around the Gladney family. Jack Gladney is the head of the Department of Hitler Studies (a discipline he has founded) at College-on-the-Hill. While his three former wives are all connected with the intelligence community and are described as lean and angular, Gladney's current wife, Babette, is a plump, earth-mother type who teaches a posture class and conspires with Gladney to hold death at arm's length by sinking into a structure of self-indulgent, preoccupied domesticity. But ironically, the very family that provides a retreat from the realities of danger and death also provides openings for its presence. For example, Jack and Babette's son Heinrich remains preoccupied with danger and death and therefore resists the house epistemology, the avoidance and distraction practiced by his parents. The ever-present television set produces news of dangers within its continuous stream of simulated experiences, dangers that present themselves through the vocalizations of the children as well as through the TV's more direct interventions into the house conversations.

Thus Jack's displacement strategies, burying himself in domesticity and in academic abstractions—adopting a keen interest in Hitler, an arch purveyor of death who had become a killer in order to deal with his preoccupation with death—do not avail him. He is assailed by dangers through the chinks in his domestic, defensive burrow by the interaction of his children with the electronic simulations produced by the commodified information order surrounding his household.

Gladney's studied inattention is further frustrated by his friend Murray, whose sophistication—"I'm from New York," he keeps saying to explain it—continually summons Gladney out of his inattention and urges him to decode modernity. "You have to learn how to look," he says, urging Gladney to find the "codes and messages."[24] In contrast with Gladney's lexical simplicity—Gladney speaks in brief fragments, expressing wonder and confusion—Murray theorizes culture, waxing eloquent, for example, on television as myth, while Gladney and Babette wonder how to insulate their children from the cultural flotsam and jetsam of TV. Meanwhile, the television monologue continues: "Dacron, Orlon, Lycra spandex" intrudes into the conversation.[25]

While Gladney and Babette press continually to burrow into family life to ward off the fear of death, their friend Murray and all the intruding cultural signs provoke confrontations with them. And, most important for the structure of the novel, "events" intrude as well. Once family and college life and their cultural contents have been portrayed in Part I, "the airborne toxic event" occurs, and the family runs from the danger, only to encounter it as Gladney is exposed to the toxicity while stepping out of his car to fill his gas tank during the exodus.

The novel then moves to the last part, the "Dylarama" where the family learns that Babette has been taking a privately produced drug, dylar, designed to overcome the fear of death. Once apprised of this, Gladney sets out to kill Babette's supplier, with whom she has been engaging in sexual encounters in return for being an experimental subject for the drug (in a TV-dominated motel room). In effect, Gladney's preoccupation with killing as a way of coping with the fear of death (represented with his Hitler obsession) comes close to actualization, although he fails both to kill the dylar man, Mr. Gray, and ultimately to push away the fear of death.

In the end, DeLillo has shown the inefficacy of all "fear-of-death inhibitors,"[26] and one character, Winnie Richards, expresses the need to incorporate fear of death into life:

> I think it's a mistake to lose one's sense of death, even one's fear of death. Isn't death the boundary we need? Doesn't it give a precious texture to life, a sense of definition? You have to ask yourself whether anything you do in this life would have beauty and meaning without the knowledge that you carry of a final line, a border or limit.[27]

And, in the same dialogue, DeLillo expresses the importance of preserving an epistemology of fear with imagery that recalls vividly the Eskimo shaman scenario developed above. Speaking of her "spacey theory about human fear," Winnie says to Gladney, as she draws him imaginatively out of his home/burrow:

> Picture yourself, Jack, a confirmed homebody, a sedentary fellow who finds himself walking in a deep wood. You spot something out of the corner of your eye. Before you know anything else, you know that this thing is very large and that it has no place in your ordinary frame of reference, a flaw in the world picture. Either it shouldn't be here or you shouldn't. Now the thing comes into full view. It is a grizzly bear, enormous, shiny brown, dripping with slime from its bared fangs. Jack, you have never seen a large animal in the wild. The sight of this grizzer is so electrifyingly strange that it gives you a renewed sense of yourself, a fresh awareness of the self—the self in terms of a unique, horrific situation. You see yourself in a new and intense way. You rediscover yourself. You are lit up for your own imminent dismemberment. The beast on hind legs has enabled you to see who you are as if for the first time, outside familiar

surroundings, alone, distinct, whole. The name we give to this complicated process is fear.[28]

This is the most important insight at which *White Noise* arrives. But *White Noise* is a novel, not a treatise on the importance of fear, and the structure of the novel, its narrative journey, its rhetorical motions, the grammars of its characters, deploy modernity's repressive politics of fear. They map the various mediating structures whose authority ("codes") inhibit both individual recognition of the place of death in identity formation and the development of public, discursive modes for problematizing danger in a way that allows people to connect everyday experience to vital questions. It is these inhibiting structures, then, that DeLillo's textual practices as well as his thematics bring into recognition.

With his style as well as with his character's remarks, DeLillo elaborates the mediating linguistic systems that drown out significant connection between danger and efficacious forms of apprehension. All that unfocused fear can discern is the noise of linguistic evasions. At one point, Babette, in the grip of fear, wonders if death is merely that estranging linguistic mediation.

"What if death is nothing but sound?"
"Electrical noise."
"You hear it forever. Sound all around. How awful."
"Uniform, white."[29]

And DeLillo proliferates the white noise with his writing. The main narrators are often interrupted, just as we expect coherence, by emissions from the postindustrial, consumer culture. One chapter's action ends with, "A woman passing on the street said, 'A decongestant, an antihistamine, a cough suppressant, a pain reliever,' " and another with the word, "Panasonic."

While DeLillo's subjectivities, in the form of linguistic fragments, reproduce the noise that drowns out self-awareness or the ability of those in modernity to locate the sources of production of the modern self, his rhetoric conveys the displacements with which the self is shielded from significant problematics connecting death and danger to life. For example, he employs a metaphor of physical bulk to show how Gladney is caught in ineffective surmises about how to ward off death. Gladney's preoccupation with Hitler is decoded by Murray, who says, "Some people are larger than life. Hitler is larger than death. You thought he would protect you. I understand completely."[30] This interpretation makes coherent the size imagery DeLillo introduces near the beginning where we learn that Gladney is comforted by his bulk; he is carrying 230 pounds on a six-foot, three-inch frame and has big hands and feet.[31] And later, Gladney is amazed that his very large colleague, Cotsakis, described as a "monolith of thick and wadded flesh,"[32] could be dead (from drowning). Gladney is incredulous and questions Murray about the death: "Poor Cotsakis, lost in the surf . . . that enormous man. . . . Dead. A big man like that . . . to be so enormous, then to die."[33]

It is also the overall structure of DeLillo's narrative that contributes to his mapping of modernity's fear and sense of death inhibitors. The story in *White Noise* is in the shape of a loop, in that it begins and ends representing quotidian family existence in the midst of the commodified, consumer culture, its characters suspended in a commercial zone saturated with consumer messages. On the very first page, as the students arrive at College-on-the-Hill, DeLillo describes the objects inside the caravan of station wagons carrying parents and students.

> As the cars slowed to a crawl and stopped, students sprang out and raced to the rear doors to begin removing the objects inside; the stereo sets, radios, personal computes; small refrigerators and table ranges; the cartons of phonograph records and cassettes; the hair dryers and styling irons; the tennis rackets, soccer balls, hockey and lacrosse sticks, bows and arrows; the controlled substances; the birth control pills and devices; the junk food still in shopping bags—onion-and-garlic chips, nacho thins, peanut cream patties, Waffelos and Kabooms, fruit chews and toffee popcorn; the Dum-Dum pops, the Mystic mints.[34]

After the narrative journey from domesticity to calamity and rash actions, the story is drawn back to the mundane venues of family life. At the very end, people are in a supermarket with a slightly altered relation to products. They are more anxious as a result of the "airborne toxic event," but their fear is not directed at environmental, life-threatening dangers; they are simply slightly less able to negotiate movement through the aisles, and their buying behavior is somewhat disoriented and suspicious.

> They turn into the wrong aisle, peer along shelves, sometimes stop abruptly, causing other carts to run into them. . . . They scrutinize the small print on packages, wary of a second level of betrayal. The men scan for stamped dates, the women for ingredients.[35]

With his narrative, DeLillo has informed us about the powerful delegating effects of modern, commercial/consumer-oriented space. Although the residents of the town have been forced out of their domestic routines by an event that should alter their relationships to themselves and life in general, they are summoned back into their old shopping haunts, and the new unease they experience remains quarantined within their relationship to consumer products.[36]

In addition to the connection with products, which absorbs much of the ideational energy of his characters, DeLillo, with his writing as well as with his thematics, presents the mediating and productive effects of television on what, for the modern person, is the "real," and, more important, what is to be feared. The TV is his window in the postmodern burrow, bringing near dangers and generating fears as well as desires. As Gladney puts it:

> Blacksmith is nowhere near a large city. We don't feel threatened in quite the same way as other towns do. We're not smack in the path of history and its contaminations. If our complaints have a focal point, it would have to be the TV set, where the outer torment lurks, causing fear and secret desires.[37]

DeLillo represents the TV role by giving it a voice throughout the novel. The narrator is often interrupted by the TV, and, at the level of thematics, DeLillo has identified here a radical entanglement between TV as informational technology and the modern constitution of danger. For example, much of the anxiety that characters in *White Noise* manifest is connected to TV weather forecasts. In a sequence about shoppers crowding the roads to avoid being out later when snow is forecast, Gladney narrates:

> Older people in particular were susceptible to news of impending calamity as it was forecast on TV by grave men standing before digital radar maps or pulsing photographs of the planet.[38]

DeLillo expresses this about TV weather with an ironic reversal. Earlier, we learn that Gladney's German teacher — tutoring Gladney who knows no German and must lead an upcoming conference on Hitler studies — is fascinated by meteorology. As a German teacher who also teaches meteorology, his strategy is to approach danger and death rather than to simply fear them. When asked how his interest in meteorology came about, he responds, "My mother's death had a terrible impact on me," and then he adds that after seeing a weather report on TV, "I turned to meteorology for comfort."[39]

DeLillo is attuned here to an important aspect of the popular culture of fear and its relationship to media. Recently, Andrew Ross has pointed out that there have been large-scale cultural transformations in weather forecasting. For example, the old "weather folklore," which was based on an "everyday cult of 'experience,' " has been replaced by a "professional ethos of "expertise,' " and that expertise, produced on TV weather forecasts, has turned increasingly toward a representation of global dangers. The modern weather report, Ross says, is danger-oriented, albeit in a displaced, commodified sense; it represents "the almost complete commodification of bodily maintenance in the face of year-round weather threats and assaults."[40]

The inhibiting effects of TV on locating danger and death, however, is the major role it plays in *White Noise*. Mr. Gray, the inventor of the death-fear inhibitor, dylar, is represented as one who speaks with a TV-like babble and is encountered in a motel room dominated by a TV, and the "airborne toxic event" is presented on TV with various fear-deflecting modes of representation, for example, "They're calling it a black billowing cloud"[41] (after having called it an "airborne toxic event"). This gap between the danger and its representation is also reflected in Gladney's conversation with a technician running a "simuvac" machine, which is another piece of forecasting technology designed to predict his life expectancy after his exposure to the toxicity.

"Am I going to die?" he asks the technician. "Not as such," is the response. "What do you mean?" asks Gladney. "Not in so many words," comes the response. "How many words does it take?" asks Gladney. The technician again: "It's not a question of words; it's a question of years. We'll know more in fifteen years. In the meantime we definitely have a situation."[42]

It is not surprising that in a modern culture with death-distancing representational practices, one cannot effect an epistemology of fear. Recognizing this, DeLillo dwells from time to time on the issue of epistemologies of belief and their inefficacy in our postmodern, anxiety-ridden burrow. We rely not on experience but "data," Gladney says. "Terrifying data is now an industry in itself."[43] "Knowledge," DeLillo recognizes, is temporarily reassuring but largely ineffective, and modern people are simply consumers of representations of danger—especially now, says Babette, who explains why her pedagogy extends to teaching a course on "Eating and Drinking: Basic Parameters":

> Knowledge changes every day. People like to have their beliefs reinforced. Don't lie down after eating a heavy meal. Don't drink liquor on an empty stomach. If you must swim, wait at least an hour after eating. The world is more complicated for adults than it is for children. We didn't grow up with all these shifting facts and attitudes. One day they just started appearing. So people need to be reassured by someone in a position of authority that a certain way to do something is the right way or the wrong way, at least for the time being. I'm the closest they could find, that's all.[44]

Conclusion

If this were a treatise that lived up to Jürgen Habermas's demand for a way to theorize the present, it would be appropriate to conclude by explicitly recognizing "the necessity of gleaning normatively substantive principles from modern experience."[45] But whatever normative force this chapter has is immanent in its style, particularly its juxtapositions of themes and thinkers, and the politics of fear I have attempted to present is not connected to the failure of the modern state to steer society in ways that retain a rational basis for policy deliberation (to paraphrase the Habermasian, somewhat state-centric problematic).

My aim has been, rather, to create a frame within which certain thinkers, through their textual practices as much as through their thematics, help us to think themes that are rarely accessible because of modernity's modes of problematizing and often obscuring danger and death. Moreover, my concern is with the recovery of *politics,* not rational steering mechanisms, where politics is understood as a recognition that we are always involved in a struggle to, as Paul Virilio has put it, "extract life from death."[46] And "life" is seen not simply as a matter of duration and "policy," thereby a matter of protection—for the "burrow" is as much a prison as it is a shelter—but an intense encounter with death; it is a living with danger rather than merely a consuming of frightening data. *White Noise* ends with neither a hopeful sign nor a lament but with Gladney in line at the supermarket, scanning the tabloid versions of the fear industry.

> Everything we need that is not food or love is here in the tabloid racks. The tales of the supernatural and the extraterrestrial, the miracle vitamins, the cures for cancer, the remedies for obesity, the cults of the famous and the dead.[47]

To end in DeLillo's spirit, then, we can look around with his kind of discernment. For example, recently there was a report of a new fear in the *Wall Street Journal*. The story begins:

> If anything can make '80s-style strivers take action, it's fear. Afraid of flab, they join health clubs. Afraid of being lonely, they deluge magazines with personal ads.
> Now there's a new fear making the rounds—the fear of forgetfulness.[48]

It is Alzheimer's that people often suspect is implicated in their memory lapses, and although "very few middle-aged worriers are actually suffering from troubles so serious" (doctors call such lapses "age-associated memory impairment"), there is a small industry developing to supply products for the worriers. As the writer puts it, "where there is fear, there are people trying to capitalize on taming that fear," and she goes on to elaborate the growing industry in adult education courses, memory-training manuals, cassette tapes, and the like.

A Harvard doctor sums up the aim of the product seekers:

> They want to eat a certain kind of food, do a certain kind of exercise to prevent mortality. . . . But the average life expectancy is still three score plus 10, which is what's written in the Bible.[49]

CHAPTER 9

Terminations
Elkin's *Magic Kingdom* and the
Politics of Death

*Hey, big deal! Death always went with the territory. I'll see you in
Disneyland.*

Richard Ramirez, AKA "The Night Stalker"

I would rather have a metaphor than a good cigar.

Stanley Elkin

*To solve political problems becomes difficult for those who allow anxiety
alone to pose them.*

Georges Bataille

In their different ways, Richard Ramirez and Stanley Elkin have used fierce
tactics to produce a pedagogy about death. Ramirez made the above statement in response to a reporter's question about whether he was concerned
that he might get the death penalty for his many grisly murders. At a simple
level, Ramirez's remark is disquieting, for it displays no ambivalence toward the fierce, remorseless, and cruel acts he perpetrated on his victims.
He is saying he is indifferent to and undeterred by the possibility of paying
for his killing with his life. Indeed he may even be welcoming his exe-
cution—the other side of the coin of his striving for intimacy with death. He
causes death and seeks to experience his own.

Apart from the sense of disquiet many experience at Ramirez's gratuitous
cruelty, his lack of concern for the consequences of his acts for either his
victims or himself, many are also doubtless disquieted by the larger aspect
of Ramirez's relation to death. When it comes to death, Ramirez is not an
avoider. He seeks intimacy with it in deed and, apparently, in word. And
whatever expectations he may have had of his interlocutors, his statement
makes of him an underground man. To those who anchor themselves to life

140

by resisting and deferring death, whose concept of the advantageous is based on distancing death, anyone who views the advantageous on the basis of death's nearness appears to be irrational.[1]

But Ramirez's statement does not merely set him apart. It reveals a sensitivity to the more common model of advantage. His "see you in Disneyland" should provoke a recognition that one can only see how central death is in all the spaces within which we associate by imagining a space where death is suspended, as in the company of the never-aging Mickey Mouse. Indeed, this different construction of temporality—a place where time stands still—is part of what sets Disneyland apart.

After Michel Foucault, we can treat Disneyland as a kind of "heterotopia."

> Places of this kind are outside of all places, even though it may be possible to indicate their location in reality. Because these places are absolutely different from all the sites that they reflect and speak about, I shall call them, by way of contrast to utopias, heterotopias.[2]

Foucault goes on to note how such heterotopias function. Among other things, a heterotopia serves as a mirror that exerts a "counteraction" on the positions people occupy.[3] This allows for the kind of reflection on space that makes our standpoints or locations contestable in contrast with the fixity they achieve within the institutionalized thought systems that help to shape them.

Such reflection, afforded by a heterotopia like Disneyland, allows for a relaxation of the ownership of those rigorously disciplined agencies that construct death within anxious discourses—the medical, insurance/actuarial, and so on. By recognizing that the grip death has on our imagination is a function of the discursive spaces within which it has been controlled, we can take Georges Bataille's instruction and not "allow anxiety alone" to pose the problem of death.

But the price of Ramirez's pedagogy is too high. His victims have paid it, and we cannot accept his ferocious methods. However, there is a more benign form of ferocity that can accomplish the kind of pedagogy that Ramirez's remark has set in motion. It is found in Stanley Elkin's "bully poetics," which, in his *Magic Kingdom,* places death on center stage. And Elkin's fantasy operates with wider vistas than does Ramirez's. He takes us to Disney World, which is several times larger than Disneyland, and his novel is far more prolix than Ramirez's brief treatment in that it relentlessly underscores many of the illusions belonging to both Disney World and the worlds it reflects. The setting of the novel is in two "magic kingdoms," England and Disney World. The former's magical qualities are highlighted by the special attention given to two of London's timeless locations: Buckingham Palace and Madame Tussaud's Wax Museum.

Before considering these magic kingdoms, however, we need some familiarity with the prototext within which Elkin developed both his notion of magic and the necessary ferocity of rhetoric. This we find in his story, "A Poetics for Bullies." "I'm Push the bully," it begins, and, with important significance for Elkin's treatment of the terminally ill and largely disabled children taken to Disney World in *The Magic Kingdom,* the bully continues,

> and what I hate are new kids and sissies, dumb kids and smart, rich kids, poor kids, kids who wear glasses, talk funny, show off, patrol boys and wise guys, and kids who pass pencils and water the plants—and cripples, *especially* cripples. I love nobody loved.[4]

Is this merely cruelty? The suggestion that it is instead a political allegory comes a few lines later when Push praises equality: "Do you know what makes me cry? The Declaration of Independence. 'All men are created equal,' that's beautiful."[5] Push is not simply terrorizing the weak; he is trying to provoke a self-consciousness about the imposed boundaries that produce such things as normal and marginal selves. To think that our discursive boundaries are part of some transcendent plan belonging to a divinely sponsored universe that hands out truths is magical thinking, a kind of thinking that Push the bully opposes. Push (and Elkin) mount this opposition with "sleight-of-mouth."

At one point, Push convinces his victim to hand over one of his arrows, saying he will magically turn the one arrow into two:

> "Trouble, trouble, double ruble!" I snap it and give back the pieces. Well sure. There *is* no magic. If there were I would learn it. I would find out the words, the slow turns and strange passes, draw the bloods and get the herbs, do the fires like a vestal. I would look for the main chants. *Then* I'd change things. *Push* would!
>   . . . But there's only casuistical trick. Sleight-of-mouth, the bully's poetics.[6]

Push (and Elkin) are courageous: "If you're a coward, get out of the business," says Push.[7] Sleight-of-mouth is not for the fearful or anxious. Elkin's bullying is rhetorical, his language is fierce, and the ferocity is aimed at encouraging an awareness where insensitivity has ruled. "I am trying to upset the applecarts of expectations and ordinary grammar," he has said, "and you can only do that with fierce language. . . . Rhetoric is here, not only to perform for us, to show its triples and barrel rolls, but to introduce significance into what otherwise may be untouched by significance."[8]

That the ferocity is rhetorical is apparent here, as Push follows a dutiful young lad who is collecting travel pamphlets from the Italian Information Center to get pictures for a special unit at his school. The language becomes fierce as Push travels, rhetorically, to the pamphlets' destinations:

I follow for two blocks and bump into him as he steps from a curb. It's a *collision*—the pamphlets fall from his arms. Pretending confusion, I walk on his paper Florence. I grind my heel in his Riviera. I climb Vesuvius and sack his Rome and dance on the Isle of Capri.[9]

In what direction is this ferocity aimed? Again, Push gives us a hint.

I have lived my life in pursuit of the vulnerable: Push the chink seeker, wheeler dealer in the flawed cement of the personality. A collapse maker. But what isn't vulnerable, *who* isn't? There is that which is unspeakable, so I speak it, that which is unthinkable, which I think. Me and the devil, we do God's dirty work, after all.[10]

Elkin speaks the unspeakable in order to tell us that life is unsponsored and flawed. He shows us our limitations and infirmities and reveals the delusional qualities in what we treat as the fixities that give us comfort. Push has an antagonist in the story, John Williams, who exemplifies high and noble visions of essential human community. He is one who rallies all the kids around him and regales them with stories, building a devoted following. It seems that Push's special ferocity toward this paragon is owed both to his democratic spirit (he refers to Williams as a "prince") and his desire to bully people out of succumbing to easy reassurances, into accepting life with its lack of guarantees, its disappointments, its unfulfilled wants. Whatever illusory forms of solidarity become the objects of people's devotion, Push overcomes (and we learn more about the significance of his name):

I can't stand them near me. I move against them. I shove them away. I force them off. I press them, thrust them aside. I *push through*.[11]

Death: The Postmodernist Rendering

In *The Magic Kingdom,* Elkin's rhetorical ferocity is aimed more specifically at the way death is sequestered in various ideational structures of reassurance—notions of temporality, reverence toward places thought of as sacred or authoritative, commitment to the ideas of a final justice and the fairness to things, and the belief in a transcendent and reasonable world. He shows, with his rhetoric, how death looks when produced differently. He speaks the unspeakability of death and dying in ferocious tones—none more cruelly enlightening than in a long, bullying soliloquy delivered by Mickey Mouse, as he taunts seven children with disfiguring, terminal diseases at the end of the story (an episode treated later in this chapter).

There is a politics immanent in Elkin's fierce, polysyllabic encounter with death and dying throughout the novel. It is partly a politics of recovery. As one critic has aptly put it, "Elkin is in the business of putting death back into dying."[12] But that recovery is not to be understood within the traditional modernist frame, which in the cases of both literary and social theory seeks a recovery of authenticity or a discovery of the ideal. Accordingly, its critical dimension, when positively cast, treats the prevailing discursive practices in terms of their movement toward the authentic or ideal and, when negatively cast, in terms of their tendency to obscure them or to produce an alienating dissimulation of them. Moreover, modernism operates within an ontology that presumes a preexisting ordered, structured, or coherent whole such that discourses of recovery are seen as recouping this obscured or lost wholeness.

The rejection of this heroic hermeneutic is represented in Elkin's bully-critique of John Williams, the paragon of "A Poetics for Bullies." And, more important, it is represented in Elkin's textual practice. His ironic cascade of images, his catalogue of similes, and his representations of the shifting discursive spaces within which such things as death are held reflect his rejection of a quest for an authentic order and the right or authentic spaces for its components. His postmodernist poetics constitutes, first, his acceptance of a world that is fundamentally disordered and, second, his use of a style that resists closure. His prose, his constantly shifting rhetorical motions and disquieting grammar, constitute a "suspensive irony."[13]

Elkin's stylistic posture does not, then, move toward closure in the representation of a proper world but conveys the multiplicity with which such things as death can be practiced and represented. Elkin is not concerned with death as ultimate limit or death as a frame for authenticity, or even death as an expression of a deeper spiritual domain or standard of temporality. Rather, he engages the ironic representation of death, which makes the ordinary ways of speaking it appear to be the result of an imperious patrolling and sacralizing of arbitrary discursive spaces.

For example, at one point, the seven terminally ill children in the novel are referred to simply within a notion of temporality as "short-timers,"[14] while in others, the linguistic frame becomes penal:

> These kids are condemned and convicted. They've been found guilty. . . .
> They've been put on the index. There's a price on their heads.[15]

This rhetoric of multiplicity is not, however, merely ironic play. A politics of death emerges as Elkin's rhetorical ferocity speaks the more unspeakable aspects of it.

This politics of death animating Elkin's story is elaborated more directly by Paul Virilio in his various writings on war. In arguing that the understanding of war has moved increasingly into the discursive space of logistics, a space within which it is treated technically rather than politically, Virilio reminds us that death and injury are what war is primarily about, as he implies in the prologue of his recent *War and Cinema,* where he quotes the Japanese maxim, "War is the art of embellishing death."[16] Given this view, along with Virilio's notion that what politics is about is deliberation and confrontation, a politics of death requires an intimate confrontation with it:

> When we see Leonardo da Vinci's discovery of death, we realize just how much the Renaissance artists—and later Delacroix, Gericault and Soutine— were fascinated by corpses. There we have a will, which is not at all morbid, to confront death. They were fascinated by death as they were fascinated by waterfalls, by lightning, by storms. . . . We mustn't turn away. *That* is political and civic virtue.[17]

Apart from his interest in putting death on the political agenda is Virilio's identification of the contemporary locus of control over death. Asserting that "it's absolutely scandalous for doctors to be the only ones confronted with the ethical problem of death,"[18] he speaks of the political space within which it should be lodged; it ought to be part of a political understanding of what kind of life we should live. And life, for Virilio, can only be understood as something that is extracted from death, for it makes sense only within an awareness of death which frames life.[19]

Elkin makes the same point ironically. During an absurd conversation about the various ways that the medical establishment determines death— the participants speak of brain death, lung death, and even finger death— someone breaks in: "There are many nice questions. There are many ethical considerations."[20] This deferral to institutionalized frames for moralizing the issue is only a slight shift in the discursive terrain, for the treatment implied by "ethical considerations" amounts to a preservation of the medicalized discursive space with some post hoc hand wringing simply added on.

The Magic Kingdom

It is with a cognizance of Virilio's attempt at a political discourse within which one can reinscribe death in life that we can approach much of the political significance of Stanley Elkin's *Magic Kingdom*. Like Virilio, Elkin understands that discursive terrains are not neutral. They are formed by scripts embodying spatial and temporal strategies. Thus, as he puts death on the agenda in his ironic, postmodernist way—not as a thing to be authentically discerned, but as a multiplicity of practices—he structures his narrative, first of all, by locating life and death in two magical domains (as noted earlier).

When the story begins in England, Eddy Bale has become England's "most recognized beggar,"[21] using the media to raise funds to cure his dying son, Liam, who has a terminal case of leukemia. When Liam dies after suffering terribly from the various standard and homeopathic "cures" to which he is subjected, Bale begins a new campaign. To compensate for Liam's suffering, he wants to do for a terminally ill group of children what he feels he should have done for Liam, make their last days pleasant instead of painful. He decides to take a group to Disney World, the "Magic King-dom."

Encouraged by having received a letter of condolence from the queen, his fund raising takes him to Buckingham Palace. During his visit there, it becomes clear that in some respects the palace is a magical place; it is deathless in the sense that time has stood still for its inhabitants. Bale is asked by a royal youngster if he is a "commoner," and a Scrabble game sitting on a table in the anteroom displays some words in a game the players have abandoned: "peasant," "serf," "primogeniture."[22] In general, most aspects of the palace are far removed from the realities of everyday life. All of the currency in Buckingham Palace is therefore symbolic, even the check for fifty pounds that the queen writes out to Bale. She tells him to show it around to stimulate donations and then to return it.

Before Liam dies, he expresses an interest in being placed in Madame Tussaud's, a place where his likeness — if not his actual life — will endure:

"Madame Tussaud's!" Liam says. "Me in Madame Tussaud's! That's a stunner. I mean no boy *wants* to die, but that's a stunner. I can almost see the expression on my mates' faces when they see me.[23]

It is clear that these two venues, the palace and the museum, constitute the centers of magical thinking about death in this kingdom.

The other place in the story, Disney World, is magical in a similar sense. It is populated with ageless characters — especially Mickey Mouse, the king of the Magic Kingdom. These magical places of illusion and the various narratives for which Eddy Bale's tour serves as a burlesque constitute, then, the kind of heterotopias that serve to direct our attention to the illusory elements of our ordinary terrains. As Foucault noted in his discussion of such places, one of their important functions is "to create a space of illusion that exposes every real space, all the sites inside of which human life is partitioned, as still more illusory."[24]

The force of this spatial strategy, in which writing and location are intertwined, operates at two levels. First, the ironic level of Elkin's writing is linked to the placement of the statements, the spaces from which they issue. For example, one of the children, Benny Maxim, whose fierce colloquial speech deploys much of Elkin's ferocity (while its content deploys Elkin's democratic spirit), is here talking to another of the youngsters about what kind of world Disney World is:

It's some tarted-up Brighton, is all. Adventureland, Tomorrowland. The bloody Never-lands! Greasy great kid stuff is what I say!"

"The Netherlands?"

What? . . . Oh. No, sweetheart. Neverland. You know, where Peter Pansy flies his pals in the pantomine. Not the *country*, not the place wif the wood gym shoes and all the boot forests. You don't talk the bull's wool do

you, Luv? Not to worry. We're all Englitch 'ere. Just little dying Englitch
boys and girls. Which is why I think we should 'ave been personally
consulted, drawn into discussion, like before they shipped us all off to
Florida and the Magic Kingdom to put us on the rides and expose us to the
dangerous tropical sun.[25]

What sets up the irony in this passage are a series of imaginative
geographies—the geopolitics that gives us England versus the Netherlands,
and the discursive practices that officially relegate Disney World, the
"amusement province," to the domain of the imaginary where, for example, "Peter Pansy flies his pals in the pantomine."

Or again, when the children are taken on a river ride on a "tiny steamer
that vaguely resembled the *African Queen*," the conversations are rendered
ironic by the ersatz, invented aspect of Disney World's places. "Nature is
amazing," says one of the children, and the boat pilot responds with, "I
learned all my lore here on the river."[26] This is not an ironic remark until
Elkin's description goes on to note how invented is the place to which the
boatman is referring. As the boatman spoke, "with a broad sweep of his
arm he indicated the rubber duckies floating on the surface of the water, the
mechanically driven, wind-up sharks, the needlework palm fronds along
the banks."[27]

This irony here, made possible by the invented nature of this particular
place, is simply more obvious than in other parts of the text. The ironic
stance is pervasive, however. It extends to all aspects of the textual strategy.
By making clear that all the spatiotemporal commitments that organize
people's lives are acts of the imagination and that the "world" in general is
an imagined set of places, Elkin is able to make irony the central trope of his
novel.

The second level at which the official divisions of the real versus the illusory are challenged comes through in episodes of awareness in which the
meanings of the different worlds are revalued through the special perceptions of the "special" children. For example, at one point Bale's charges are
watching a parade in Disney World. The official parade, predicated on a
radical separation between the Disney characters from the amusement province and the visitor/tourists from elsewhere (the "real" provinces), is about
to begin. However, the children turn away and focus on the spectators,
mostly senior citizens, who present a parade of humanity caught in a process of decrepitude—"lamb turning to mutton," as one of the children puts
it.[28]

They see "a pot bellied, slack breasted man, his wife with bad skin, wrin-
kled, scarred, pitted as scrotum," and they see how "bellies swell up and
muscles go down," how "hips and thighs widen like jodhpurs."[29] Not being able to stop watching the crowd instead of the official parade of cartoon
characters, they end up crying, *"This, this, is the parade!"* and continue to

gawk at such bizarre scenes as "an ancient woman in a rubber Frankenstein mask for warmth," with her nurse "feeding her cigarettes" as she is "venting her smoke through a gap in the monster's jaws."[30]

In watching the parade, the "special" children begin to feel less special. By focusing on the ravages of time and the visible disabilities and personal peculiarities of the elderly visitors, Elkin undermines the effects of the rhetorics within which the terminally ill children—the "short-timers"—are to be pitied. In effect, he points out that the particular narrative for moving toward death represented by the "normal" life cycle, with its extended process of decrepitude, is not necessarily to be preferred.

This revaluing is made especially evident through one of the children, Charles Mudd-Gaddis, whose disease produces a more rapid process of decrepitude. His failing cognitive abilities have spared him the preoccupation with cosmetics, subtle prostheses, and the other accoutrements favored by those with gerontophobia.

The standard temporal model for moving toward death is also explicitly impugned in an early conversation between Bale's son, Liam, and one of his doctors. Liam says "My life is hard." The doctor remarks, "Everyone wants to live. We all love the sunshine and we all love the rain. Only the nutcase thinks life is hard. Hard? It's softer than silk pajamas."[31]

When Liam explains that he is only twelve and doesn't want to die, the conversation proceeds:

> "Yes, and you weren't always sick. You've kicked the football in your time I'll be bound. You've jumped into the header." Liam smiled. "Sure. And I'll bet the baby you know how to swim, that you've been to the baths, maybe even to the sea itself. Maybe even to Brighton. And Blackpool. Brighton and Blackpool! And you tell me life is hard."[32]

Life is hard for short-timers, it seems, only if they insist on holding onto traditional models of temporality. And the short-timer's sojourn that Elkin invents has the effect of contesting life's standard temporally driven narratives.

To organize this resistance, the movement of the story follows (and burlesques) two traditional narratives, one based on historical episodes, the healing trips to Lourdes, and the other on a folktale, the story of Snow White and the Seven Dwarfs, which has been produced in many forms, including a Walt Disney cartoon version.

One narrative, then, is an anachronistic, historical one, which Elkin uses to undermine the belief in the magical/spiritual powers of a special place. He employs a Nietzschean reversal, figuring Disney World as a "reverse Lourdes;"[33] it offers no pretense of healing but serves instead as a venue of last wishes. A rivalrous atmosphere develops as the terminally ill from all over the globe pour in:

Each day Eddy, the kids see other damaged children: Americans of course, but there is a family from Spain, a contingent from South America. There were African kids with devastating tropical diseases. He's heard that a leper or two is in the park. It's a sort of Death's invitational here . . . the new style is to deal reality the blows of fantasy.[34]

And Elkin has many of his own blows to deliver against the fantasies through which death is segregated from life, represented, among other ways, in the segregation of terminally ill children — the short-timers — from the full-termers.

There is another important dimension to the Lourdes pilgrimage narrative. Those who fail to accept death as intimately connected to life in Elkin's story treat early death as unjust. Disney World is a Lourdes with the function of providing a measure of amusement to redress the imbalance caused by the existence of children from whom years are stolen. In contrast with the force of this narrative, the children themselves seem to think that it's not a matter of justice. Early death is not something to correct for. Early or late, death's appearance is a matter of chance; it's all a gamble, and one of the children, Benny Maxim, produces this understanding. When asked where he would go on his "dream holiday," he answers "Monte Carlo."[35]

As it is put later in the story, "Benny was a gambler . . . wise to the ways — at least so he thought — of house odds." So instead of buying the terminating scenario, "he lived with hope."[36]

Elkin's other narrative vehicle addresses various dimensions of the segregation of the children from others. *The Magic Kingdom* contains what is essentially a burlesque of the Snow White story. And, like burlesque in general, the narrative element mocks the solemn lessons that are thought to organize the pedagogy of the more standard versions of the story.

Mary Cottle, a nurse accompanying the children, is Elkin's Snow White. In place of the poisoning that puts the fabled Snow White to sleep, Mary has a poisoned womb; its chemical brew is such that she can only have deformed children, and her reaction to this has been to break her engagement with her fiancé and to give up heterosexual sex altogether. In its place, she masturbates whenever she gets a chance to be alone.

If we heed the major ethical axes of traditional versions of the Snow White story, Elkin's burlesque narrative can be seen to display some fidelity to the fable's structure. Among other things, the Snow White tale is a caution against the evils of self-love (all the mirror gazing of the wicked witch/mother) and a celebration of "true" love (Snow White awaking to conjugal bliss with the prince).[37]

Elkin's Snow White, Mary Cottle, undergoes the same change. At the end of the story she and Eddy Bale have sexual intercourse, just as the sojourn with the seven terminally ill children (the Seven Dwarfs) is coming to an end. Thus, one strand of Elkin's text follows the tale's chronicling of the awakening of a dormant heterosexual sexuality.

The seven children/dwarfs are explicitly identified by Mickey Mouse, who names them in a vicious, bullying monologue. For example, after six are named he equates the seventh, whose skin is blue from a heart defect, with "Grumpy."

> Which left the blue kid, who'd given him that sullen, half-hearted response and who, more importantly, was the very color of choler. Grumpy to life! So *something* to do with death.[38]

As the story takes on all of the Snow White analogues, the text reflects more explicitly on death. But what has suggested this particular narrative vehicle? There are two dimensions of the Snow White structure that play into Elkin's hands (or perhaps better, into his sleight-of-mouth). The first and most significant are the temporal tropes that organize the Snow White story and produce the major impetus of the critical dimension of Elkin's treatment.

The seven children are "dwarfs," in the sense that they are marginalized and set apart because of their status as "short-timers." They exist in death's grip because it is thought that their time span is dwarfed. And Elkin's story militates against this view continually. In addition to the above-quoted passage in which Liam is told by his doctor that his life is not hard just because he has less time, there are numerous places where restricted views constituting the children's special identity are overturned. In particular, the idea that terminally ill children must avoid sexuality is lampooned. It becomes clear that all the restrictions on the children, justified as protecting them, are what is damaging. Thus, for example, they are finally allowed out in boats on a lake, and there is talk of making sure that these already-near-death children wear life jackets. The young man in charge of the boats objects to the children going out: "But these kids are dying," and the response comes: "They'll wear life jackets."[39]

Most significant, however, is the overcoming of the limitation on the children's sexuality. It is not sex or any other particular form of exuberance that is the cause of death. Life is the cause of death, so it may as well be lived fully. Any aspect of life can terminate in death. One child who had applied to go on Bale's trip had Che'diak-Higashi disease, and upon eagerly tearing open the envelope, which he recognized as coming from Bale, cut himself and died because the paper had produced an invasion of white blood cells.

One of the children on the trip dies of something more exciting than a promising mail call—of love. Rena Morgan tells Benny Maxim she loves him, and after saying, "Oh Benny, the good die young," she dies because of what her emotion has unleashed into a system overburdened with the effects of cystic fibrosis:

It was her respiration, her terribly heavy breathing that had caused her spasms and loosed the poisons in her chest, the mucus and biles, the clots of congestion hanging together and preserving her life by the strings of the ordinary. The great prognostication had simply failed to factor her desire into the equation. He had missed his prognosis because he hadn't taken her sighs into account, the squalls, blasts, and aerodynamics of passion, all the high winds and gale-force bluster of love.[40]

Within the story, the "great prognostication" is a prediction about whether Rena Morgan will survive the trip, but in relation to the more general thematic on death, it implies that standard, anxious orientations toward death fail to take life's passions into account and thus encourage an overly cautious practice of life. Those on the trip finally realize this. Rena Morgan stops treating her "disease" as a restriction on life and gives into her passions. And Mary Cottle/Snow White abandons her restriction to self-love (masturbation) and exuberantly copulates with Eddy Bale. If the children can embrace life despite their weaknesses and deformities, why can't Mary Cottle risk producing more of these types from her poisoned womb?

Rena Morgan's openness to desire, her refusal to capitulate to a model of hedging against an early demise, echoes Elkin's rejection of the death-defying model of temporality that has animated Eddy Bale's compensatory pilgrimage. And Mary Cottle's cries, as she and Bale are in the throes of passion, underline this. The time to live is "now."

Thinking *Now Now Now Now Now Now* and inviting all the cock-eyed, crook-backed, tortuous bandy deformity out of the bottle, calling forth fiends, calling forth bogies, rabid, cow-head bloody bones. *Now* she thinks, *now!*[41]

She has decided to live and therefore love in the "now," and to accept with love all those that might result.

God's ugly, punished, customers, his obscene and frail and lubberly, his gargoyle, flyblown hideosities and blemished, poky mutants, all his throwbacks, all his scurf, his doomed, disfigured invalids, his human slums and eldritch seconds, the poor relation and second-best, watered, bungled being, flied ointment, weak link, chipped rift, crack and fault and snag and flaw, his maimed, his handicapped, his disabled, his crippled, his afflicted, delicate cachexies with their provisional, fragile, makeshift tolerances.[42]

The effect of Elkin's burlesques of the Lourdes and Snow White stories is to rob these and other narratives of their privilege in connection with how death is to be understood and, through the characters who manage to avoid complicity in them, to articulate a position in which death becomes an intimate part of life rather than an alien force to be refused immigration rights.

Thus, Rena Morgan insists on playing "dangerous games" by braving public spaces that can cause anxiety and make her cystic fibrosis more threatening than usual,[43] and Mudd–Gaddis, "the little geriatric," with his untimely decrepitude, resists the marginalization that ordinary models of temporality would impose on him:

> "I've never felt special. I've never felt marked. Singled out, I mean. What I've lived was just"—and here the little geriatric paused, struggled for the exact words—"a life."[44]

When a physician objects to Mudd–Gaddis's blurring of the distinction between himself and others—"Just a life?"—Mudd–Gaddis points out that the doctor is caged in by a formulation of his medical language, the discourse on symptoms:

> Symptoms make a difference to you. I've my fingerprints of course, and my eyes are probably their own shade of blue. And I sit on a different bum than the rest, my own special customized behind, but so does everyone. . . . I mean we all know that bit about no two snowflakes, and when we first hear it it's news of a sort. Of a sort it is. We think, we think, "All this *stuff* in the world and no two leaves exactly alike? No two thumbs or signatures?" Make-work for the handwriting experts, the forgery detectives. But what difference does a difference make?[45]

Mudd–Gaddis's refusal to let the medical discourse's notion of symptoms govern the meaning of his life has a significant political impetus; it represents the thoroughgoing commitment to democracy that Elkin affirms in his bully story. This democratic orientation is not articulated directly in *The Magic Kingdom*. There is no explicit "politics of death" argued for. But Elkin's relentless irony, applied to all the discursive practices within which death is lodged, calls into question all pretensions to authority, all attempts at ownership.

His most ferocious rhetorical attack is on medicine's implicit claim to own the significance of death. To be terminally ill can be thought of as a fact of life if we recognize, with Elkin, that life is the cause of death and that in a fundamental sense—in the broad sweep of things—we are all "short-timers." It is only within the medical discourse upon which modern culture has conferred speaking rights that a given difference in terms of speed of movement toward death becomes the type of difference that will authorize the expression "terminally ill."

When Eddy Bale is assembling his seven children/dwarfs, he is impressed with "the fact that none of these children was under the care of a pediatrician."[46] They had all been handed over to specialists who diagnosed and treated them, "if you could call their courses of experimental drugs and dollops of nuclear medicine and being zapped by lasers treatment."[47]

They were tortured not into health . . . but into at best brief periods of remission. They died in pain, language torn from their throats, or what little language they had left, turned into almost gangster argot, uncivilized, barbaric as the skirls and screaks of bayed prey.[48]

While at a more literal level, medicine's domination is here represented by the weaponry with which it assaults the dying bodies, the more significant rhetoric of the passage evokes the ownership of speech. Against medicine's steadfast attempt to own speech about the children's conditions, throughout the story the children struggle to legitimate their own ability to speak about what and who they are—as in Mudd-Gaddis's simple statement, "What I've lived was just . . . a life," as he reacts to talk about "symptoms." And, in a moment of fierce mocking of medical concepts, the love that Rena Morgan dies of is referred to as an "unforeseen complication."[49]

But there is more than medical discourse with which Elkin's ironic discourse is in contention. There are various ethical discourses within which objects such as "the deserving dead" emerge (as the children are being chosen). And death is shown to be lodged in elaborate rhetorics that evoke the ideas of justice and fairness. At one point, for example, Eddy Bale addresses his dead son, Liam, as he explains the excursion to Disney World as fair compensation for the children's imminent early demise.

I'm trying to make it up to them, you see. For being so sick, I mean. For having these catastrophic diseases. For having to die before their time.[50]

Elkin also figures the imminent deaths of the children within a penal discourse—as when one of Bale's staff says, "These kids are condemned and convicted. They've been found guilty, Mister Bale. They've been put on the index. There's a price on their heads."[51]

There is also the rhetoric of chance applied to death. In addition to the above-quoted remarks of Benny Maxim, "the gambler," is the perspective of one of the doctors, a former casualty ward physician, who thought of himself as "one of the best diagnosticians in the world," yet who avoided making public claims about when to expect this or that person to expire.

It was out of neither modesty *nor* fear that he failed to offer his strong suit. It was good, honest prudence. The fact was his gift was a curse. He knew outcomes. He knew people would die. He handicapped death.[52]

Elkin's ironic sweeps of the rhetorical clutter within which death is understood take on the avant-garde, the intellectual, as well as the official and popular constructions. For example, there is a conversation in which Kübler-Ross's narrative of death denial is mocked, as a death specialist visits one of the terminally ill children:

"Don't you see, Noah," she told the eleven-year-old boy when she called round at his house to ask him to die, "You're denying the facts. Don't you see how typical your behavior is? Kübler-Ross tells us that denial, rage, bargaining, and acceptance is the classic pattern of people in your circumstance. *You* can't get past even the first stage. How do you expect to come to terms with your situation?"

"Well, if I don't," Noah Cloth said, "I won't die then, will I?"

"That's bargaining," the woman said, pouncing cheerfully. "No," Noah Cloth said evenly, "It's rage."[53]

The woman leaves a pamphlet, and when Noah's father picks it up and inquires if Noah knows what it is about and if he would like to have it read to him, Noah says, "No," and tells him that "there's better stories on the telly."[54]

The Political Economy of Death

What is left after Elkin has savaged the various discourses of death? As noted above, he is not involved in the modernist intellectual project of stripping away ideological or inauthentic discursive coverings to reveal what death really is. Rather, his focus is on life, showing us how we limit and constrain life's exuberance by the way we construct death. The linguistic economies within which we officially or unofficially give meaning to life and death have a paralyzing effect; we become stingy and afraid to spend—that is, to live. Our different discourses of death—juridical, medical, even statistical/chance—are all discursive economies within which death is a force to be held off by the exercise of a kind of parsimony. And this conceptual parsimony, along with the strictures on perception and conduct it implies, prevents a vision and a conduct of life as exuberant expenditure. It cedes authority and control to the agents who own and operate the various departments of constraint and restraint.

This understanding of the anxiety-driven discursive economies that structure thought about the significance of death provides access to an elaborate theoretical lens through which we can view the pedagogy emerging from *The Magic Kingdom,* for it evokes the theory of political economy of Georges Bataille, the spirit of whose bold position is evinced in his remark, noted earlier, that "to solve political problems becomes difficult for those who allow anxiety alone to pose them."[55]

Against the scarcity-parsimony, saving and hoarding view of economy, Bataille posits a situation of growth and excess that produces an abundant play of energy over the surface of the globe. This excess has to be dissipated, for life is exuberance, and economy is organized around the expenditure of this exuberance. For Bataille, the expenditure produced by this exuberance is represented not only in the squandering of wealth through sacrificing, gift giving, and the ritual destruction of value but also in erotic/sexual forms of expenditure and consumption (and, ultimately in the process of dying, the consumption of one's life in the process of living). As Bataille has put it, "Eroticism, it may be said, is assenting to life up to the point of death."[56]

There is also an important temporal view expressed in Bataille's notion of economy that is consumption driven and based on an excess of exuberance; it is the view that one does not hoard for the future but lives in the present, an ethic of temporality that, as already noted, organizes the reversals of value the children in the story manage to effect during their sojourn to Disney World. As Bataille asserts:

> If I am no longer concerned about "what will be" but "what is" what reason do I have to keep anything in reserve? I can at once, in disorder, make an instantaneous consumption of all I possess. This useless consumption is *what suits me,* once my concern for the morrow is removed. And I thus consume immoderately, I reveal to my fellow beings that which I am *intimately:* consumption is the way in which *separate* beings communicate.[57]

Once we heed this view of "economy," many of the details of Elkin's story take on a coherence beyond that provided by the Lourdes and Snow White narratives. For example, after Rena Morgan dies in an expenditure of passion, another of the children, Noah Cloth, engages in another form of expenditure. He asks for the balance of a stipend being held for him and proceeds to squander it—stuffing money in game machines, soda machines, whichever machines are unoccupied at the moment. When he finally runs out of money, one of his peers summarizes, "Now *that* was a shopping spree!"[58]

And the shopping spree is only one of the final expenditures once the constraints on the exuberance of the traveling party are relaxed. The death of Rena Morgan and the erotic encounter between Eddy Bale and Mary Cottle are not unconnected within the frame provided by Bataille's notion of general economy. The concept of a fundamental separation that humans try to overcome is central here. For Bataille, persons are separate discontinuous beings motivated in their various forms of expenditure to overcome this discontinuousness. Just as consumption in general becomes a mode of restoring intimacy and connectedness (as Bataille expressed in the above passage), both death and sexual intercourse serve to overcome disconnectedness as well. "Death, in that it destroys the discontinuous being, leaves intact the general continuity of existence outside ourselves." And, according to Bataille, eroticism is the desire to replace isolation with a feeling of continuity.[59]

Thus, when Rena Morgan dies, the continuity of life, for which death is a temporal guarantee, is reaffirmed, for in Bataille's terms, "Death distributes the passage of generations over time."[60] Those that remain experience this continuity and are moved to the erotic act, another manifestation of continuity and an overcoming of isolation as well as a received permission to dissipate energy in erotic exuberance.

Just before Eddy Bale and Mary Cottle have intercourse, Mary keeps saying, "We lost one," and then, eschewing any form of birth control and rejecting her former anxiety about reproducing miscreants, she is driven to the dual continuity of the erotic coupling and the possibility of reproducing life, in whatever size or shape it might appear.

> She positions herself to take Bale's semen, to mix it with her own ruined and injured eggs and juices to make a troll, a goblin, broken imps and lurching oafs, felons of a nightmare blood, fallen pediatric angels, lemures, gorgons, cyclopes.[61]

Elkin's story thus articulates well with Bataille's political economy based on the expenditure of exuberance, but there is an additional implication manifested in the ferocity of Elkin's prose as it catalogs and figures life's uglier specimens. It is, once again, Elkin's bully poetics, with its democratizing drive to overturn the discursive practices with which life's administered boundaries distribute eligibilities and ineligibilities. The children and all marginalized beings are eligible to *live* to spend their exuberance, but they have to be bullied into a recognition of this.

Elkin chooses the king of the Magic Kingdom to do the rhetorical honors for the final bullying. This calling upon Mickey Mouse is reflected in Mary Cottle's thoughts as she prepares to bring miscreants into being.

> Now, now, now, now, now, she thinks, and calls upon the famous misfits, upon centaurs and satyrs and chimeras, upon dragons and griffins and hydras and wyverns. Upon the basilisk, the salamander, and the infrequent unicorn. *And upon, at last, a lame and tainted Mickey Mouse.*[62]

This end to the genealogy of Mickey Mouse, from the early cartoon character, through the genial host at the Magic Kingdom, to bullying rhetorician, and finally as one who joins the tainted multitude, is the end of the summons that Elkin serves to have Mickey perform his bullying sleight-of-mouth (before even he cannot maintain a difference from those he verbally assaults). Before Mary Cottle's evocation, Elkin's Mickey Mouse becomes a "rat," a fierce rhetorical provocateur whose obscene stream of invective affronts the children rather than coddling and protecting them, an affront that ultimately provokes their recognition of their eligibility for participation in life (in the expenditure of exuberance). Mickey, in short, becomes Elkin (or vice versa).

Mickey first turns to the child with a hole in her heart and blue skin. "Let's see if that shit washes off!" (He tosses her a damp washcloth.)[63] And he goes on: "You guys are something else . . . the faded follies, I love it." He points to another child, "How long they give you to live?" The child shrugs, and Mickey presses on, "An hour? A day? . . . Because if it's less than a day you can forget about Rome. Know why? . . . *Because Rome wasn't built in a day!*[64]" One of the children says, "Is he crazy? Why's he saying these things? Why's he bullying sick children?"[65] I think we know.

Notes

Chapter 1. Language and Power: The Spaces of Critical Interpretation

1. Michel Foucault's genealogical orientation is, among other things, a reaction against "interpretation," where it is conceived as an attempt to locate the depth lying beneath the surface. This is most dramatically brought out in his approach to discourse, which he produced before he conceived of his approach as genealogical. He asserted that, among other things, the analysis of a discursive formation involves weighing the value of statements, a value that is "not gauged by the presence of a secret content." *The Archaeology of Knowledge*, trans. A. M. Sheridan Smith (New York: Pantheon, 1972), p. 120.

2. Michel Foucault, "Nietzsche, Genealogy, History," in *Language, Counter-Memory, Practice*, ed. Donald F. Bouchard and trans. Sherry Simon (Ithaca, N.Y.: Cornell University Press, 1977), p. 139.

3. Ibid., p. 148.

4. Michel Foucault, "The Order of Discourse," in *Language and Politics*, ed. Michael J. Shapiro (New York: New York University Press, 1984), p. 127.

5. Michel Foucault, *Politics, Philosophy, Culture: Interviews and Other Writings*, ed. Lawrence D. Kritzman and trans. Alan Sheridan (New York: Routledge, 1988), p. 156.

6. Orvar Lofgren, "Our Friends in Nature: Class and Animal Symbolism," *Ethnos* 50, III–IV (1985), p. 207.

7. Ibid., p. 208.

8. Ibid., p. 210.

9. Ibid.

10. Ibid.

11. Henri Lefebvre, "Reflections on the Politics of Space," *Antipode* 8 (May 1976), p. 31.

12. Ibid.

13. Arthur Miller, *Timebends: A Life* (New York: Harper and Row, 1987), p. 175.

14. Ibid., pp. 175–76.

15. Ibid., p. 143.

16. Ibid., p. 144.

17. Ibid., p. 236.

18. This quotation is from Stephen Holmes, "Truths for Philosophers Alone?" *Times Literary Supplement*, December 1–7, 1989. Holmes's essay is nominally a review of *Leo Strauss: The Rebirth of Classical Political Rationalism*, ed. Thomas Pangle (Chicago: University of Chicago Press, 1989), p. 1320, but it is, rather, a thoroughgoing analysis of the Straussian position on the separation of philosophy from everyday life and its encouragement of an esoteric, obscure form of prose. As Holmes puts it, in one of his more ironic statements about Strauss's writing, "He apparently thought he was protecting the community by his indigestible prose."

19. For the various positions Habermas has articulated over the years, see his *Knowledge and Human Interests*, trans. Jeremy J. Shapiro (Boston: Beacon Press, 1971), and his more recent *Theory of Communicative Action*, vol. 1, trans. Thomas McCarthy (Boston: Beacon Press, 1984), and *The Philosophical Discourse of Modernity*, trans. Frederick Lawrence (Cambridge: MIT Press, 1987).

20. This position is articulated in Habermas, *The Philosophical Discourse of Modernity*.

21. Pierre Bourdieu, *In Other Words*, (Cambridge: Polity Press, 1990), p. 15.

22. This part of Habermas's argument can be found in *The Philosophical Discourse of Modernity*, pp. 299ff.

23. For Jacques Derrida's critique of this view that a speaker is wholly present to the meaning of an utterance see, for example, "Signature Event Context," *Glyph* 1 (1977), pp. 172–97.

24. Stanley Elkin, *The Magic Kingdom* (New York: Dutton, 1985), p. 66.

25. Ibid.

26. Foucault, "Nietzsche, Genealogy, History," p. 155.

27. Michael J. Shapiro, *Language and Political Understanding: The Politics of Discursive Practices* (New Haven, Conn.: Yale University Press, 1981), p. 186.

28. Michel Foucault, "Governmentality," *Ideology and Consciousness,* no. 5 (1979), p. 17.

29. Michel Foucault, "Of Other Spaces," trans. Jay Miscowiec, *Diacritics* 16 (Spring 1986), p. 22.

30. See A. J. Gurevich, *Categories of Medieval Culture,* trans. G. L. Campbell (London: Routledge and Kegan Paul, 1985), p. 302.

31. See Donald Lowe, *History of Bourgeois Perception* (Chicago: University of Chicago Press, 1982), pp. 63ff., for an elaboration of this point.

32. Adam Smith, *The Wealth of Nations,* vols. 1 and 2, ed. W. B. Todd (Oxford: Clarendon Press, 1976).

33. Ibid.

34. Foucault, "Governmentality," p. 11.

35. Ibid., p. 17.

36. These distinctions between heterodox positions versus belonging to an unstated doxa belong to Pierre Bourdieu, *Outline of a Theory of Practice,* trans. Richard Nice (Cambridge: Cambridge University Press, 1977), p. 168.

37. Foucault, "Governmentality," p. 11.

38. Ibid., p. 21.

39. Michel Foucault, "War in the Filigree of Peace," *Oxford Literary Review* 4 (Autumn 1979), pp. 17–18.

40. Maurice Blanchot, *The Space of Literature,* trans. Ann Smock (Lincoln: University of Nebraska Press, 1982), p. 79.

41. Ibid., p. 3.

42. Foucault, "Nietzsche, Genealogy, History," p. 148.

43. Nietzsche, *Human, All Too Human,* I, p. 719.

44. Foucault, "Of Other Spaces," p. 27.

Chapter 2. Politicizing Ulysses: Rationalistic, Critical, and Geneological Commentaries

1. A. J. Gurevich, *Categories of Medieval Culture,* trans. G. L. Campbell (London: Routledge and Kegan Paul, 1985), p. 302.

2. For an analysis of the subversive, antiofficial culture impetus of Rabelais's "carnivalesque" style, see M. M. Bakhtin, *Rabelais and His World,* trans. Helene Iswolsky (Bloomington: Indiana University Press, 1984).

3. Michel Foucault, "The Order of Discourse," *Language and Politics,* ed. Michael J. Shapiro (New York: New York University Press, 1984); Hans Blumenberg, *Work on Myth,* trans. Robert M. Wallace (Cambridge: MIT Press, 1985).

4. See the section on Dante in Hans Blumenberg, *The Legitimacy of the Modern Age,* trans. Robert M. Wallace (Cambridge: MIT Press, 1983), pp. 338–40.

5. See the discussion in Blumenberg's *Work on Myth,* p. 79.

6. This expression belongs to Hugh Kenner, *Ulysses* (Baltimore, Md.: Johns Hopkins University Press, 1987).

7. Jon Elster, *Ulysses and the Sirens* (Cambridge: Cambridge University Press, 1979), p. 39.

8. Ibid., p. 77.

9. Jon Elster, *Logic and Society* (New York: John Wiley, 1978), p. 50.

10. Elster, *Ulysses and the Sirens*, p. 49.

11. Jon Elster, *Making Sense of Marx* (London: Cambridge University Press, 1985), p. 15.

12. Elster, *Ulysses and the Sirens*, p. 102.

13. Elster, *Making Sense of Marx*, p. 388.

14. Andrew Parker, "Futures for Marxism: An Appreciation of Althusser," *Diacritics* 15 (Winter 1985), p. 64

15. Elster, *Logic and Society*, pp. 21–25.

16. Norbert Elias, *Power and Civility*, trans. Edmund Jephcott (New York: Pantheon, 1982), pp. 230–31.

17. Jürgen Habermas, *Theory and Practice*, trans. John Viertel (Boston: Beacon Press, 1973), p. 255.

18. Max Horkheimer and Theodor Adorno, *The Dialectics of Enlightenment*, trans. Jon Cummings (New York: Herder and Herder, 1972), p. xiv.

19. Elster, *Logic and Society*, pp. 60ff.

20. Horkheimer and Adorno, *The Dialectics of Enlightenment*, p. 24.

21. Ibid., p. 14.

22. Ibid., p. 44.

23. Ibid., p. 49.

24. Theodor Adorno, *Prisms*, trans. Samuel and Shierry Weber (Cambridge: MIT Press, 1981), p. 31.

25. Theodor Adorno, *Negative Dialectics*, trans. E. B. Ashton (London: Routledge and Kegan Paul, 1973), pp. 146–48.

26. Theodor Adorno, "Sociology and Psychology," trans. Irving N. Wolfarth, *New Left Review* 46 (1967) and 48 (1968), pp. 69–70. My discussion here of Adorno's style has benefited from the treatment in Gillian Rose, *The Melancholy Science: An Introduction to the Thought of Theodor W. Adorno* (London: Macmillan, 1978), chap. 2.

27. Ibid., p. 73.

28. Friedrich Nietzsche, *On the Genealogy of Morals*, trans. Walter Kaufman and R. J. Hollingdale (New York: Vintage, 1969), p. 80.

29. Theodor Adorno, "Society," trans. F. R. Jameson, *Salmagundi* nos. 10–11 (Fall–Winter, 1969–70), p. 147.

30. Ibid.

31. Michel Foucault, "Nietzsche, Genealogy, History," in *Language, Counter-Memory, Practice*, ed. Donald F. Bouchard (Ithaca, N.Y.: Cornell University Press, 1977), p. 139.

32. See Gilles Deleuze's chapter, "The Overman against the Dialectic," in his *Nietzsche and Philosophy*, trans. Hugh Tomlinson (New York: Columbia University Press, 1983).

33. Foucault, "Nietzsche, Genealogy, History," p. 148.

34. Friedrich Nietzsche, *Human, All Too Human*, I, p. 719.

35. For the development of this argument see Michel Foucault, *The History of Sexuality*, trans. Robert Hurley (New York: Pantheon, 1978), and "Two Lectures," in *Power/Knowledge*, ed. Colin Gorden and trans. Colin Gorden, Leo Marshall, John Mepham, and Kate Soper (New York: Pantheon, 1980), pp. 78–108.

36. Michel Foucault, "Of Other Spaces," trans. Jay Miscowiec, *Diacritics* 16 (Spring 1986), p. 22.

37. Ibid., p. 23.

38. Ibid., p. 27.

39. Friedrich Nietzsche, *Thus Spoke Zarathustra*, trans. Walter Kaufman (New York: Viking, 1966), p. 131.

40. Ibid., p. 132.

41. Ibid., p. 48.

42. Ibid., p. 49.

43. Ibid., p. 138.

44. Ibid.

45. Jacques Derrida, "Otobiographies," trans. Avital Ronnel, in *The Ear of the Other,* ed. Christie V. McDonald (New York: Schocken, 1985), p. 35.

46. Franz Kafka, "The Silence of the Sirens," in *The Complete Stories,* ed. Nahum N. Glatzer (New York: Schocken, 1976), p. 431.

47. Ibid.

48. Ibid.

49. Ibid.

50. Ibid., p. 432.

51. The escape route imagery to locate Kafka as a writer is elaborated in Gilles Deleuze and Flix Guattari, *Kafka: Toward a Minor Literature,* trans. Dana Polan (Minneapolis: University of Minnesota Press, 1986).

52. Franz Kafka, "Josephine the Singer, or The Mouse Folk," in *The Complete Stories,* ed. Glatzer, p. 361.

Chapter 3. Weighing Anchor: Postmodern Journeys from the Life-World

1. For a discussion of the difference between radical and conservative forms of postmodernist thinking, see Hal Foster, "(Post)Modern Polemics," *New German Critique,* no. 33 (Fall 1984), pp. 67–78.

2. See Jean-François Lyotard, *The Postmodern Condition,* trans. Geoff Bennington and Brian Massumi (Minneapolis: University of Minnesota Press, 1984); and Seyla Benhabib, "Epistemologies of Postmodernism," *New German Critique,* no. 33 (Fall 1984), p. 114.

3. Benhabib, "Epistemologies of Postmodernism," p. 115.

4. The relevant work is John Austin, *How to Do Things with Words* (Cambridge, Mass.: Harvard University Press, 1962).

5. Gerard Raulet, "Structuralism and Post-Structuralism: An Interview with Michel Foucault," trans. Jeremy Harding, *Telos,* no. 55 (Spring 1983), p. 206.

6. Michel Foucault, "About the Concept of the Dangerous Individual in Nineteenth Century Psychiatry," *International Journal of Law and Psychiatry* 1 (1978), pp. 1–18.

7. Ibid., p. 1.

8. Ibid., p. 2.

9. Ibid., p. 12.

10. Jacques Derrida, *Speech and Phenomena,* trans. David Allison (Evanston: Northwestern University Press, 1973), p. 78.

11. Jacques Derrida, "The Supplement of Copula: Philosophy before Linguistics," in *Textual Strategies,* ed. Josué Harari (Ithaca, N.Y.: Cornell University Press, 1979), pp. 82–120.

12. See Michel Foucault, *Discipline and Punish: The Birth of the Prison,* trans. Alan Sheridan (New York: Pantheon, 1977).

13. Hans-Georg Gadamer, *Truth and Method* (New York: Seabury Press, 1975).

14. See Clifford Geertz, *Negara* (Princeton: Princeton University Press, 1980), p. 122.

15. For an elaboration of this position see Clifford Geertz, "The Politics of Meaning," in *The Interpretation of Culture* (New York: Basic Books, 1973).

16. Michel Foucault, "Nietzsche, Genealogy, History," in *Language, Counter-Memory, Practice,* ed. Donald Bouchard (Ithaca, N.Y.: Cornell University Press, 1977), p. 145.

17. This particular point is made in Michel Foucault, "Two Lectures," in *Power/Knowledge,* ed. Colin Gorden and trans. Colin Gorden, Leo Marshall, John Mepham, and Kate Soper (New York: Pantheon, 1980), pp. 78–108.

18. Foucault, "Nietzsche, Genealogy, History," p. 153.

19. Raulet, "Structuralism and Post-Structuralism: An Interview with Michel Foucault," p. 202.

20. Richard Rorty, "Habermas and Lyotard on Postmodernity," in *Habermas and Modernity,* ed. Richard J. Bernstein (Cambridge: MIT Press, 1985), p. 174.

21. Ibid., p. 172.

22. Ibid., p. 171.

23. Ibid., p. 172.

24. For the argument that Foucault fails to provide a critical position, see Jürgen Habermas, "The Genealogical Writing of History: On Some Aporias in Foucault's Theory of Power," trans. Gregory Ostrander, *Canadian Journal of Social and Political Theory* 10, nos. 1–2 (1986), pp. 1–9.

25. See Jürgen Habermas, *The Philosophical Discourse of Modernity,* trans. Frederick Lawrence (Cambridge: MIT Press, 1987), chapter 11.

26. Jürgen Habermas, *The Theory of Communicative Competence,* vol. 1, *Reason and the Rationalization of Society,* trans. Thomas McCarthy (Boston: Beacon Press, 1984), p. 295.

27. Rorty, "Habermas and Lyotard on Postmodernity," p. 171.

28. For a similar rejoinder to Rorty's argument, see Jonathan Arac, "Introduction," in *Postmodernism and Politics,* ed. Jonathan Arac (Minneapolis: University of Minnesota Press, 1986), p. xviii.

29. Raulet, "Structuralism and Post-Structuralism: An Interview with Michel Foucault," p. 206.

30. Michel Foucault, "The History of Sexuality," in *Power/Knowledge,* ed. Colin Gorden, p. 191.

31. See Michel Foucault's discussion of the commentary in "The Order of Discourse," in *Language and Politics,* ed. Michael Shapiro (New York: New York University Press, 1984), pp. 114–16.

32. See Michel Tournier, *Vendredi ou les limbes du Pacifique* (Paris: Gallimard, 1967). All quotations are from the English edition: *Friday or the Other Island,* trans. Norman Denny (Harmondsworth: Penguin, 1974). My discussion of the novel benefits from the excellent reading by Anthony Purdy, "From Defoe's 'Crusoe' to Tournier's 'Vendredi': The Metamorphosis of a Myth," *Canadian Revue of Comparative Literature,* June 1984, pp. 216–35.

33. Ian Watt, "Robinson Crusoe as Myth," in *Robinson Crusoe: An Authoritative Text, Backgrounds, and Sources of Criticism,* ed. Michael Shinagel (New York: Norton, 1975), p. 315.

34. Ibid., p. 322.

35. Karl Marx, *Capital,* vol. I., trans. Eden and Cedar Paul (New York: International Publishers, 1929), p. 52.

36. Michel Foucault, *The Order of Things* (New York: Vintage, 1973), p. 262.

37. Jean Baudrillard, "Beyond Use Value," in *For a Critique of the Political Economy of the Sign,* trans. Charles Levin (St. Louis, Mo.: Telos Press, 1981), p. 140.

38. Baudrillard's extended critique of this aspect of Marx's position is in his *Mirror of Production,* trans. Mark Poster (St. Louis, Mo.: Telos Press, 1975).

39. Baudrillard, "Beyond Use Value," p. 141.

40. Ibid.

41. Tournier moves the Robinson Crusoe story from the seventeenth to the eighteenth century. The change in time does not enter my reading but is analyzed in depth in Purdy's treatment (noted above in note 33). Among other things, the change in period allows Tournier to imply a Benjamin Franklin parody in Crusoe's determined accumulation ethic.

42. Tournier, *Friday or the Other Island,* p. 96.

43. Ibid., p. 99.

44. For an extensive treatment of the feminization of the island theme, see Alice A. Jardine, *Gynesis* (Ithaca, N.Y.: Cornell University Press, 1985), pp. 218–23.

45. Tournier, *Friday or the Other Island,* p. 143.

46. Ibid., p. 141.

Chapter 4. Political Economy and Mimetic Desire in *Babette's Feast*

1. Pierre Bourdieu, *Outline of a Theory of Practice,* trans. Richard Nice (Cambridge, Mass.: Cambridge University Press, 1977), p. 172.

2. Karl Marx, *Capital,* vol. 1, trans Ben Fowkes (New York: Vintage, 1977), p. 126.

3. Ibid., p. 195.

4. Ibid., p. 211.

5. For a good discussion of the inevitable mediation of representation, see Jacques Derrida, "Sending: On Representation," *Social Research* 49 (1982): 294–326.

6. Jean Baudrillard, "The Ideological Genesis of Needs," in *For a Critique of the Political Economy of the Sign,* trans. Charles Levin (St. Louis, Mo.: Telos Press, 1981), p. 63.

7. Ibid., p. 73.

8. Ibid., p. 75.

9. Jean-Joseph Goux, "Banking on Signs," *Diacritics* 18 (Summer 1988), pp. 15–37.

10. Marcel Mauss, *The Gift,* trans. Ian Cunnison (London: Cohen and West, 1970), p. 1.

11. Bourdieu, *Outline of a Theory of Practice,* and *Distinction: A Social Critique of the Judgement of Taste,* trans. Richard Nice (Cambridge, Mass.: Harvard University Press, 1984).

12. Bourdieu, *Distinction,* pp. 99–168.

13. Georges Bataille, *The Accursed Share,* vol. 1, trans. Robert Hurley (New York: Zone Books, 1988).

14. Sigmund Freud, "Three Essays on the Theory of Sexuality," *Standard Edition of the Complete Psychological Works of Sigmund Freud,* ed. and trans. James Strachey, vol. 7, pp. 135–36.

15. Ibid., pp. 147–48.

16. This contradiction is analyzed in Arnold Davidson's masterful deconstructive reading of the essays. See his "How to Do the History of Psychoanalysis: A Reading of Freud's *Three Essays on the Theory of Sexuality,*" in *The Trial(s) of Psychoanalysis,* ed. Françoise Meltzer (Chicago: University of Chicago Press, 1988), pp. 39–64.

17. See Jacques Lacan, *Ecrits,* trans. Alan Sheridan (New York: Norton, 1977), p. 311.

18. Ibid.

19. René Girard, "Delirium as System," in *To Double Business Bound* (Baltimore: Johns Hopkins University Press, 1978), p. 90.

20. Ibid., p. 91.

21. Ibid., p. 89.

22. André Orléan, "Money and Mimetic Speculation," trans. Mark R. Anspach, in *Violence and Truth: On the Work of René Girard,* ed. Paul Dumouchal (Stanford: Stanford University Press, 1985), p. 101.

23. Lawrence Birken, *Consuming Desires* (Ithaca, N.Y.: Cornell University Press, 1988), p. 31.

24. Orléan, "Money and Mimetic Speculation," p. 102.

25. For a chronicle of this change in the structure of space as it has influenced the commodification of music, see Jacques Attali, *Noise: The Political Economy of Music,* trans. Brian Massumi (Minneapolis: University of Minnesota Press, 1985); for a treatment of the political implications of the replacement of territorial space with electronic transmission, see Paul Virilio, *Speed and Politics* (New York: Semiotext[e], 1986).

26. Gianni Vattimo, *The End of Modernity,* trans. Jon R. Snyder (Cambridge: Polity Press, 1988), pp. 9–10.

27. This effect of Marco Polo's travels is analyzed in Benedict Anderson, *Imagined Communities* (London: Verso, 1983), pp. 23–24.

28. Isak Dinesen, "Babette's Feast," in *Babette's Feast and Other Anecdotes of Destiny* (New York: Vintage, 1988). Dinesen's story takes place in a small Norwegian village, while the 1987 film, written, produced, and directed by Gabriel Axel, is situated in a Danish village.

29. Dinesen, "Babette's Feast," p. 7.

30. Ibid., p. 8.

31. Ibid., p. 3.

32. Ibid., p. 9.

33. Ibid., p. 6.

34. Ibid., p. 21.

35. Bataille, *The Accursed Share,* p. 122.

36. Dinesen, "Babette's Feast," p. 3.

37. Ibid., pp. 30–31.

38. Bourdieu, *Distinction,* p. 163.

39. Dinesen, "Babette's Feast," p. 12.

40. Ibid., p. 22.

41. Ibid., p. 27.

42. Ibid., p. 41.

43. Lacan, *Ecrits,* p. 299.

44. See Bataille, *The Accursed Share,* p. 34.

45. Ibid.

46. Susan Stewart, *On Longing* (Baltimore, Md.: Johns Hopkins University Press, 1984), p. 135.

47. Dinesen, "Babette's Feast," p. 38.

48. Ibid., p. 46.

49. Ibid., p. 47.

Chapter 5. American Fictions and Political Culture: DeLillo's *Libra* and Bellah et al.'s *Habits of the Heart*

1. Robert Bellah, Richard Madsen, William M. Sullivan, Ann Swidler, and Steven M. Tipton, *Habits of the Heart* (New York: Harper and Row, 1986).

2. Mailer coins this expression as a subtitle in his *Executioner's Song* (New York: Warner Books, 1979), a novelistic biography of Gary Gilmore.

3. Don DeLillo, *Libra* (New York: Viking, 1988). It is undoubtedly the case that Mailer's *Executioner's Song,* among others (e.g., *Why We Are in Vietnam*), provides a prototype, as well as appearing as part of the intertext, for *Libra*.

4. The idea of a "mythic plot," which suppresses the diversity of everyday life in order to emphasize what is transcendental or universal, is elaborated in Frank Kermode, "Secrets and Narrative Sequence," *Critical Inquiry* 7 (Autumn 1980), p. 85.

5. Don DeLillo, "American Blood: A Journey through the Labyrinth of Dallas and JFK," *Rolling Stone,* December 8, 1983, p. 22.

6. Ibid., p. 24.

7. See the "author's statement" at the end of *Libra*.

8. Arthur Miller, *Timebends: A Life* (New York: Harper and Row, 1987), p. 510.

9. DeLillo, *Libra,* p. 15.

10. DeLillo, "American Blood," p. 24.

11. Ibid.

12. Ibid., p. 27.

13. DeLillo, *Libra,* p. 77.

14. Bellah et al., *Habits of the Heart,* p. vi.

15. See ibid., p. 334, for a summary of this combination.

16. Ibid., p. 11.

17. Fredric Jameson also remarks on the impoverished narratives in *Habits*. See his "On *Habits of the Heart*," *South Atlantic Quarterly*, (Fall 1987), pp. 545–65.

18. DeLillo, Libra, p. 221.

19. This point is also made in Jameson, "On *Habits of the Heart*," p. 549.

20. Bellah et al., *Habits of the Heart*, p. 80.

21. These alternative models of the self come, of course, primarily from the modern poststructuralist literature exemplified in the writings of Foucault, Derrida, Deleuze, and Baudrillard, among others.

22. Bellah et al., *Habits of the Heart*, p. vii.

23. Michel Foucault, *The Order of Things* (New York: Random House, 1970). See especially sec. 4, "Character," in chap. 5, "Classifying."

24. Ibid., p. 263.

25. Bellah et al., *Habits of the Heart*, p. vii.

26. Foucault, *The Order of Things*, p. 263.

27. Bellah et al., *Habits of the Heart*, p. 295.

28. Ibid., p. 175.

29. Ibid., p. 192.

30. DeLillo, *Libra*, p. 137.

31. Ibid., p. 94.

32. Ibid., p. 108.

33. Ibid., p. 100.

34. Michel Foucault, *Discipline and Punish: The Birth of the Prison*, trans. Alan Sheridan (New York: Pantheon, 1977), pp. 138–39.

35. DeLillo, Libra, p. 353.

36. Ibid., p. 354.

37. Ibid.

38. Bellah et al., *Habits of the Heart*, p. 50.

39. Ibid.

40. Ibid., p. 51.

41. DeLillo, *Libra*, p. 320.

42. Ibid., p. 319.

43. John Gardner, *The Wreckage of Agathon* (New York: Ballantine, 1970), p. 218.

44. Ibid., p. 316.

45. Ibid., p. 40.

46. Ibid., p. 321.

47. Ibid.

48. Ibid., p. 330.

49. Ibid., pp. 147–48.

50. Ibid., p. 148.

51. Bellah et al., *Habits of the Heart*, p. 39.

52. Ibid., p. 247.

53. DeLillo, *Libra*, p. 221.

54. Don DeLillo, *Americana*, p. 73.

55. Bellah et al., *Habits of the Heart*, p. 280.

56. Ibid., p. 282.

57. DeLillo, *Libra*, p. 5.

58. Ibid., p. 76.

59. Ibid., p. 178.

60. Ibid., p. 264.

61. Ibid., pp. 250–51.

62. Ibid.

63. Ibid.

64. M. M. Bakhtin, "Discourse and the Novel," in *The Dialogic Imagination,* ed. Michael Holquist and trans. Caryl Emerson and Michael Holquist (Austin: University of Texas Press, 1981), pp. 272–73.

65. Ibid., p. 291.

66. See Leonard Davis, *Resisting Novels* (New York: Methuen, 1987), p. 54, for this point of view.

Chapter 6. Spatiality and Policy Discourse: Reading the Global City

1. Paul Virilio, *L'espace critique* (Paris: Christian Bourgois, 1984).

2. Robert Reinhold, "The Los Angeles Life, but on New York Time," *New York Times,* Style section, March 6, 1988, pp. 1–3.

3. Virilio's concept of chronospace is developed in Paul Virilio and Sylvere Lotringer, *Pure War* (New York: Semiotext[e], 1983).

4. Jean Baudrillard, "The Art Auction: Sign Exchange and Sumptuary Value," in *For a Critique of the Political Economy of the Sign,* trans. Charles Levin (St. Louis, Mo.: Telos Press, 1981), p. 122.

5. The expression "ground plan" belongs to Martin Heidegger. See "The Age of the World Picture," in *The Question Concerning Technology,* trans. William Lovett (New York: Harper and Row, 1977).

6. For a discussion of the failure of contemporary social theory to treat spatialization as practice, see Edward Soja, "Modern Geography, Western Marxism, and the Restructuring of Critical Social Theory," in *The New Models in Geography,* ed. Richard Peet and Nigel Thrift (London: Allen and Unwin, 1987).

7. This is why Gilles Deleuze has called Foucault, whose analyses are focused primarily on discourses, a "cartographer." See his *Foucault,* ed. and trans. Sean Hand (Minneapolis: University of Minnesota Press, 1986), pp. 23–44.

8. Jacques Derrida, *Speech and Phenomena,* trans. David Allison (Evanston, Ill.: Northwestern University Press, 1973), p. 78.

9. Anthony Giddens, *A Contemporary Critique of Historical Materialism* (Berkeley: University of California Press, 1981), p. 90.

10. Ibid., p. 93.

11. Ibid., pp. 93–94.

12. Michel de Certeau, "Practices of Space," in *On Signs,* ed. Marshal Blonsky (Baltimore, Md.: Johns Hopkins University Press, 1985), p. 124.

13. Both expressions belong to de Certeau, ibid.

14. De Certeau, "Practices of Space," p. 127.

15. The quotation is from Edward Soja, "The Socio-Spatial Dialectic," *Annals of the Association of American Geographers,* no. 70 (June 1980), p. 210.

16. For an excellent summary of the production of merchandising space in nineteenth-century France, see Richard Terdiman, *Discourse, Counter-Discourse* (Ithaca, N.Y.: Cornell University Press, 1985), pp. 136–38. See also Michael B. Miller, *The Bon Marché* (Princeton: Princeton University Press, 1981), pp. 165–230.

17. See Daniel Boorstin, *The Americans: The Democratic Experience* (New York: Vintage, 1974).

18. Aldous Huxley, *The Grey Eminence* (London: Chatto and Windus, 1944), p. 292.

19. Ibid., p. 11.

20. Michel Foucault, "Of Other Spaces," trans. Jay Miscowiec, *Diacritics* 16 (Spring 1986), pp. 22–27.

21. Huxley, *The Grey Eminence,* p. 11.

22. Foucault, "Of Other Spaces," p. 23.

23. Michael Walzer, "Liberalism and the Art of Separation," *Political Theory* 12 (August 1984), p. 315.

24. Ibid.

25. See Gilles Deleuze and Félix Guattari, *Anti-Oedipus*, trans. Robert Hurley, Mark Seem, and Helen A. Lane (New York: Viking, 1977). The quotation is from an application of their concepts by Klaus Theweleit in *Male Fantasies*, vol. 1, trans. Stephen Conway (Minneapolis: University of Minnesota Press, 1987), p. 264.

26. Deleuze and Guattari, *Anti-Oedipus*, p. 35.

27. Walzer, "Liberalism and the Art of Separation," pp. 317–20.

28. Michel Foucault, "War in the Filigree of Peace," *Oxford Literary Review* 4 (Autumn 1979), p. 18.

29. This treatment of discursive practices as assets is found in Michel Foucault, *The Archaeology of Knowledge*, trans. A. M. Sheridan Smith (New York: Pantheon, 1972), p. 120.

30. Walzer, "Liberalism and the Art of Separation," p. 323.

31. Foucault, "Of Other Spaces," p. 23.

32. Michel Foucault, *Discipline and Punish*, trans. Alan Sheridan (New York: Pantheon, 1977), pp. 257–92.

33. Ibid., p. 277.

34. Henri Lefebvre, "Reflections on the Politics of Space," trans. Michael J. Enders, *Antipode* 8 (May 1976), p. 33.

35. Ibid., p. 31.

36. Jacques Attali, *Noise: The Political Economy of Music*, trans. Brian Massumi (Minneapolis: University of Minnesota Press, 1985), pp. 117–18.

37. Ibid., p. 47.

38. Ibid., p. 119.

39. Norbert Elias, "Introduction," in *Quest for Excitement: Sport and Leisure in the Civilizing Process*, Norbert Elias and Eric Dunning (New York: Basil Blackwell, 1986).

40. See E. P. Thompson, "Patrician Society, Plebeian Culture," *Journal of Social History* 7 (Summer 1974), p. 403, and "The Moral Economy of the English Crowd in the Eighteenth Century," *Past and Present* 50 (February 1971), pp. 76–136.

41. On gambling's shaping effects on sport, see Dennis Brailford, *Sport and Society: Elizabeth to Anne* (London: Routledge and Kegan Paul, 1969), p. 213.

42. On the implications for the city of the development of broadcasting space, see Virilio and Lotringer, *Pure War*, p. 87.

43. This use of the concept of tendency belongs to Paul Virilio in *Pure War*.

44. Charles Lockwood and Christopher B. Leinberger, "Los Angeles Comes of Age," *Atlantic* 26 (January 1988), pp. 31ff.

45. The turning of the idea of a problem into the more critical concept of "problematization" is central to Foucault's strategy in his genealogical analyses. For a good summary of how he views this strategy, see the "Introduction" in his *Use of Pleasure*, trans. Robert Hurley (New York: Pantheon, 1985).

46. Lockwood and Leinberger, "Los Angeles Comes of Age," p. 32.

47. On the globalization of Los Angeles's economy, see Edward Soja, "Taking Los Angeles Apart: Some Fragments of a Critical Human Geography," *Society and Space* 4 (1986), pp. 255–72; and Mike Davis, "Chinatown, Part Two? The 'Internationalization' of Downtown Los Angeles," *New Left Review*, no. 164 (March/April 1987), pp. 65–86.

48. Zaitech is discussed in Davis, "Chinatown, Part Two?" pp. 72–73.

49. Soja, "Taking Los Angeles Apart," pp. 260–61.

50. The Third World labor pool theme is elaborated in Davis, "Chinatown, Part Two?"

51. Ibid., pp. 73–75.

52. See Foucault, *Discipline and Punish*, pp. 293–308.

53. Glenn C. Loury, "The Family as Context for Delinquency Prevention: Demographic Trends and Political Realities," in *From Children to Citizens*, ed. James Q. Wilson and Glenn C. Loury (New York: Springer-Verlag, 1987), pp. 3–26.

54. Ibid., p. 4.

55. Anthony Giddens, *The Constitution of Society* (Berkeley: University of California Press, 1984), pp. 183–84.

56. Michel de Certeau, *The Practice of Everyday Life*, trans. Steven F. Rendell (Berkeley: University of California Press, 1984), pp. xviii–xx.

Chapter 7. Strategic Discourse/Discursive Strategy: The Representation of "Security Policy" in the Video Age

1. For recent accounts of this subculture, see Jonathan Kwitney, *The Crimes of Patriots: A True Tale of Dope, Dirty Money, and the CIA* (New York: Norton, 1987); and Edith Holleman, Andrew Love, et al., *Inside the Shadow Government* (Washington: Christic Institute, 1988).

2. Karl Marx, *Capital*, vol. 1, trans. Ben Fowkes (New York: Vintage, 1977), chap. 1, "The Commodity."

3. Ernest Mandel, *Late Capitalism*, trans. Joris De Bres (London: NLB, 1975), chap. 9, "The Permanent Arms Economy of Late Capitalism."

4. Anapong Chaiyarit, *Business Post* (Bangkok), October 28, 1988, p. 1.

5. For an almost pure version of such geopolitical thinking, see Zbigniew Brzezinski, *Game Plan* (Boston: Atlantic Monthly, 1986).

6. Michel Foucault, "Of Other Spaces," trans. Jay Miscowiec, *Diacritics* 16 (Spring 1986), p. 22.

7. Ibid.

8. See the account of the events leading up to the Thirty Years' War in Aldous Huxley's *Grey Eminence* (London: Chatto and Windus, 1944), for a powerful representation of the contention between the medieval and modern geopolitical mentalities represented respectively by the novel's main characters, Father Joseph and Cardinal Richelieu.

9. Michel Foucault, *The Archaeology of Knowledge*, trans. A. M. Sheridan Smith (New York: Pantheon, 1972), p. 120.

10. Michael J. Shapiro, "Introduction: Textualizing Global Politics," in *International/Intertextual Relations*, ed. James Der Derian and Michael J. Shapiro (Lexington, Mass.: Lexington Books, 1989), pp. 11–22.

11. This expression belongs to Michael Walzer, "Liberalism and the Art of Separation," *Political Theory* 12 (August 1984), p. 315.

12. This expression is Brad Klein's in his "Hegemony and Strategic Culture," *Review of International Studies* 14 (1988), p. 141.

13. Abram de Swaan, "Terror as Government Service," in *Repression and Repressive Violence*, ed. Marjo Hoefnagels (Amsterdam: Swets and Zeitlinger, 1977).

14. Ibid., p. 40.

15. Ibid., p. 44.

16. Reported in Raymond Williams, *Writing in Society* (London: Verso, 1983), p. 71.

17. Reported in Paul Fussell, *The Great War and Modern Memory* (New York: Oxford University Press, 1975), p. 13.

18. Ibid., p. 12.

19. Ibid., p. 17.

20. This is described in Donald Emmerson, " 'Southeast Asia': What's in a Name?" *Journal of Southeast Asia Studies* 15 (March 1984), pp. 1–21.

21. Joseph Kruzel, "Perspectives 1986," in *The American Defense Annual, 1987–1988*, ed. Joseph Kruzel (Lexington, Mass.: Lexington Books, 1987), p. 1.

22. The more sophisticated analyses are in, among other places, Kwitney, *The Crimes of Patriots,* and in the Christic Institute's *Inside the Shadow Government.*

23. Kruzel, "Perspectives 1986," pp. 1–2.

24. Ibid., p. 7.

25. John J. O'Connor, "The Real World Impinges on 'Miami Vice,' " *New York Times,* October 19, 1986, sec. 2, p. 31.

26. Ibid.

27. Fredric Jameson, *Sartre: The Origins of a Style* (New York: Columbia University Press, 1984), p. 17.

28. .See Molière, "The School for Wives," trans. Miles Malleson (London: Samuel French, 1954).

29. Robert Karl Manoff, "Some Notes on the News: John McWethy Reports on SDI," unpublished paper delivered at the Second Institute for Global Conflict and Cooperation (IGCC) Conference on Discourse, Peace, Security, and International Society, Ballyvaughan, Ireland, August 1988.

30. Ibid.

31. Ibid.

32. Avishai Margalit, "The Kitsch of Israel," *New York Review of Books,* November 24, 1988, p. 20.

33. Ibid.

34. Ibid.

35. Quoted in Joseph C. Goulden, *Truth Is the First Casualty: The Gulf of Tonkin Affair — Illusion and Reality* (Chicago: Rand McNally, 1969), p. 23.

36. See Goulden, *Truth Is the First Casualty,* chap. 2, "Mr. Johnson's resolution," pp. 48–79.

37. *Newsweek,* February 13, 1989, p. 9.

Chapter 8. The Politics of Fear: DeLillo's Postmodern Burrow

1. Franz Kafka, "The Burrow," trans. Willa and Edwin Muir, in *The Complete Stories,* ed. Nahum N. Glatzer (New York: Schocken, 1971), p. 325.

2. Ibid., p. 357.

3. Manuel Puig, *Betrayed by Rita Hayworth,* trans. Suzanne Jill Levine (New York: Dutton, 1971).

4. The expression comes from a review of DeLillo's *White Noise.* See Pico Iyer, "A Connoisseur of Fear," *Partisan Review* 53 (1986), pp. 292–97.

5. Michel Foucault, *The History of Sexuality,* trans. Robert Hurley (New York: Pantheon, 1978), p. 25.

6. Barry Lopez, *Arctic Dreams: Desire and Imagination in a Northern Landscape* (New York: Scribners, 1986), p. 201.

7. This particular formulation of the Foucauldian question is suggested in James W. Bernauer, "Michel Foucault's Ecstatic Thinking," in *The Final Foucault,* ed. James Bernauer and David Rasmussen (Cambridge: MIT Press, 1988), p. 46.

8. Don DeLillo, *White Noise* (New York: Viking-Penguin, 1985), p. 162.

9. Nevil Shute, *On The Beach* (New York: Morrow, 1957).

10. Don DeLillo, "American Blood: A Journey through the Labyrinth of Dallas and JFK," *Rolling Stone,* December 8, 1983, p. 27.

11. Fredric Jameson, "The Politics of Theory: Ideological Positions in the Postmodernist Debate," *New German Critique,* no. 33 (Fall 1984), p. 53.

12. DeLillo, "American Blood," p. 27.

13. Don DeLillo, *Running Dog* (New York: Vintage, 1978), p. 93.

14. DeLillo, *White Noise,* pp. 294–95.

15. For a detailed exegesis of DeLillo's fiction based on systems theory and the general argument that DeLillo's writing attacks closed systems, see Tom LeClair's extensive study, *In the Loop: Don DeLillo and the Systems Novel* (Urbana: University of Illinois Press, 1987).

16. Tom LeClair, "An Interview with Don DeLillo," in *Anything Can Happen: Interviews with Contemporary American Novelists,* ed. Tom LeClair and Larry McCaffery (Urbana: University of Illinois Press, 1983), p. 83.

17. Ibid., p. 81.

18. Bruce Bawer, "Don DeLillo's America," *New Criterion* 3 (April 1985), p. 37.

19. Don DeLillo, *Players* (New York: Vintage, 1984), p. 104.

20. Ibid., p. 110.

21. DeLillo, *White Noise,* p. 143.

22. Ibid., p. 26.

23. Ibid., p. 27.

24. Ibid., p. 51.

25. Ibid., p. 52.

26. Ibid., p. 228.

27. Ibid., pp. 228–29.

28. Ibid.

29. Ibid., p. 198.

30. Ibid., p. 287.

31. Ibid., p. 32.

32. Ibid., p. 69.

33. Ibid., p. 168.

34. Ibid., p. 3.

35. Ibid., p. 326.

36. The idea that narrations or stories exemplify spatial practices is developed by Michel de Certeau. See "Spatial Stories," chapter 9 in *The Practice of Everyday Life,* trans. Steven F. Rendell (Berkeley: University of California Press, 1984), pp. 115–30.

37. DeLillo, *White Noise,* p. 85.

38. Ibid., p. 167.

39. Ibid., p. 55.

40. Andrew Ross, "The Work of Nature in the Age of Electronic Emission," *Social Text,* Winter/Spring 1987/88, p. 120.

41. DeLillo, *White Noise,* p. 115.

42. Ibid., p. 140.

43. Ibid., p. 319.

44. Ibid., pp. 171–72.

45. Jürgen Habermas, "The New Obscurity: The Crisis of the Welfare State and the Exhaustion of Utopian Energies," trans. Phillip Jacobs, *Philosophy and Social Criticism* 11 (Winter 1986), p. 1.

46. Paul Virilio and Sylvere Lotringer, *Pure War,* trans. Mark Polizotti (New York: Semiotext[e], 1983), p. 139.

47. DeLillo, *White Noise,* p. 326.

48. Pamela Sebastian, "As Baby Boomers Age, Many Become Forgetful—and Often Assume the Worst," *Wall Street Journal,* June 22, 1988, sec. 2, p. 27.

49. Ibid.

Chapter 9. Terminations: Elkin's *Magic Kingdom* and the Politics of Death

1. See Fyodor Dostoyevsky, *Notes from the Underground,* trans. Serge Shishkoff (New

York: Crowell, 1969), p. 25ff. for his treatment of the underground man's reversal of the idea of the advantageous.

2. Michel Foucault, "Of Other Spaces," trans. Jay Miscowiec, *Diacritics* 16 (Spring 1986), p. 24.

3. Ibid.

4. Stanley Elkin, "A Poetics for Bullies," in *Criers and Kibitzers, Kibitzers and Criers* (New York: Random House, 1965), p. 197.

5. Ibid.

6. Ibid., pp. 198–99.

7. Ibid., p. 198.

8. Scott Sanders, "An Interview with Stanley Elkin," *Contemporary Literature* 16 (Spring 1975), p. 133.

9. Elkin, "A Poetics for Bullies," pp. 199–200.

10. Ibid., p. 206.

11. Ibid., p. 217. For a similar reading of "A Poetics for Bullies" that has influenced my account, see Peter J. Bailey's discussion in his *Reading Stanley Elkin* (Urbana: University of Illinois Press, 1985) pp. 1–20.

12. Michael Martone, "Believe It: Stanley Elkin and the Out-Jesusing of Fiction," *Denver Quarterly* 20 (Summer 1985), p. 121.

13. This characterization of Elkin's postmodernist form of irony belongs to Alan Wilde, *Horizons of Assent* (Baltimore, Md.: Johns Hopkins University Press, 1981), p. 10. In Wilde's terms, Elkin's suspensive irony embodies a vision of "multiplicity, randomness, contingency." It abandons a "quest for paradise" and accepts a disordered world.

14. Stanley Elkin, *The Magic Kingdom* (New York: Dutton, 1985), p. 257.

15. Ibid., p. 122.

16. Paul Virilio, *War and Cinema: The Logistics of Perception,* trans. Patrick Camiller (New York: Verson, 1989).

17. Paul Virilio and Sylvere Lotringer, *Pure War,* trans. Mark Polizotti (New York: Semiotext[e], 1983), p. 108.

18. Ibid., p. 128.

19. Ibid., pp. 139–40.

20. Elkin, *The Magic Kingdom,* p. 37.

21. Ibid., p. 6.

22. Ibid., p. 8.

23. Ibid., p. 30.

24. Foucault, "Of Other Spaces," p. 27.

25. Elkin, *The Magic Kingdom,* pp. 47–48.

26. Ibid., p. 66.

27. Ibid.

28. Ibid., p. 227.

29. Ibid., p. 223.

30. Ibid., p. 224.

31. Ibid., p. 28.

32. Ibid.

33. Ibid., p. 182.

34. Ibid.

35. Ibid., p. 48.

36. Ibid., p. 176.

37. For an interpretation of the standard versions of the Snow White tales, see N. J. Girardot, "Initiation in the Tale of Snow White and the Seven Dwarfs," *Journal of American Folklore* 90 (1977), pp. 274–300.

38. Elkin, *The Magic Kingdom,* p. 284.

39. Ibid., p. 252.

40. Ibid., p. 296.

41. Ibid., p. 316.

42. Ibid., pp. 316–17.

43. Ibid., p. 132.

44. Ibid., p. 99.

45. Ibid.

46. Ibid., p. 7.

47. Ibid., p. 4.

48. Ibid.

49. Ibid., p. 301.

50. Ibid., p. 87.

51. Ibid., p. 122.

52. Ibid., p. 242.

53. Ibid., p. 46.

54. Ibid.

55. Georges Bataille, *The Accursed Share*, vol. 1, trans. Robert Hurley (New York: Zone Books, 1988), p. 54.

56. Georges Bataille, *Death and Sensuality: A Study of Eroticism and the Taboo* (New York: Ballantine Books, 1962), p. 5.

57. Bataille, *The Accursed Share*, p. 58.

58. Elkin, *The Magic Kingdom*, p. 313.

59. Bataille, *Death and Sensuality*, pp. 9–10.

60. Ibid., p. 34.

61. Elkin, *The Magic Kingdom*, p. 316.

62. Ibid., p. 317.

63. Ibid., p. 281.

64. Ibid., p. 285.

65. Ibid.

Index

Michael J. Shapiro is professor of political science at the University of Hawaii. He is the author of numerous articles and books including, most recently, *The Politics of Representation: Writing Practices in Biography, Photography, and Policy Analysis* (1988) and *International/Intertextual Relations: Postmodern Readings of World Politics* (1989; coedited by James Der Derian).